LEGENDS OF THE TRACK

Great Moments in Stock Car Racing

LEGENDS OF THE TRACK

Great Moments in Stock Car Racing

DUANE FALK

MetroBooks

MetroBooks

An Imprint of Friedman/Fairfax Publishers

©2001 by Michael Friedman Publishing Group, Inc.

Library of Congress Cataloging-in-Publication Data

Falk, Duane.
    Legends of the track / Duane Falk.
        p. cm.
    Includes bibliographical references (p.) and index.
    ISBN 1-58663-071-7 (alk. paper)
        1. Stock car racing—United States—History. 2. Racetracks (Automobile racing)—United States—History. 3. Automobile racing drivers—United States—History. I. Title.

    GV1029.9.S74 F34 2001
    796.72'0973—dc21

                                    00-049621

Editor: Nathaniel Marunas
Art Director: Kevin Ullrich
Designer: Paul Taurins
Photo Editor: Lori Epstein
Production Manager: Richela Fabian Morgan

Color separations by Fine Arts Repro House Co., Ltd.
Printed in England by Butler & Tanner Ltd.

10 9 8 7 6 5 4 3 2 1

For bulk purchases and special sales, please contact:
Friedman/Fairfax Publishers
Attention: Sales Department
230 Fifth Avenue
New York, NY 10010
212/685-6610 FAX 212/685-3916

Visit our website:
www.metrobooks.com

DEDICATION

In memory of my parents, Arthur and Elinor Falk

ACKNOWLEDGMENTS

I would like to thank Nathaniel Marunas for his help and support in getting the book on track, and the rest of the crew at MetroBooks who did such a great job with the photo research, design, and layout. Special thanks are due to the staffs and "old-timers" at the many tracks who so kindly provided background and first-person perspectives, as well as to the race-team members who were kind enough to take time from their grueling schedules to answer questions. Thanks also to my friends and coworkers for their excitement and encouragement. Most of all, I would like to extend a grateful thank-you to my wife, Cindy, and to my children—Amy, Duncan, and Lisa—for their patience through this project; I promise you'll see more than the back of my head at the computer now that it's done.

FRONT ENDPAPER: The 1954 race at Oglethorpe Speedway, Georgia.
BACK ENDPAPER: Pole-sitter Bobby Labonte (number 18) and Mike Skinner (number 31) lead the field under threatening skies at the 1999 Cracker Barrel 500 (at Atlanta).
TITLE PAGE: Mark Martin at Sears Point, 1999.
OPPOSITE: Crews line up in front of their pit stalls, forming a colorful color guard as the National Anthem is sung before the 1999 race at Sears Point.

Contents

Next time you watch a Winston Cup race at, say, Darlington Raceway, think about the competition your favorite driver faces. The most obvious is the field of forty-two other drivers he'll vie against throughout the afternoon. If his car is not running well, you'll see him battle his vehicle as well—by now, cockpit cameras have made familiar the sight of a driver sawing the steering wheel back and forth as he struggles to maintain control of his ride.

> ## "Auto racing, bullfighting and mountain climbing are the only real sports...all others are games."
>
> ## —Ernest Hemingway

But there's one other opponent that every driver in the race must beat—the speedway itself. And at Darlington Raceway, the track is the toughest challenge any driver will face that weekend. It's easy for racing fans, even knowledgeable ones, to forget that before a crew and driver begin to figure out how to beat the other teams in the garage, they must first assess the track they're running on. While television gives us a bird's-eye view of the close competition among the drivers, running their cars inches off of each other's fenders and bumpers, it cannot convey the essence of automobile racing: the feeling of the car on the track. Certain sensations form the basic vocabulary of the stock car racer: the tires gripping asphalt or sliding through dirt; the G-force as a car sails into a tight turn; the vertigo of slipping over the edge of control.

Winston Cup teams today face twenty-one different tracks in a season, each with its own idiosyncrasies and challenges. Some are benign and some wicked. Over the course of its more-than-fifty-year history, the premier series of NASCAR (Grand National, now Winston Cup) has been raced on more than 150 tracks, ranging from ⅕-mile (320m) dirt bullrings to huge, high-speed motordromes to winding road courses. Races have been held in thirty-five of the United States, and overseas in two foreign

PAGES 6-7: The field closes up heading into turn 1 at New Hampshire during the 1997 race. Jeff Burton (not visible in this photo) began a 3-year winning streak at the flat track with that event. OPPOSITE: Close quarters in the Martinsville Speedway garage. There's not much infield at the half-mile track, so the haulers and garage stalls of the forty-three race teams that qualified for this 1999 event are packed in tight.

countries. And each of those speedways has a personality shaped as much by the locale and the spectators as by its surface and banking.

NASCAR racing is about the fans as well as the contestants, and the fans' impressions of the sport are often dictated by the speedway itself. After each race, sportswriters and broadcasters report on the fight for the top qualifying spot, the battles for the lead, the pit stops, and the wrecks, but the families who committed the time and money to make the trip to the track will remember much more about the experience than that. The traffic they sit in on their way to the race, the food, the restrooms and concessions (and prices thereat), and the comfort of the seat they spend five hours sitting in (or standing on)—all of these facets of the racetrack experience are part of the fans' memories, regardless of what happens on the track itself.

> ## "You win some. You lose some. You wreck some."
>
> ## —Dale Earnhardt

While this book certainly covers the cars and stars of stock car racing, it really focuses on the tracks of NASCAR. Included are racetracks that characterize the different eras of NASCAR history, from the dirt tracks of the 1940s and '50s to the superspeedways of the '60s to the many new tracks built since then. You will find plenty of hard facts about those hard surfaces, but you will also share some of the countless memorable moments and races, which are included to give readers a feel for the character of the places that are so fundamental to this thrilling sport.

Hopefully this book will give you a fresh perspective on your favorite raceway and even inspire you to mark the places where a gutsy pass was made, a championship won, or the underdog pulled off a miraculous comeback. It might also provide an opportunity to take a step back from the slick presentation and fast pace of today's typical race weekend and appreciate the qualities of the sport that have historically imbued it with both humanity and dignity.

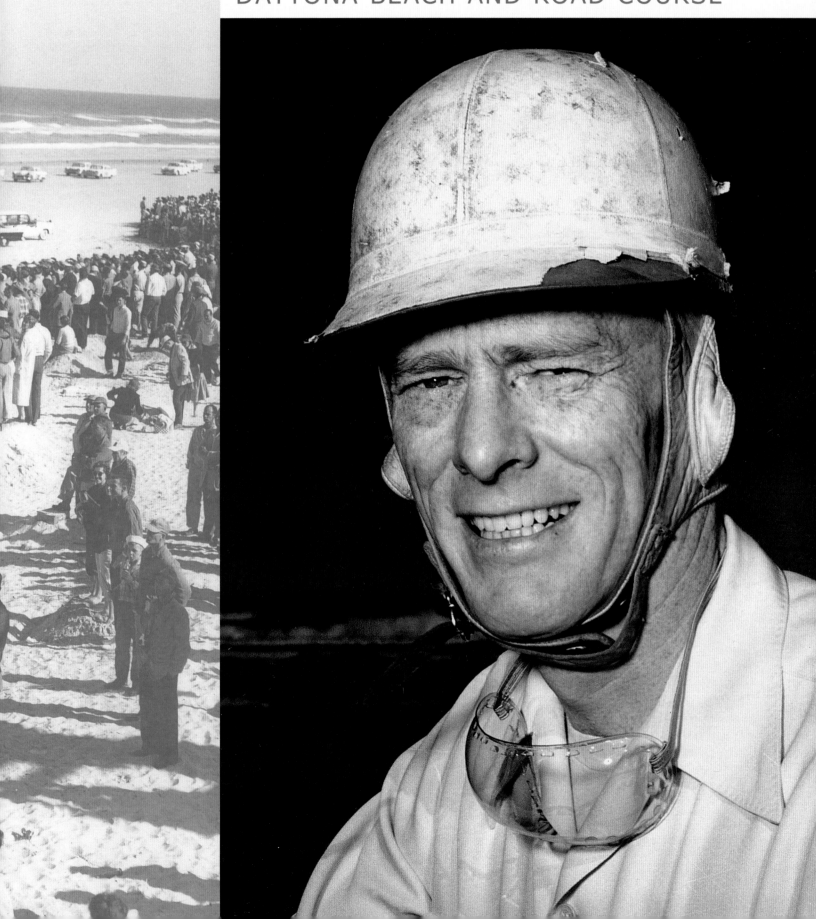

I f there's one place identified with NASCAR, it's Daytona Beach, Florida. The Daytona International Speedway, with its premier Daytona 500 event, is an icon of stock car racing, but Daytona and NASCAR were synonymous even before the superspeedway was built. NASCAR was founded in that municipality, and grew directly out of William Henry Getty "Big Bill" France's involvement with races run on a very special course there.

The association of fast cars and the beaches around Daytona goes back even further, all the way to the beginning of the twentieth century. Right after there were automobiles, there were automobile speed records, and Daytona and Ormond beaches were where early records were set. There was plenty of room for would-be record-setters to accelerate up to top speed (and then slow back down), and the wide lane of smooth, hard-packed sand was the best surface available at the time for speed runs.

One of the pioneers at Daytona was the venerable Random E. Olds (creator of the Oldsmobile and founder of REO Motor Company). Olds had the first certified speed record there, a dizzying 50 mph (80kph) in a prototype vehicle, *The Pirate*. (At that time just about every vehicle was a prototype.) The venue caught on, and 1904 saw the first official "Speed Week" at Daytona. By 1910, top speeds had climbed dramatically: Barney Oldfield exceeded 131 mph (209.6kph) that year. Over the next twenty years, automotive speedsters from around the world arrived at Daytona in search of the elusive

"LSR" (land speed record). In 1928, Sir Malcolm Campbell first brought his *Bluebird* to the beaches, leaving with a record of 206.96 mph (330.9kph). Not to be outdone, his fellow countryman Henry "the Mad Major" Seagrave drove his *Golden Arrow* to 231.45 mph (370.1kph) the following year, wowing an estimated 100,000 spectators and earning him a knighthood.

During the next five years, Campbell would aggressively push for the 300-mph (479.7kph) mark in the sands of Daytona. In 1931, he reached 246.09 mph (393.5kph); in '32, 253.97 mph (406.1kph); and on March 7, 1935, he topped out at 276.82 mph (442.9kph). At these speeds, though, it became clear that the beach surface was too short, too narrow, and too unpredictably bumpy. Racing at more than 275 mph (440kph), a speedster was also extremely susceptible to

PAGES 10–11: Daytona Beach, 1957. PAGE 11: Robert "Red" Byron was NASCAR's first champion. Actually, he was the first champion twice: he took the trophy for the Modified series in 1948, NASCAR's first year, and then the Strictly Stock championship in that series' first season, 1949. Not a bad record, considering he raced in only fifteen Grand National events from 1949 through '51. TOP: Barney Oldfield was a showman and a consummate racer. An inaugural inductee into the Motorsports Hall of Fame, Oldfield started out racing bicycles, then motorcycles. He became Ford's top auto racer in the early 1900s, and in 1910 set the world speed record at Daytona Beach: 131.724 mph (210.8kph). BOTTOM: Ransom E. Olds was the man who started the action on the beach, first bringing his speedster, *The Pirate*, to Daytona in 1902. Here, H.T. Thomas poses in that vehicle in 1903. The prototype, later renamed the *Olds Flyer*, topped out at about 60 mph (96kph).

In 1935, British racer Sir Malcolm Campbell became the first person to break the 300-mph (479.7kph) land-speed barrier. Doing so, he surpassed the records he himself had set in the 1920s, established in the *Bluebird*, shown here. This photo is from a 1928 run during which he clocked in a 16.76-second mile, for an average speed of 215 mph (344kph).

winds blowing in from the ocean. As a result, the fast crowd moved to the famed Bonneville salt flats, where Campbell reached the 300-mph mark late in '35.

DAYTONA BEACH & ROAD COURSE

LOCATION: *Daytona Beach, Florida*
RACE LENGTH: *160-200 miles (256-320km) on a 4.1–4.2 mile (6.6–6.7km) beach/road course*
NUMBER OF RACES RUN: *Ten Strictly Stock and Grand National, between July 10, 1949, and February 23, 1958*
SPEED RECORD (AVERAGE FOR AN ENTIRE RACE): *101.541 mph (162.5kph), on February 17, 1957*

The city fathers were concerned that the loss of Speed Week would leave Daytona just another beachside town, so they decided to hold an auto race. Sig Haugdahl, an ex-racer who was in the area, helped them lay out a course. It was one of the most unique racecourses ever run, and certainly the most unusual for stock cars. The "track" ran north along a portion of the famous beach, for about 1.5 miles (2.4km). It then cut across the dunes (the north turn) over to the parallel Highway A1A and ran back the same distance before cutting back through to the beach (the south turn). The overall course was 3.2 miles (5.1km) long, dictated by the necessity of using the easiest places to cut between beach and high-

way. The first race was run on March 8, 1937, and featured twenty-seven cars that had qualified in time trials.

The race was unique not only for the course, but for the cars, which were not modified roadsters but "stock" cars—that is, street-legal family cars. Unfortunately, the race lost money by virtue of poor crowd control, and the sand in the turns was so soft that cars bogged down and blocked the course. The city council vowed never to repeat the experiment.

The Birth of NASCAR

That first Daytona race event had included Bill France, a mechanic and sometime racer from the Washington, D.C., area who had stopped in Daytona Beach a few years earlier with his family, perhaps to watch Sir Malcolm Campbell set a speed record. He saw potential in the beach races and convinced the local Elks club to take a stab at the Daytona course. France organized a race for Labor Day of 1937, and though he was only able to scrape up $100 for the purse, the track conditions were much better (he had bulldozed shell rock from the beach into the turns to harden them) and the event was better managed. Even so the Elks claimed to have lost money and pulled their hats (or antlers) out of the ring.

France was persistent, though, and convinced local restaurant owner Charlie Reese to put up the pot for another go. This event, held in July 1938, actually made money and France was "off to the races." France had even participated in the race, finishing second. The winner (Smokey Purser) had driven off immediately after taking the checkered flag—to return his car to stock condition, as it turned out, which earned him a disqualification. France, in second place, should have inherited the win, but thought that would look suspicious, so promoted third-place runner Lloyd Mooney to first place.

Besides the race purse, France arranged prizes for the leaders on certain laps. Local businesses sponsored these prizes: a case of motor oil, a box of cigars, a $2.50 coupon for a local men's store, and $25 off a used car from the local lot. France continued to run beach races over the next few years, honing his organizational and promotional skills and crystallizing his ideas about how stock car racing should be run. Then U.S. involvement in World War II intervened in 1941, putting an end to racing through the first half of the '40s.

After the war, France picked up where he had left off, with beach races in 1946 and '47. He'd learned some valuable lessons and had developed strategies to help stock car racing rise above the challenges posed by multiple sanctioning bodies and conflicting championship schemes and racing rulebooks. France decided to apply his organizational talent to more than just the beach races, and create his own racing league. The result was the formation of NASCAR, which took place at the Streamline Hotel in Daytona Beach, in 1947. The Strictly Stock division would be its mainstay, and the fledgling organization's race schedule would include the beach and road course at Daytona.

The very first season for NASCAR was 1948, during which only the Modified division (which was set up along with the Strictly Stock and Roadster divisions) ran. France found that as a result of shortages imposed by the war, there were too few new cars out on the streets to run a stock division. The very first NASCAR race, in February '48, was run on the Daytona beach and road. The race was run on a shorter course—2.2 miles (3.5km). Marshall Teague and Fonty Flock took turns at the point, but "Red" Byron was the eventual winner. Byron brought the same success to the Modified Division crown that year, becoming NASCAR's first champion.

By 1949, the Detroit factories had cranked up production enough that a season of Strictly Stock car racing was tenable. France may have planned for the beach course to be the first race in that schedule as well, but circumstances dictated that the season start off in Charlotte. The schedule started halfway through the year, so the circuit rolled into Daytona in July.

The Strictly Stock division went back to a longer course for its race—4.15 miles (6.64km). The shorter track used the previous year wasn't holding up well in the corners, and anyway the long course was already set up for motorcycle races run there each year. With minor variations in the length—it eventually ended up at 4.1 miles (6.56km)—that was the course used for the remainder of the races.

A tableau from an earlier era: the flagman stands ready to mark the beginning of Barney Oldfield's 1910 speed record run. The *Blitzen Benz* was up to the task, and Oldfield managed to raise the bar to 131.724 mph (210.8kph). Oldfield, the first man to break the mile-a-minute barrier in an automobile, died in 1946.

Before he became a race organizer, "Big" Bill France was a racer. His on-track career started well before his famous trip to Daytona. As a teenager, France raced midgets at tracks in the Maryland-Washington-Pennsylvania region. In Florida, he took part in most of the beach events in the 1930s and '40s. In a transitional period between racer and promoter, he's shown here following a 1938 race he both promoted and won.

A Nice Place to Visit, but I Wouldn't Want to Race There

Daytona was a tough, tough course. On the beach side, drivers needed to find the right line to run—to avoid the too-soft sand near the "infield" and stay out of the ocean on the outside. The sand at the edge of the surf was wet and hard-packed and gave the tires a better bite, so it was the fastest place to run. Over the course of the race, though, ruts developed that could send a car shooting off to one side, or catch the tires and flip the car right over. Visibility was nil: the spray from the surf, wet sand thrown up by cars in front, and seagull droppings (or feathers and blood if the birds got too close to the speeding vehicles) coated the windshield in a sticky slurry.

Tim Flock, a two-time winner on the course, described the technique he used to make his way through the traffic: "You'd actually feel the car over here—you couldn't see him—move over a little bit and try to hold it straight." Running too close behind another car could actually sandblast your windshield. Some teams used plastic sheets taped over the windshield (much like today's tear-off strips), which could be removed on a pit stop to give the driver, briefly, a clear view.

At the north end of the beach was a sharp cut over to the highway. With the poor visibility, drivers often couldn't tell where to make the turn. The beach was lined with spectators, though, and according to champion Buck Baker, "when you ran out of people, you turned left." In the 1956 race, Johnny Beauchamp used a particular family of fans on the

beach to mark his place: when he saw them out his side window, he knew he was at the turn. Well, at some point in the race, his unwitting signposts got up and moved. Beauchamp came along the next lap, didn't see them, kept going and drove right off the end of the course.

Every NASCAR fan knows that race days are at the mercy of the elements. If it rains (or snows), the race is postponed. On the early Daytona course, there was another force of nature that often affected the races—the tides. The start times were set to allow as much time as possible with the tide out. More than once the race had to be abbreviated because it was running long and the incoming tide left no room for the cars on the beach.

The north turn was a transition from sand to asphalt. To slow down, the drivers would throw their cars sideways going into the turn. The brakes on the cars, like everything else, were stock, and would often overheat and fade by the end of the second or third lap. To cool them down, racers would often run in the surf so the spray would shoot up under the cars and onto the hot brakes.

The biggest crowds of spectators were in that north turn, but fans lined up all along the long course. Unlike today's self-contained facilities, this was a huge, open area. To make any profit from the race, NASCAR had to have a way to control crowd entry (i.e., through the ticket sellers). Since he couldn't ring the course with fencing, France used a bit of psychology to keep interlopers at a minimum. The area around the course was plastered with signs warning " Watch Out for Snakes!!" There was enough truth to the

Where it All Started—The Daytona Beach and Road Course

Where it All Started—The Daytona Beach and Road Course

warning that most folks stuck to the paths and paid their entry fee rather than slog through the supposedly snake-infested underbrush.

Coming out of the north turn, the cars sped onto the asphalt ribbon of Highway A1A. Ribbon is probably exactly what it looked like to the racers—it was a narrow two-lane road, down which they'd run at speeds up to 140 mph (224kph). If a competitor came up on a slow car he had to hope that car stayed in his lane, because there was nowhere to dodge! Side-by-side racing was a game of chicken to see who would back off as the cars came up on a breakdown, or plowed into the south turn. As brakes began to fail, the veteran racers used a trick to slow themselves down at the last moment going into that turn. They'd drop the wheels on one side off the edge of the asphalt and "cross the car up," basically throwing it into a sideways slide to lose speed. Around the south turn, they were back on the long stretch of beach. There was no fast way through those corners, so the key to the race was power. Ace mechanics, like Raymond Parks and Smokey Yunick, would gear the car to get the best speed down the straightaways and rely on the drivers to keep it on the course through the turns.

Early Grand National Races

The first Grand National race on the beach and road course was held on July 10, 1949. NASCAR collected ticket money from 5,000 of the fans that came to watch the twenty-eight-car field run forty laps. The race was a romp for the Oldsmobile contingency (the ghost of old Ransom E. Olds must have been smiling down on his former playground that day). That model swept the top four positions and also took sixth through eighth. Gober Sosebee, in an Olds, held the lead from the green flag, but with six laps to go drove off the north end of the course, dropping to eighth place. Red Byron was in the catbird seat and took the win. The race was notable in that there were no cautions and also that there were three women in the field. The Flock brothers (Fonty, Tim, and Bob) were joined by their sister, Ethel Flock Mobley (driving her husband's Cadillac); Sara Christian and Louise Smith also competed.

The field blossomed in 1950 to forty-one cars (the race was won by Harold Kite in his first NASCAR competition), then in 1951 to fifty-four cars, including thirteen different makes. One of those models made its first impression on the stock car racing world that day. Marshall Teague, in his number 6 Fabulous Hudson Hornet, took the first of his five wins that season and began a four-year-long winning tradition for Hudson. The Hudsons weren't overpowering on the straightaways, but with a lower center of gravity than other models, they had a decided advantage through the turns. In the hands of masters like Teague, Herb Thomas, and Tim Flock, Hudsons won at Daytona in 1951, '52, and '54, and scored a total of seventy-nine wins through the '55 season (the Hudson's last in Grand National).

PAGES 16–17: The NASCAR nativity scene. Big Bill France (center) heads a meeting of racing professionals gathered in the Ebony Room of the Streamline Hotel, Daytona Beach. The group hammered out the foundations of the organization over two days in December 1947. France was nominated the president of the new group and "Cannonball" Baker its first commissioner of racing. ABOVE: In 1928, spectators come to the rescue of record-setter Frank Lockhart. Lockhart designed and built the streamlined *Stutz Black Hawk* racer (one of the first cars ever tested in a wind tunnel) and eclipsed the 200-mph (320kph) mark in it on the sands of Daytona. He drifted off course during the run, though, and flipped into the surf. He lost his life in the same car in another crash during the second run; he blew a tire and the car went tumbling end-over-end, this time fatally.

Where it All Started—The Daytona Beach and Road Course

The "First Ladies" of NASCAR: Louise Smith (top left), Sarah Christian (top right), and Ethel Flock Mobley (bottom). These women ran in only the first few seasons of the circuit and had only one top-five finish among them, but as female pioneers in a sport dominated by men, the significance of these drivers extends far beyond their track records.

That first win for Teague and his Hudson was actually a gift from another team. At the start of the last lap, Teague was running in second place, more than three minutes behind Tim Flock. Flock needed to make a quick pit stop for gas to finish the race, and it cost him the win. There was plenty of time for him to gas up and still maintain his lead, except that his pit crew had begun celebrating the victory a bit too soon and wasn't prepared for the stop. By the time they found a can of gas for the car, Teague had made up the entire margin and pulled ahead to take the win. Flock finished in second place. "I lost the Daytona Beach race in 1951 because my pit crew was drunk!" Flock later declared.

There was no question about Teague's win in 1952, though. He and Hudson running mate Herb Thomas (driving another "Teaguemobile") took first and second places,

respectively. Teague was able to finish without making a pit stop because the race was red-flagged after thirty-seven laps due to incoming tides.

Fonty Flock also lost the race on gas, in 1953. He had taken the lead in the opening lap and was in first place when he took the white flag. Then he ran out of gas. Teammate Slick Smith pushed him back to the pits, where he fueled up. Ultimately, he finished the race in second place, behind Bill Blair, who put Olds back in the winner's circle. On a side note, Fonty and pole-sitter Bob Pronger had a bet as to which of them would lead the first lap. The two drove door-to-door up the beach and into the north turn. The more experienced Flock hit the brakes at the last instant and slid around the turn, but Pronger never let up, and at full speed sailed through the guardrail and over a dune, landing on an access road at the bottom of the stands. Flock won the bet, if not the race.

Due to interleague rivalries, Marshall Teague, the previous year's Daytona winner, did not even compete at Daytona in 1953. In its early years NASCAR was very sensitive to the possibility of losing its stars to other racing organizations so was strict about not allowing its drivers to participate in events sponsored by other sanctioning bodies. In '52, Teague had raced in AAA events and so had to pay a fine to get into the '52 Daytona race. In '53, he returned to AAA and never came back to the Grand National League.

Tim Flock was once again cheated of a Daytona win in 1954. This time he took the checkered flag, but was disqualified following the postrace inspection. NASCAR said his car had polished carbs. Flock had a different viewpoint. The Ernest Woods team had been experimenting with two-way radios in the car, and there was a pole with an antenna in their pits, along with an antenna and a variety of other equipment on the car. According to Flock, the car had so much stuff on it that Bill France was "after him before the race even started." Regardless of the reason, the penalty was applied, and a disgruntled Flock slammed the door in France's face (literally and figuratively), quitting NASCAR.

🏁 The 1955 Daytona Beach Race

Tim Flock didn't race at all the rest of 1954, but did come down to Daytona with friends before the '55 season started, to relax and watch the teams practice. As they watched, a gleaming white Chrysler, numbered 300, roared by. Flock, impressed with the car's performance told his companions, "If I had that car, I'd win the race." As fate would have it, an acquaintance of the car's owner was standing nearby and overheard the remark. Recognizing Flock, he brought driver and car owner Carl Kiekhafer together. That meeting led to an association that brought Flock twenty-one wins over the next two years.

In 1955, Kiekhafer had descended on NASCAR and, as he did with any endeavor to which he put his mind, dominated it. Sensing Flock's potential, Kiekhafer put the driver behind the wheel of the 300 Chrysler for the '55 Daytona race, a 160-mile (256km) event. NASCAR made the driver pay a good faith deposit before they'd allow him to qualify for the race. As the song goes, "You don't tug on Superman's cape"—you also don't thumb your nose at Big Bill France.

The Chrysler was fast: Flock put it on the pole for the event and set a new speed record (by more than 7 mph [11.2kph]) of more than 130 mph (208kph). But the car had been set up with an automatic transmission, and Flock expressed his concerns about not having a manual shift to Kiekhafer before the race. "Do you want to race the car or not?" was the reply, and Flock agreed to drive the car as was.

Fireball Roberts (in the Fish Carburetors M-1 car) jumped out to the lead right from the first lap and kept his

Tim Flock took the number 300 Chrysler to victory lane eighteen times on his way to the 1955 Grand National championship trophy (shown here). The porcelain-white dynamo was up front most of the year, leading thirty-three of thirty-nine races and more than half the total laps (3,500 out of 6,200).

Buick there for all thirty-nine circuits, with Flock flagged in second place. Fate smiled on the young Georgian for a change, though. In the postrace inspection, the NASCAR officials determined that the rods on the M-1 car had been modified by the team's mechanic, Red Vogt; as a result, the officials punted the team to the rear of the finishing order. Tim Flock, in his first ride with the new team (indeed the team's first race), was awarded the win. That was just the start. He went on to eighteen wins that year (the record at the time, and second in NASCAR history only to Richard Petty's twenty-seven wins in 1967).

End of an Era

Kiekhafer and Flock repeated the Dayton win in 1956. Flock took the lead from Jim Paschal on the twenty-seventh lap and held it until the race was red-flagged on the thirty-seventh lap (the tide had begun washing in over the beach side of the course).

By 1956, Kiekhafer was fielding a slew of cars in each race. At Daytona, he had six teams, including one for driver Charlie Scott, the first black driver ever to compete in NASCAR. The '56 race was also remarkable for an episode involving Junior Johnson. Johnson flipped his car in the surf and was photographed running down the beach *ahead* of the still-rolling car. Junior was never able to explain how he managed that trick.

Having won two consecutive championships, Kiekhafer pulled out of NASCAR as suddenly as he had arrived. Despite his short tenure, the sport definitely had been changed by his involvement. He showed the racing community that a scientific approach and careful organization could play as big a part in achieving victory as grit and raw talent.

The Detroit auto manufacturers were solidly into backing race teams in 1957. Pontiac's efforts paid off with Cotton Owens' win on the beach that year. The contest was a duel between Owens and Paul Goldsmith, in a Chevy, that ended with the latter's engine blowing with only eight laps to go. The race was also the first time the average speed of a NASCAR event exceeded 100 mph (160kph) (it was clocked at 101.541 mph [162.5kph]).

That was also the year Harley J. Earle unveiled his concept car, *The Firebird Two*, which would later be immortalized in a silver replica mounted atop the Daytona 500 trophy. The speedster, representing streamlined speed, tops what is now known as the Harley J. Earle Trophy.

The last beach race, in 1958, proved to be the most exciting. Curtis Turner, in a Holman-Moody Ford, and Paul Goldsmith, in a Smokey Yunick Pontiac, battled for the lead through most of the race. It looked like Goldsmith would walk away with the win when Turner, trapped behind a slow car, spun out on the beach and fell far behind. But the race wasn't over.

On the last lap, the visibility had become so bad that as Goldsmith reached the end of the beach straightaway, he kept going along the beach rather than making the turn. He caught his mistake right away and did a 180°, heading back to the course. Turner took advantage of Goldsmith's excursion to close in. As Goldsmith's number 3 Pontiac slid back onto the track for the last turn, Turner's Ford was in sight and bearing down. As it turned out, Goldsmith had corrected his error just in time, and was able to hang on to a five-car-length lead over Turner right to the finish line. It was the closest finish ever on the course.

This thrilling race was the last one NASCAR ran on the beach course. Bill France had been after the Daytona city fathers to build a permanent course for many years, and finally got the backing he needed to proceed. Accordingly, in 1959 the circuit would shift to what at the time was the newest and biggest superspeedway in the United States—the Daytona International Speedway. With the opening of that marvelous racecourse, NASCAR moved into a new era.

And Daytona Beach today? The former course is high-priced real estate. Still a tourist attraction, the area is now the site of hotels and shops rather than grandstands and grease monkeys.

More than 37,000 spectators showed up for the 1957 running of the Daytona Beach race. There weren't many facilities, but there was plenty of room around the edge of the big course. Cotton Owens and Pontiac earned their first trips to Grand National victory lane that day.

When you think of today's NASCAR, there are many images that come to mind. Brilliantly colored cars festooned with logos and polished to mirror sheen. The full-throated crescendo, like the scream of a wing of fighter jets, as forty-three racecars dive into the first turn. Acrid scents of rubber, gasoline, and smoke offset by the enticing aroma of "track food." The panoramic view of showcase facilities that support fast, tight racing and service a city's worth of fans. This richly sensual panoply of sights, sounds, and smells is indeed today's Winston Cup. Those of NASCAR in the 1950s—when the organization and the sport were in their infancy—were considerably different.

The main thing that the early generation of drivers had in common with today's drivers was a fierce desire to win. Those men—and women—were pioneers of the sport, and like all pioneers, they had to make do with what equipment and resources they could manage. The cars they drove were often their family sedans. The only modification NASCAR allowed in the first few seasons was a reinforcing plate on the front right wheel to keep the lug nuts from tearing through from the stress of constant, hard left-hand turns. It wasn't until the mid-1950s that "severe usage packages" were approved to beef up the cars and better insure the drivers' safety.

The racetracks of the day were as far from today's carefully planned speed palaces as you could get. For its first decade, the fledgling organization had to rely mostly on existing tracks to fill its schedule. It didn't yet have the popularity to entice, and certainly not the authority to compel, developers to invest in new facilities. Luckily, there were numerous tracks, already extant—enough to pack the forty-to-sixty race schedules of the 1950s and '60s.

Those tracks were, with very few exceptions, small affairs, built around the show grounds of the county or state fair or on rural property in order to host the local hot rod heroes and a hometown crowd of spectators. So NASCAR ran its first schedules on such humble facilities. Most tracks were a ½ mile (0.8km) or less (a ⅕-mile [.32km] track fit nicely around the outside of a high-school football field) and most were made of dirt. If the drivers and fans were lucky, the proprietor would oil the dirt or use calcium chloride to keep the dust down. Fans quickly learned not to go to the races dressed in their Sunday best.

Track layouts varied from place to place. Most were oval, or roughly so. Many, like Martinsville, in Virginia, had little or no banking in the turns, while others had a steeply sloped lip that served to lift cars right out of the track if they were unlucky enough to slip that far out of the groove. Photos often show spectators ringing the outside of the track to watch the race, though most tracks had some sort of grandstand for fans along the front stretch. On the other side of the track, the pit row and infield were makeshift affairs. Pit boxes were often just the inside lane of the front straightaway, with no fence or wall to separate them from the racing action a few feet away. Teams didn't require much by way of fancy track facilities—haulers, mobile "pit headquarters," and the like—so could easily set up their toolboxes, gas cans, and tow vehicle (if they hadn't just driven their racecar to the track) anywhere in the open infield.

What is truly amazing when you look at the early schedules is the diversity of locales where Grand National races were run. Traditionally, most people associate NASCAR exclusively with the Southeast, and indeed many of the premier tracks are located there. Over its history, though, NASCAR races have been run on almost as many tracks in the "non-southern" states as it has in Dixie. North Carolina leads the list for the number of tracks, but New York and California are next. The first Strictly Stock season held three of its eight races in Pennsylvania and New York. Tracks in Arizona, Washington state, and Canada were all part of the series in the 1950s.

Taking the show on the road across the country didn't propel NASCAR to the nationwide prominence it enjoys today—that required the attention of the major television networks—but it did have an impact on the teams trying to run the schedules. Bread-and-butter racers, like Lee Petty, who depended on running and finishing week-in and week-out to support their families, had a tough time crisscrossing the country to participate in every race. Instead, many drivers cherry-picked the races that paid the most, were most prestigious, or simply were near home. By the early 1960s, the situation had gotten out of hand.

The 1964 season had more than sixty races, most of which were under 100 miles (160km). There were even occurrences where more than one Grand National race was run on the same day—in different parts of the country. Despite these concerns, NASCAR's goal was continued growth. In addition, the France family showed admirable loyalty to the tracks that had been with them through thick and thin, so the expansion continued (that is, until the advent of R.J. Reynold's involvement in 1971 drastically winnowed the schedule and produced the Winston Cup series).

The style of racing in the early days fit the venues as well. In many cases, short track races were only fifty laps long, so there wasn't time to play your cards close to the vest. Instead, the sport was characterized by hard-chargers who ran their equipment full-bore, on the edge. They either won by enormous margins, or broke down and fell out. Race fans today like to speculate about how a Curtis Turner or Junior Johnson would stack up against a Dale Earnhardt and Jeff Gordon, given equally sturdy equipment. One suspects that a driver like Turner could push the limits of even a 1999 Ford Taurus.

Some of the tracks that hosted NASCAR's first decade are still on the circuit. Martinsville

PAGES 22–23: Bowman-Gray Stadium, 1954.
PAGE 23: A pleased Dick Rathman holds the checkered after a win at Langhorne in 1953.

Short Tracks and Bullrings

and Richmond have changed over the years, but still retain their essential character, and form a vital link to the rich history that makes up the sport. Nor were short tracks strictly a feature of the early years of the sport. Bristol Raceway, still one of the most popular tracks on the circuit, was not added to the schedule until 1961. The very last new short track to host a Grand National race was Meyer Speedway in Texas, just a year before the dawning of the modern era, in 1971.

Highlighted here are a few of those tracks, each of which has its own personality and stories.

Hoping to expand NASCAR's popularity by attracting nationally known racing personalities, Big Bill France himself sponsored Bill Holland (the 1949 Indy 500 winner) in seven races during the '51 season. Holland didn't have much luck in stock cars (with only one top-five finish), but the handsome Connecticut driver proved France's marketing acumen by garnering plenty of press coverage.

LOCATION: *Charlotte, North Carolina*
RACE LENGTH: *150 miles (240km) on a ¾-mile (1.2km) dirt oval*
NUMBER OF RACES RUN: *Twelve Strictly Stock and Grand National, between June 19, 1949, and October 17, 1956*
SPEED RECORD (AVERAGE FOR AN ENTIRE RACE): *72.268 mph (115.6kph), set on October 17, 1956*

Charlotte Speedway, a regular stop in the early years of stock car racing, was not really a remarkable track, but it earned a special place in NASCAR history. It served as the location of the first Strictly Stock points race in the series' inaugural season.

Today, Charlotte is the epicenter for stock car racing in the United States, but in 1949 it seemed an unlikely venue to host the leadoff event of the new series. Bill France probably wanted to begin the Strictly Stock season at Daytona (as he had with the previous year's Modified series), but saw an advantage to having it in Charlotte instead. France was aware that the National Stock Car Racing Association (NSCRA)—a rival racing organization based in Charlotte—was gunning for many of the same drivers he hoped would race in NASCAR events. Not wanting to lose the top talent to a rival organization, Big Bill felt the best way to beat them to the punch was to demonstrate NASCAR's potential right in NSCRA's home territory. As a result, the first Strictly Stock car race was held at Charlotte, North Carolina.

Charlotte was a typical short track of the time. It was a ¾-mile (1.2km) dirt oval built by the Charles family on leased property near what is now the Charlotte Airport. The facility was built in 1948 and hosted a handful of Modified races before the big Strictly Stock event in 1949. Heavy dust and tire-snagging ruts were among the challenges racers faced as they slid through the flat (nonbanked) turns. The corners were edged with a packed dirt curb, topped with a rough-made, uneven, wooden fence. In the event a car went through that nominal barricade, it would roll down embankments outside of the turns. A waist-high wooden barrier separated the track from the unfinished infield, along the front chute. The flagman enjoyed the safety of a flag stand on the inside of the front straightaway. On the other side of the track, a post-and-wire fence provided protection for the fans in the stands. The track also featured grandstands along the front straight, which accommodated a relatively large number of fans, an important point for the young series.

The 1949 150-Miler at Charlotte

The summer race was announced only a couple of months in advance, but since the field would be made up mostly of family sedans, France had little doubt that he'd

Otis Mann pulls his number 19 Ford ahead of third-place qualifier Red Byron (number 22) in the inaugural race of the first Strictly Stock season, 1949, at Charlotte. Byron ended up where he started, in third. The eventual winner of the event, earning a spot in racing history, was Jim Roper, who had started in twelfth place.

have enough applicants. Nor was he disappointed. Most of the big names from the Modified circuit turned out, though several Modified series regulars were missing from the field. Buddy Shuman, Speedy Thompson, and Ed Samples were on probation (and therefore unable to participate) for allegedly spreading thumbtacks on the track at a previous race.

Not all of the drivers had a suitable ride available when they arrived. Bob and Fonty Flock brought cars to the race, but younger brother Tim showed up without a ride. Bob pointed out a couple watching the practice runs at the track from a new Olds 88, a solid and somewhat hard-to-find car at the time. Bob suggested that Tim ask the fellow if he could borrow his car. The owner, Buddy Elliott, despite the sensible advice of his wife, brought the car back the next day for Tim to race in.

The contestants qualified based on trial laps the day before the race. Bob Flock led a field of thirty-three with a fast lap of 67.958 mph (108.7kph), driving a 1946 Hudson Hornet. The adventurous Elliotts' Olds, with Tim Flock aboard, came in second, and the 1948 Modified champion, Red Byron, came in third. Altogether the field featured nine different makes of cars.

A sizable crowd of 13,000 paid to watch the 200-lapper on Sunday, June 19, 1949 (and many more nonpaying fans turned out at the track, causing the state troopers quite a headache). As is still the case, every fan was on his feet when flagman Alvin Hawkins gave the field the green flag.

A thick fog of dust quickly obscured both ends of the track as the pack roared through the first few turns. Bob Flock took the early lead but was overtaken after five or so laps by eighth-place starter Bill Blair. Masterfully broad-sliding his number 44 Lincoln through the turns, Blair picked off one position after another, lapping the entire field. Pole-sitter Flock was one of the many drivers—at least a third of the

field—who dropped out of the race with an overheated engine, oil leak, or some other mechanical snafu.

Surprisingly there was only one crash in that race. A new face to racing, Lee Petty, got "out of shape" (or lost control) going into the third turn on lap 107. His number 38 Buick (he switched to his signature number 42 for his next race), actually the Petty family car, rolled end over end, finally coming to rest on its wheels facing oncoming traffic. Petty climbed up to sit at the berm of the track. Petty later said, "I was just sitting there thinking about having to go home and explain to my wife where I'd been with the car."

Three quarters of the way through the race the radiator on leader Blair's car blew, forcing him to park for the afternoon. Glenn Dunnaway, in Hubert Westmoreland's number 25 Ford, picked up the lead and stayed there to take the checkered flag. Three laps behind, Jim Roper was flagged in at second place in a crippled Lincoln.

NASCAR officials were suspicious about the winning car, though. They noticed that it handled exceptionally well through the rutted turns and Dunnaway freely admitted that the car was a bootlegger belonging to Westmoreland. NASCAR found that the reason for its stability was a set of beefed-up rear springs, a clear violation of the strictly stock rules. They disqualified the car, and Dunnaway was moved to last place in the finishing order. Car owner Westmoreland was irate at the ruling and actually took NASCAR to court over it. The clear definition of the stock rules was unequivocal, though, and the state court threw out the case. Dunnaway took the reversal philosophically—he had won the first race, whether they disqualified him or not.

But what really took the sting out of the disqualification was the fact that Dunnaway left the track with more money than if he'd actually been paid for first place. A number of the other drivers, knowing that Glenn had been unaware of the illegal enhancements (Westmoreland had offered him the ride at the track), chipped in to give him a pot rivaling the $2,000 winner's award.

Jim Roper entered the books as the winner. Fonty Flock took second place and $1,000. Red Byron was in third, and Sam Rice fourth. Tim Flock safely returned the Elliotts' Olds after taking a respectable fifth place.

Adieu, Sweet Charlotte

The Charlotte dirt track remained on the Grand National circuit until 1956, hosting twelve races altogether. Tim Flock earned his first win there in 1950. The aggrieved Hubert Westmoreland was back in '51 with Bill Holland, the '49 Indy 500 winner. Holland had been suspended by the AAA for running a charity event without charging a fee so decided to try his hand at NASCAR. Westmoreland was again disappointed as Holland flipped and demolished his Plymouth. For those who get a chuckle every time contemporary driver Dick Trickle's name comes up, try the name of the April '53 race winner: Indianapolis driver Dick Passwater (in his only NASCAR win). Buck Baker extended owner Carl Kiekhafer's winning streak at the track to three in a row when he took the last NASCAR race there in '56.

The Charlotte track remained substantially unchanged since that historic first race in 1949, and with the lack of significant improvement and growing competition from other nearby raceways, it was dropped from NASCAR schedule after the '56 season. The track closed down shortly thereafter.

LANGHORNE SPEEDWAY

LOCATION: *Langhorne, Pennsylvania*
RACE LENGTH: *150–300 miles (240–480km) on a 1-mile (1.6km) dirt circle*
NUMBER OF RACES RUN: *Seventeen Strictly Stock and Grand National, between September 11, 1949, and September 15, 1957*
SPEED RECORD (AVERAGE FOR AN ENTIRE RACE): *85.850 mph (137.4kph), set on April 14, 1957*

Poll any of the old-timers on which track they think was the toughest of all time and Langhorne is sure to be at or near the top of the list. Daytona Beach was a unique combination of surfaces, and the "Lady in Black," as Darlington Raceway is known, has the rep as the toughest track to tame, but as Tim Flock recalled in *The Last Lap:* "Langhorne Speedway was the hardest track to win on. If you could win at Langhorne you were one hell of a race driver, cause you run flat out and never did lift." A trophy from the eastern Pennsylvania speedway was one of the most coveted awards among stock car racers of the early years.

The track opened as the Philadelphia Speedway in 1926. It was a narrow, circular track fittingly nicknamed the "Great Left Turn." The dirt surface was heavily oiled to keep dust from filling the air, but this meant that black gook would cover the fronts of the cars, often fouling their radiators and sidelining them. Like most tracks at that time,

Herb Thomas was an impoverished sharecropper who went from barely making ends meet to being a racing hero. Thomas was a smart driver who knew how to pace himself during a race, a technique that really paid off: during his career, Thomas earned forty-eight wins in only 230 starts (from 1949 to '62) as well as two championships (in '51 and '53). Thomas was well on his way to a third title in '56 when his career was derailed by critical injuries suffered in a crash at that year's Cleveland County Fairgrounds race.

the pits were just off to the side of the front straight. There was plenty of room around the sizable track for spectators, including a large grandstand and open space atop the hill

that made up the inside border. You wouldn't want to stand around the outside of this track, though: the barricade was just a low metal guardrail that separated the cars from a steep embankment that at points dropped as much as 30 feet (9.1m).

The stress on the cars and drivers of constantly turning left led to frequent accidents. It probably didn't help that the starting lineups for some of the races exceeded sixty cars. Langhorne quickly acquired a reputation as a very dangerous place to race as well as a new nickname: "The Track That Ate the Heroes." Records of the races at Langhorne read like casualty lists. In 1950, John Schelesky was hospitalized when his car fell 20 feet (6.1m) down an embankment. In 1951, spectacular crashes left two drivers injured, one critically (Fritz Holzman was rushed to Mercer Hospital with head injuries). In the 1952 spring race, George Fleming flipped six times during practice and was taken to the hospital with back injuries; in the fall race, Larry Mann became the first Grand National driver killed during a race, succumbing to head injuries sustained when his Hornet flipped. In 1953, Frank Artford was killed while attempting to qualify; Ray Duhigg crashed during the race, suffering a broken neck. In 1954, in a crash-filled race, Harvey Eakins went through the guardrail and dropped 30 feet (9.1m) to an access road and was hospitalized with back injuries. In 1955, Leslie Young was taken to the hospital with a concussion in the spring race; Axel Anderson suffered a fractured skull in the fall race. In 1956, John McVitty died of internal injuries sustained by rolling his car during the qualifying round.

Though the track accommodated large crowds (gate counts of more than 20,000 were usual), the toll on drivers and equipment was high. And though the track remained open for many years—it was paved in 1965 and hosted USAC sprint car races—the series did not return after the '57 season. After '71, the area was redeveloped and is now a shopping center.

There were many high points in the track's history as well. Curtis Turner had the toughness and determination it took to master the raceway and won the first two events there, in 1949 and '50. In the first race, he was joined in the winner's circle by an honorary co-winner. Sara Christian, the highest-ranking woman in NASCAR history (thirteenth in the '49 points standing), finished sixth in the grueling 200-lap event. Her spectacular effort prompted track officials to honor her along with Turner.

The June 1953 race was called the International 200 and was one of the few NASCAR races open to foreign as well as domestic cars. It didn't matter what kind of car you were driving that day, though, unless it happened to be the number 120 Hudson. Dick Rathman led the first lap from his outside pole position and never relinquished the point— his second such performance there. He followed it up with another win in the fall race as well.

TOP: It wasn't just the Grand National drivers who had a tough time of it at Langhorne. During this 1951 Sportsman race, a twelve-car pileup and fire brought the event to a screeching halt. BOTTOM: Dick Rathman earned three wins at Langhorne, including this one, the 1953 International 200. Rathman (born Jim, but he switched his name and identity with his brother, and fellow racer, as a teenager) captured twenty-eight wins in only 128 races (for a winning percentage of almost 22 percent), from '51 to '55.

Short Tracks and Bullrings

Junior Johnson passed more cars in the September 1954 race than most drivers do in two or three races. Engine troubles had put him in last place, laps down, at the very start of the race, which was particularly bad since the race featured sixty-four cars. In an amazing effort, he worked his way back up to the fifteenth spot, while Herb Thomas took one of his three career wins at the track.

A robust crowd of 31,000 watched Paul Goldsmith motor to a seven-mile (11.2km) winning margin in the first of his nine Grand National wins in 1956. In '57, Gwyn Staley, driving a Chevy convertible, won the last race at Langhorne. It was the first win by a convertible in the mixed ragtop/hardtop format.

MARTINSVILLE
SPEEDWAY

LOCATION: *Martinsville, Virginia*
RACE LENGTH: *100–250 miles (160–400km) on a ½-mile dirt oval (paved in 1955)*
NUMBER OF RACES RUN: *104 Strictly Stock, Grand National, and Winston Cup, between September 25, 1949, and October 1, 2000*
SPEED RECORD (AVERAGE FOR AN ENTIRE RACE): *82.223 mph (131.6kph), on September 22, 1996*

The NASCAR community lost a cherished friend in 1999 with the passing of H. Clay Earles, founder and owner of Martinsville Speedway. Earles had been part of NASCAR since its very earliest days. Shortly after World War II, Earles took a gamble and invested $10,000 of his savings in a partnership with Bill France to build a raceway in southern Virginia. The bill ended up being closer to $60,000, but the racetrack ended up a winner. Earles was always an innovator when it came to his business, and was a warm and caring friend to the racing community. Earles' approach—always take care of the fans—continues to manifest itself in innumerable ways at Martinsville, from the immaculate track and beautifully manicured grounds to the delicious red hot dogs that can't be found anywhere but the concession stands at the Virginia track.

Martinsville first opened in 1947 and was the sixth race on the inaugural Strictly Stock schedule in '49. The ½-mile (0.8km) track is the only original speedway still on the premier series circuit and has hosted more than one hundred Strictly Stock, Grand National, and Winston Cup races in the intervening decades.

The track is currently measured at 0.526 miles (0.84km), making it the shortest track on the circuit today. It's a very flat track, with only 12 degrees of banking in the turns and none at all on the straights. The track is often described as paper clip shaped, with long straights and tight, short turns. The configuration lends itself to fast acceleration, with speeds reaching up to 120 mph (192kph), followed by hard braking going into the corners as drivers scrub off half that speed. The inside lane in both turns is made of concrete to better withstand the stress of heavy cars braking and then accelerating again. One key to success there is to keep the brakes intact through 500 circuits and to be able to quickly accelerate out of the turns without spinning the wheels or breaking the back end loose. One of the most vivid images provided by the in-car (or under-car) cameras today is that of glowing cherry-red brake rotors as the driver stomps "hard on the binders" (brakes) at the end of the straightaway.

Martinsville Speedway hasn't changed all that much from this 1968 aerial view. There are more stands and more parking now, but the oldest and smallest track on the schedule still provides tight, exciting racing.

Martinsville is essentially a one-lane track, at least toward the beginning of a race. The goal of every driver on the opening lap is to stay at the bottom, if already there, or to get there if he started on the outside. When cars slide or are bumped out of that bottom groove, they don't just lose one spot but ten or twenty as the whole field conga-lines by to the inside. As a result, the racing at Martinsville is tight and close and usually involves contact. Few cars leave a 500-lapper there without some sheet-metal damage. The track is relatively narrow, so a minor incident can quickly block the whole track and involve many cars.

ABOVE: Look at that face—is he a coal miner or racecar driver? Clearly, dirt-track racing in the 1940s put the driver intimately "in touch" with the track. Red Byron, a decorated WWII veteran and a familiar face on the stock car scene in the '40s (not to mention NASCAR's first champion), is seen here in '47 after (it seems) the first race at Martinsville, a Modified series event. Byron, for one, knew how to maintain a good relationship with the dirt tracks of the day. OPPOSITE: Always a short track, Martinsville was built with pit stalls and pit roads along both its front- and backstretches. Pitting on the backstretch posed a significant disadvantage to the teams relegated there. In 1999, the front-stretch pit road was extended into the turns to allow all teams to pit there. Here, Dale Earnhardt's number 3 crew goes to work during the '99 Goody's Body Pain 500 near the head of the new pit road.

Earles opened the dirt track, then measured at 0.500 mile (0.8km), in 1947 and hosted the Modified tour. The first race was won by the ubiquitous Red Byron, driving a Raymond Parks Ford. In an early show of multicar team strength, Byron's teammate, Bob Flock—also driving for Parks—took second place. Parks and Byron repeated their success in the first Strictly Stock race at the track in September '49. He sewed up the championship with the win, taking the lead for good from Fonty Flock when Flock's Buick lost a wheel.

Over the years, Earles went to great efforts to make Martinsville a quality racing venue. The track was paved in 1955, and the next year the two Grand National races (the second event was added in '50) were extended to 500 laps. Since then, countless chapters of NASCAR history have been written at Martinsville (far too many to recount here), a couple of which are included below.

The 1987 Goody's 500

Richard Petty is the king at Martinsville, as else-where, with fifteen victories at the track between 1960 and '79. Darrell Waltrip, who is second to Petty with eleven wins, earned one of them in a memorable last lap move in the September 27, 1987, race.

Waltrip was in his first season with owner Rick Hendrick and had yet to see victory lane. He started the September Goody's 500 halfway back in the field, well behind pole-sitter Geoff Bodine. Bodine had won Martinsville races in both the Modified and Busch Grand National series and had earned his first Winston Cup win (with Rick Hendrick) at the track in 1984. Bodine set a new track record for qualifying speed in the '87 race and jumped out to an early lead. He stayed at the front for seventy-one laps, but was then caught up in an accident among the lapped cars of Bobby Hillin, Jimmy Means, and Richard Petty.

As the race wound down, only Waltrip, who had steadily moved up over the laps, Dale Earnhardt, and Terry Labonte were still on the lead lap, with Dale's number 3 Chevy in the lead. A caution flag came out with only six laps left, and the three contenders lined up for a shootout when the race resumed with three laps to go.

On the last lap, Labonte tried a daring pass outside of Earnhardt but scraped the wall and careened down the back-stretch. Waltrip saw an opportunity to slide under the number 11 car going into turn three, but tagged Labonte's back end, sending him up into Earnhardt. As Terry and Dale slid up the track trying to regain control, Waltrip slipped under them both and scooted out of turn four to the checkered flag. Earnhardt recovered quickly and followed him for second, but Labonte was nailed by Bobby Allison as the pack came around for the flag. While Waltrip drove to the winner's circle, the number 11 and number 3 teams stormed to the NASCAR trailer to protest, but to no avail.

PAGES 32–33: The view from high in the stands of the April 9, 2000, race at Martinsville. The track is considerably more developed than it was in the late '60s (compare with photo on page 29), but it retains the welcoming feel it has had since its dirt-track days. ABOVE: The Skoal Bandit crew pulls away damaged sheet metal after a crash in the 1991 Goody's 500 at Martinsville threatened the team's chances at their fourth consecutive win that season. They pulled the metal off, keeping the number 33 on the lead lap and in position to challenge for the win. The crumpled quarter panel may actually have helped, opening up more airflow to cool the brakes (a critical consideration at a small track).

"Bridesmaid" Harry Finally Gets the Girl

Harry Gant was one of a few top NASCAR drivers who earned his first win at Martinsville. In 1981, Gant hooked up with celebrities Burt Reynolds and Hal Needham as driver of the Skoal Bandit number 33 team and ripped off a string of second-place finishes.

"Bridesmaid" Harry started in the April 1982 Virginia National Bank 500 with ten runner-up finishes behind him but no wins. Terry Labonte, Darrell Waltrip, and Sportsman series star Butch Lindley took turns at the point through the race. Meanwhile, Gant remained in the hunt even though he was driving a damaged car (the result of a fender-bender earlier on in the event). Labonte's engine expired and Waltrip spun out, leaving the battle to the finish to Gant and Lindley. It turned into a contest for gas mileage as the drivers tried to stretch their fuel over the final 180 laps. In the end, Lindley ran dry and Gant made it to the end, taking his first Winston Cup win.

The 1991 Goody's 500

Harry Gant was at the center of another very special moment at Martinsville, this time on September 22, 1991. Beginning with the Southern 500 several weeks earlier, Gant had won everything in sight through the month of September, both in the Winston Cup and Busch series. Going into the Goody's 500, the fifty-one-year-old had set the record as the oldest NASCAR winner and was aiming to tie the modern-era (post-1972) record of four consecutive wins. The funny thing was that everyone, even the other drivers, was rooting for him. As Dale Earnhardt said, "He's given us all a new lease on our careers." Pre-race coverage by ESPN featured old-timers Ned Jarrett and Benny Parsons begging Gant for a turn in his four-wheel fountain of youth.

Though Gant started the race in twelfth place, the number 33 team was unconcerned. Gant's previous two wins had come from starting spots of tenth and thirteenth and the driver was famous for coming up from mid-pack to challenge late in the race. He repeated that pattern again at the ½-mile track. The green and white Skoal Bandit car was visibly faster through the turns than any other team, and moved up steadily through the field to take the lead by lap 196. Gant stayed in the lead for most of the next 200 laps. The only serious challenge came from Rusty Wallace, and that challenge ended badly. Wallace tried to cut under Gant going into turn three and nudged him, sending them both spinning into the wall. The normally even-tempered Gant later admitted he was "mad as a bull" for the first few laps after the wreck, though he didn't think Wallace had intentionally spun him.

Andy Petree and the number 33 crew managed to keep the Taylorsville, North Carolina, veteran on the lead lap but Gant restarted the race back in twelfth—last in line. It didn't look promising for the damaged Olds, and broadcaster Benny Parsons lamented that there seemed to be no way Harry would win his fourth straight. Gant hadn't made that concession, though. The fans at the track and at home stayed on their feet from that point on as Gant moved up the line, steadily picking off the eleven cars ahead of him. Shepherd, Schrader, Rudd, Wallace, Irvan, and Earnhardt all receded into the rearview mirror before Gant finally took the lead from a hopeful Brett Bodine on lap 454 and then went on to his fourth win in a row. Not bad for a grandpap.

The next week at North Wilkesboro it looked as though "Mr. September" would set a modern-era record with five in a row. Gant dominated the race from the pole until a 10-cent part broke, rendering the car brakeless with only a few laps left. The hobbled car fell victim to Earnhardt, stalking the lead in the number 3 car, and the magic streak was over. The four wins were enough to move Gant from twelfth to fourth place in the points chase, his best finish in many years.

Other Thrillers at Martinsville

Martinsville played a role in another winning streak in 1998 when Ricky Rudd, trying to extend his string of consecutive winning seasons to sixteen, showed the world just how much of an athlete a race car driver has to be. Rudd had not fared well so far that year but had a strong car going into the September NAPA Automotive 500. Rudd shared the lead through the race with Ernie Irvan, Sterling Marlin, and Jeff Burton, but hung on to the point from lap 405 forward to take the win. What made it a special performance was that the cooling system in Rudd's car had malfunctioned early in the race, and with temperatures at the track exceeding 90 degrees Fahrenheit (32°C), the Virginia native was literally baking in the cockpit. Despite heat exhaustion and dehydration, he hung in there to earn a well-deserved win by half a second over a charging Jeff Gordon.

There have been many exciting races at Martinsville, but the most spectacular, according to Mr. Earles himself, happened in 1981 at the finish of a race that wasn't even a Winston Cup race. Ritchie Evans and Geoff Bodine were battling on the last lap of a Modified race at the track and tangled coming off turn four. Evans' number 61 rode up over Bodine's car and onto the outside retaining wall. The car was nearly on its side, with the right-side wheels on the top of the wall, but Evans never let up on the throttle and drove it along the fence toward the finish line. Just before the flagstand, the car dropped down to the track, and Evans spun across the line with only three wheels left on the car.

Dave Marcis (number 71) leads Richard Petty and James Hylton on the way to his first Winston Cup win in the Old Dominion 500 at Martinsville. "We had the breaks and the brakes," said Marcis of his win. His closest competitor, Benny Parsons, slowed near the end of the race as his brakes faded due to heavy usage.

LOCATION: *North Wilkesboro, North Carolina*
RACE LENGTH: *100–200 miles (160–320km) on a ½-mile dirt oval (paved in 1957)*
NUMBER OF RACES RUN: *Ninety-three Strictly Stock, Grand National, and Winston Cup, between October 16, 1949, and September 29, 1996*
SPEED RECORD (AVERAGE FOR AN ENTIRE RACE): *107.360 mph (171.8kph), on October 5, 1992*

When Enoch Staley built a speedway in the backwoods of North Carolina, he told the bulldozer operator to level the property "from this rock down to that tree." Well, the 'dozer driver didn't quite get the job done, and North Wilkesboro Speedway became the only track on the circuit with a slant: a downhill front straight and an uphill back straight.

North Wilkesboro was built in 1947 and was a very popular dirt track in the 1940s and '50s. The 0.625-mile (1km) circuit hosted six races in NASCAR's '48 Modified series schedule and the last race of the year in '49's Strictly Stock season. The early races at the track were 100 to 125 miles (160–200km), but in 1957 the surface was paved and shortly after the race length was extended to 400 laps, or 250 miles (400km). The track was a regular stop in the Grand National and Winston Cup circuits until it closed in 1996.

Bob Flock won the battle in that first stock race in 1949, taking the checkered flag, but Red Byron won the championship war by edging out Lee Petty that day. Bob Flock's win was one of four for the Flock family at the track (two

for Fonty and one each for the other two brothers). The 1950 race was won by Leon Sales (driving for Hugh Westmoreland), Sales' first NASCAR win, unusual because it came in his very first NASCAR start.

Richard Petty holds the record at the track with a total of fifteen wins. His first came in the 1962 Gwyn Staley 400. A bit of added excitement occurred during the race when fuel trucks ran out of gasoline halfway through the race. A caution flag was raised to allow a tanker to go for more fuel, but it never made it back to the track. Crews scurried around the infield siphoning gas from passenger cars and track vehicles to finish the race. In 1967, North Wilkesboro was the site of Richard Petty's seventy-fifth win; the October win was also his tenth straight, a record that may never be broken.

NASCAR stalwart Junior Johnson had a special fondness for Wilkesboro, his home track, and his teams had a lot of success there over the years. Driving Junior Johnson's number 26, Darel Dieringer won just one race at the track, but did so in dominating fashion—Dieringer led every one of the 400 laps of the April 1967 event. Johnson, a native of nearby Ronda, North Carolina, was honored in 1976 when a grandstand at the track was named for him; to put an exclamation point on the day's events, another of Johnson's drivers, Cale Yarborough, won the race by more than a lap over Richard Petty (despite a plastic banner that blew in from the infield and covered his grille, necessitating a last-minute pit stop). After the win, Johnson christened his new grandstand with a bottle of "Wilkes County Champagne," a.k.a. moonshine.

The short-track style of racing at North Wilkesboro was never more evident than in the 1991 First Union 400. The race was a doozy and saw a total of seventeen caution flags. Partway through the event, NASCAR parked driver Geoff Bodine in the wake of several incidents involving him and Davey Allison. Dale Jarrett summed up the racers' frustrations: "People don't pass you anymore, they just knock you out of the way." Winston Cup director Dick Beatty was kept busy all day long handing out warnings to the line of drivers and crew chiefs outside his trailer. Darrell Waltrip survived to finally win the race.

Despite pressure through the 1990s to add race dates at new, larger facilities at the expense of the short tracks, NASCAR stayed true to its old friends and North Wilkesboro remained on the schedule—at least until 1997. The co-owning Staley and Combs families sold their shares of the track to Bob Bahre and O. Bruton Smith, who reassigned the North Wilkesboro races to their other tracks, New Hampshire and Texas. The fall 1996 race, won by Jeff Gordon, was the last at the track, which closed permanently in '97.

A recent poll of NASCAR fans asked which track should get the next new date on the schedule. What do you think—Homestead, Texas, Kansas City? No, in a tribute to the old short track's popularity, 37 percent of those polled voted for North Wilkesboro.

Darel Dieringer, with trophy and beauty queen, after his Gwyn Staley 400 win in 1967. Dieringer drove Junior Johnson's number 26 Ford from green flag to checkered flag, leading every lap along the way, despite caution flags that bunched the field six times during the event. The North Wilkesboro win was Dieringer's only one with Johnson and the last of his career.

TOP: Jim Paschal romps over the field in the 1966 Gwyn Staley Memorial at North Wilkesboro Speedway, beating second-place finisher G.C. Spencer by six laps. BOTTOM: The Rainbow Warriors perform flawlessly in the last pit stop of the 1996 Tyson Holly Farms 400 at North Wilkesboro. It was the last Winston Cup race run at the track that year, and solid pit stops helped Jeff Gordon add his name to the list of winners at the old raceway.

Short Tracks and Bullrings

W ith the wealth of data available from fifty-one years of NASCAR racing, you could fill whole chapters just with speedway records. Instead, this sidebar hits some of the high (or low) points. Note: The records listed here refer only to races run in the premier NASCAR series.

Long & Short

LONGEST TRACK: Daytona Beach and Road course—4.17 miles (6.7km)

SHORTEST TRACK: The Islip Speedway—0.2 miles (0.3km)

HIGHEST BANKING: Bristol Motor Speedway—36 degrees in the turns (since 1969)

LONGEST RACE (DISTANCE): The World/Coca-Cola 600 at Charlotte (1960 to present)

SHORTEST RACE (DISTANCE): 100-lap race at the ¼-mile (0.4km) Buffalo Civic Stadium (July 19, 1958)

LONGEST RACE (TIME): 1952 Southern 500 at Darlington—6 hours, 42 minutes

LONGEST SEASON: 1956—from November 13, 1955, to November 18, 1956

SHORTEST SEASON: 1949—from June 19, 1949, to October 16, 1949

Fast & Slow

FASTEST QUALIFYING LAP: 212.809 mph (340.5kph)—by Bill Elliott in the 1987 Winston 500

FASTEST RACE (AVERAGE FOR AN ENTIRE RACE): 186.288 mph (298.1kph)—1985 Winston 500 at Talladega, May 5, 1985

SLOWEST RACE (AVERAGE FOR AN ENTIRE RACE): 35.398 mph (56.6kph)—100-mile (160km) race at Wilson Speedway, North Carolina, September 28, 1952

SLOWEST TOP SPEED AT A TRACK HOSTING MORE THAN ONE RACE: 49.308 mph (78.9kph)—Canfield Fairgrounds, Ohio

Most & Least

RACE WITH THE MOST CAUTIONS: Valleydale Meats 500 at Bristol Motor Speedway—20 yellow flags, April 9, 1989; Food City 500 at Bristol Motor Speedway—20 yellow flags, April 13, 1997

MOST CARS IN A RACE: 82—1951 Southern 500 at Darlington Raceway, September 3, 1951

FEWEST CARS STARTING A RACE: 12, at multiple races at Rambi Racetrack, Richmond, Nashville, Hickory, and Savannah Raceways

The longest NASCAR track ever, the Daytona Beach and Road Course. In this view, Paul Goldsmith keeps his number 3 Smokey Yunick Pontiac two car-lengths ahead of a charging Curtis Turner as they slide through the north turn in the last lap of the 1958 race (the last ever on that course configuration).

RACE WITH MOST LEAD CHANGES: 1984 Winston 500 at Talladega, May 6, 1984—75 lead changes in 188 laps

TRACK HOSTING THE MOST RACES (THROUGH 1999): Daytona International Raceway—105

MOST RACES IN A SEASON: 62–1964

LEAST RACES IN A SEASON: 8–1949

MOST WINS AT A TRACK BY A DRIVER: 15–Richard Petty, at both Richmond and North Wilkesboro

MOST CONSECUTIVE WINS AT A TRACK: 7–Richard Petty, at Richmond (1970–1973); 7–Darrell Waltrip, at Bristol (1981–1984)

MOST DISTANT TRACK: Suzuka and Motegi Courses, Japan (non-points)

Young & Old

OLDEST TRACK ON NASCAR CIRCUIT: Martinsville Speedway (since inaugural 1949 season)

NEWEST TRACK ON NASCAR CIRCUIT: Miami-Homestead (since 1999)

OLDEST WINNING DRIVER: Harry Gant—52 years, 219 days (1992 Champion Spark Plug 400 at Michigan, August 16, 1992)

YOUNGEST WINNING DRIVER: Donald Thomas—20 years, 120 days (1952 100-mile race at Lakewood Speedway, Georgia, November 16, 1952)

Number of NASCAR Tracks by State (and Canada)

North Carolina, 27	Nevada, 2
California, 15	Arkansas, 1
New York, 15	Connecticut, 1
Georgia, 12	Delaware, 1
Pennsylvania, 10	Iowa, 1
South Carolina, 10	Kentucky, 1
Virginia, 9	Louisiana, 1
Florida, 8	Maine, 1
Alabama, 7	Maryland, 1
Tennessee, 6	Massachusetts, 1
New Jersey, 5	Nebraska, 1
Ohio, 5	New Hampshire, 1
Michigan, 4	Oklahoma, 1
Arizona, 3	Oregon, 1
Indiana, 3	South Dakota, 1
Texas, 3	Washington, 1
Canada, 2	West Virginia, 1
Illinois, 2	Wisconsin, 1

States that never hosted NASCAR: New Mexico, Utah, Colorado, Missouri, Mississippi, Montana, Rhode Island, Vermont, Minnesota, North Dakota, Kansas, Alaska, Hawaii, Wyoming, Idaho

TOP: The 2000 season was Darrell Waltrip's last behind the wheel of a Winston Cup car. During his twenty-nine-year career, he earned eighty-four wins (fourth on the all-time win list) and three championships. Waltrip remains in racing, though, having become a television announcer beginning in 2001. ABOVE: Davey Allison, son of ace racer Bobby Allison, was one of the few rookies to win a race in his first season. Allison won two (at Talladega and Dover) in 1987 on his way to Rookie of the Year honors. The talented driver then lost his life in a helicopter crash in 1993.

Robert "Junior" Johnson, a determined and shrewd racecar driver and one of the best ever in NASCAR history, was dubbed the "Last American Hero" by writer Tom Wolfe. Johnson usually ran a full-throttle style, but with uncharacteristic restraint he managed to miss all eight of the crashes in this 100-mile (160km) race at Columbia Speedway in 1958 and went on to win by eight laps. It was one of his six wins that year.

COLUMBIA SPEEDWAY

Location: *Columbia, South Carolina*
Race length: *100 miles (160km) on a ½-mile dirt oval (paved in 1971)*
Number of races run: *Forty-three Grand National, between June 16, 1951, and August 27, 1971*
Speed record (average for an entire race): *76.514 mph (122.4kph), set on April 7, 1971*

Like so many of the bullrings of the 1950s, the ½-mile dirt track in Columbia, South Carolina, was a rough track to handle—one slip and you were immediately out of shape. But tough old drums like Ralph Earnhardt earned their living plying their skills on tracks like this one.

The track opened in 1932, but the first Grand National race didn't take place there until 1951. Frank Mundy won his first NASCAR race that day in a Studebaker, which was the first time in victory lane for the car manufacturer, too.

Buck Baker earned his first Grand National win at Columbia as well, in 1952. The race was halted at one point for a caution involving E.C. Ramsey's Ford and a spectator's car. The witless fan had attempted to drive his automobile across the track while the race was in progress. After the

collision, the infuriated Ramsey climbed out of his car and proceeded to beat the daylights out of the fan, until the police settled Ramsey down and hauled away the interfering would-be contestant.

Later, as a result of Gober Sosebee's crash in the March 1955 race, there was no official time record and a somewhat questionable final rundown. Gober's car was one of four involved in a crash that sent his number 51 Olds into the scoring stand and wiping out the timing equipment.

Junior Johnson showed uncharacteristic patience and care in avoiding the eight crashes in the June 1958 race to take the victory by a margin of eight laps. What's perhaps most impressive about that is that he first took the lead with only forty-four laps remaining.

Ned Jarrett had three victories at Columbia, including a come-from-behind win in 1964. He could have had four wins there if his car hadn't run out of gas in 1961 with only four laps left in the race, despite a pit stop not long before. Jarrett vowed that there would be someone pouring gas in his car on every pit top from then on—whether he needed it or not.

In 1966, Curtis Turner was on a comeback (after the ban from NASCAR for his involvement with the Teamsters Union was lifted—see "Asheville-Weaverville Speedway"), driving for Junior Johnson. Turner, who had a reputation for being a partygoer and carouser, wore a three-piece suit to drive the number 26 in the August event. Turner said that team sponsor Holly Farms "...wanted me to be a gentleman driver and I figured this was the first step. You gotta look good, you know!"

Neil "Soapy" Castles used his quarter panel to express his political views in one of the final races at the track, in 1971. His car was painted with the words "The free Lt. Calley Special" in reference to military trials underway following the My Lai Massacre in the Vietnam War.

The Columbia track was paved in 1971 for the final two races, but fell victim to the shortening of the Grand National schedule in 1972. The track closed in 1977.

As a last note, Columbia was also the site of Richard Petty's very first auto race, in 1958 in the Convertible division. He finished a respectable sixth in a field that included Fireball Roberts and Joe Weatherly, despite being hit in the head by an airborne piece of wood when another car crashed through the fence. Petty went on to take the track record with seven Grand National wins there.

for membership in the Federation of Professional Athletes." Upon hearing of this challenge, NASCAR president Bill France declared, "We'll fight this union to the hilt." Reports were that the Teamsters would appear at Weaverville to back the unionization plans, and that there would be more than race-car fenders banging that day.

The expected pyrotechnics never occurred. The Teamsters, Turner, and Flock didn't make an appearance at the track, so the race was able to proceed without incident, at least at the start. As it turned out, the condition of the track itself made the race exciting enough. The race was scheduled as a 500-lap event, but not long after the start the surface of the track began to disintegrate. On lap 208 the race was red-flagged to clean up after a crash involving Bunk Moore's number 58 car (surprisingly the first caution of the day). NASCAR officials took the opportunity to assess the situation. As track workers filled the holes around the track with loose debris and chunks of pavement, NASCAR's executive manager Pat Purcell told drivers that the race would be

ASHEVILLE-WEAVERVILLE SPEEDWAY

LOCATION: *Weaverville, North Carolina*
RACE LENGTH: *100–250 miles (160–400km) on a ½-mile (0.8km) dirt oval (paved in 1958)*
NUMBER OF RACES RUN: *Thirty-four Grand National, between July 29, 1951, and August 24, 1969*
SPEED RECORD (AVERAGE FOR AN ENTIRE RACE): *83.360 mph (133.4km), set on March 5, 1967*

The ½-mile track at Weaverville, North Carolina, was a banked dirt track that was billed as the "fastest half-mile in the country." No doubt the pace looked pretty fast to the occupant of Herb Thomas' car there in July 1954: promoter and former driver Joe Littlejohn had a passenger seat installed in the car and rode around with Thomas on the qualifying laps. Weight distribution was much less of a factor back then and the duo took the pole for the race.

The 1961 Western North Carolina 500

Asheville-Weaverville had perhaps its biggest crowd ever on August 13, 1961, when more than 10,000 spectators showed up for the 500-lap race. Unfortunately, they'd come not just for the race, but also for the expected fireworks—between NASCAR and the Teamsters Union. Earlier that month driver Curtis Turner had approached the Teamsters Union with a deal to obtain financing for the Charlotte Motor Speedway he was building with Bruton Smith. The deal was that Turner and fellow driver Tim Flock would help the union organize NASCAR drivers in return for financial help. On August 8, Turner released a news bulletin that said: "A majority of the drivers on the Grand National Circuit have signed applications and paid initiation dues of $10

Bobby Isaac swept the 1969 races at the Asheville-Weaverville Speedway, the last two NASCAR events ever held at the track. Isaac had hooked up full-time with the Nord Krauskopf number 71 team that year, during the course of which the combo picked up an amazing seventeen wins. They scored eleven more the following year, along with the Winston Cup championship.

shortened and there would be a 50-lap dash after the green flag to finish it. That would take the race to 258 laps, just past the halfway point, and make it official.

The teams raced the final segment, competing against the obstacles on the track as much as with each other, and Junior Johnson came out on top, three laps ahead of second-place finisher Joe Weatherly. The race was red-flagged at lap 258 and would not resume. But the fun didn't end there. Nearly 4,000 spectators, many of whom had perhaps come more for the anticipated confrontation than for the racing, remained after the race and began to protest the shortening of the event. The situation quickly got out of hand. One of the fans parked across the entrance to the infield, preventing the race teams from leaving. "I paid five bucks to see a 500-lap race. Somebody owes me some laps or some money," hollered one of the belligerents.

The teams were pretty much on their own. The NASCAR officials had left the track before the ruckus started. Several of the trapped infield occupants tried to reason with the crowd—more a mob by this point—but were thrown over a fence into a nearby pond. Neither the local sheriff's office nor the state highway patrol was able to bring the crowd under control.

As evening fell, the confrontation came to a head. Six-foot-six (2m) Pops Eargle, one of the crewmembers on Bud Moore's number 8 team, took charge of the "negotiations" when one of the mob leaders poked at him with a stick of lumber. Pops grabbed the stick and smacked the fan across the head. Sensing a change in the initiative, the crowd

dispersed, and the team members were eventually able to leave. Unfortunately, the stamina and skill of the drivers in dealing with a treacherous track were overshadowed by the ugly postrace events. The battle between NASCAR and the Teamsters never materialized, either at Asheville-Weaverville or any other venue.

Hot Races at Asheville-Weaverville

Ned Jarrett blazed past the competition in the February 1965 race, while a fire broke out in the brush lining the speedway along the backstretch. Spectators fought the flames until a caution came out halfway through the race. When it appeared the fire was under control, the green flag flew again. The speeding cars actually fanned the flames, though, spreading the conflagration all along the back straight. Fans and track workers managed to extinguish the fire by the time the race concluded.

During the 1967 race at Asheville-Weaverville, Bobby Allison and Richard Petty fanned the flames of their rivalry. The close competition between the drivers resulted in twenty-two lead changes through the 500 lap event, with Allison making the one that counted. Only four other cars out of the thirty-car lineup finished the race.

One of the most amazing performances on a short track was Bobby Isaac's come-from-behind win in the August 1969 race. And we're not talking coming from a lap down to win—Isaac had fallen five laps off the pace when his car ran out of gas on lap 324 of the 500-lapper. It only took him sixty laps to get back to the front, and he never let up.

Many of the small tracks that characterized NASCAR's early years remained essentially unchanged (i.e., unimproved) as the series moved into its second decade, dooming them. Asheville-Weaverville's ½-mile (0.8km) dirt track (shown here in 1959) was one such track, falling victim to changing times when it was dropped from the Grand National schedule in 1971.

Short Tracks and Bullrings

RICHMOND INTERNATIONAL RACEWAY

LOCATION: *Richmond, Virginia*

RACE LENGTH: *Various lengths on a ½-mile (0.8km) (lengthened to ¾-mile [1.2km] in 1988) dirt oval (paved in 1968)*

NUMBER OF RACES RUN: *Eighty-nine Grand National and Winston Cup, between April 19, 1953, and September 9, 2000*

SPEED RECORD (AVERAGE FOR AN ENTIRE RACE): *109.047 mph (174.5kph), set on September 6, 1997*

When Paul Sawyer invested his savings in stock car racing in the mid-1940s, he couldn't have imagined where it would lead him. His buddy Joe Weatherly lured him into the race-promotion business, and Sawyer soon found himself running the Wilson Speedway in North Carolina and the Strawberry Hill Speedway at the Virginia State Fairgrounds in Richmond. Weatherly went on to concentrate on driving, and Sawyer decided to focus his efforts on the Richmond facility.

The Virginia Fairgrounds track had pretty humble beginnings as a rough ½-mile (0.8m) clay bullring. Sawyer had a golden rule that he worked by—dedication to the race fan—and he has lived by that rule through the years, improving the facility to turn it into the premier raceway it is today.

Things haven't always been smooth, though—especially the track surface. For the first Grand National race in 1953, the track conditions were so poor that the pole qualifying speed was less than 50 mph (80kph). Tim and Fonty Flock held off going out to qualify until later in the day, expecting track workers to make improvements. By the time they realized things weren't going to get any better, they were told they were too late to qualify and would have to start at the back of the field. Instead, they packed up and left.

Rain has played a big part in many events at Richmond. When the qualifying round for the April 1962 race was rained out, competitors drew lots to determine starting positions. Herman "the Turtle" Beam drew the pole position, but on the pace laps, he pulled to the inside and allowed the field to move past him for the actual start of the race. When questioned later about this unusual strategy, he said he "didn't like being up front with all of those hot dogs!" Some races, such as the March '64 Richmond 250, were split over two days when rain intervened. Dave Marcis earned his favorite win, by his account, at the track in '82 due to rain. Fans today often see Dave stay on the track an extra lap when a caution flag comes out in order to lead a lap and gain valuable bonus points (and sponsor exposure). That tactic paid off in the February '82 Richmond 400. When leader Joe Ruttman spun on lap 245, all of the lead-lap drivers pitted—except Marcis. The rain started and the race was

Paul Sawyer, seen here in 1965, first dipped his toes into the racing waters as a car owner, buying two stock cars with savings from his stint in the U.S. Army. His career grew from there, and the Richmond speedway that he built and operated has grown and prospered since its 1946 opening.

called five laps later, with Marcis notching the last win of his career (at this writing).

The track was lengthened several times over the years, but the most drastic improvements came in 1968, when the surface was paved, and in 1988, when the track was completely reconfigured. Gone was the fairground ½-mile, replaced by the smallest "superspeedway" on the circuit—a ¾-mile D-shaped gem. Davey Allison continued the Alabama Gang's history of strong finishes at Richmond by winning the first event on the new configuration. Lights were added in 1991, and Harry Gant earned number two in his streak of four-in-a-row by passing Davey Allison with a handful of laps left to win the first night race held there.

Though the facility has changed greatly, racing at Richmond still has much of the character it's had since the early days. Terry Labonte reminded everyone of that by taking the lead from Dale Jarrett late in the 1998 Pontiac Excitement 400 in old-fashioned, short-track style. With only two laps to go after a restart, Labonte ducked low under Jarrett in turn three, slid his Kellogg's Chevy up the track, and slapped sheet metal with the number 88, nudging that car out of the groove. As the two battled for the lead, another car

In the early 1970s, teams with corporate sponsorship had a tremendous advantage. Bobby Allison, with Coca-Cola backing, was able to write his own ticket and enjoyed solid seasons with Junior Johnson and Roger Penske, and later with his own operation, through the first half of the decade. Solid work from Bill Hamner, the number 12's new crew chief, kept Allison up front in this February '74 Richmond race, while a pit miscue took competitor Richard Petty out of the chase.

crashed along the front-stretch, bringing out the race-ending yellow flag. Labonte had a car-length on Jarrett at the line, and got the win.

The 1972 Capital City 500

Richard Petty and Bobby Allison traded paint on many occasions on the short tracks of the Grand National schedule, including the Fairgrounds oval. Indeed, the most spectacular of Petty's wins at Richmond happened on September 10, 1972, at the Capital City 500 after just such a duel.

Allison was at the top of his game that year, with eight wins already going into the fall race. He looked strong again as he put his red and gold Coca-Cola machine on the pole for the 500-lapper. Bobby held the lead for the first forty laps, but then the real show started. Petty made a pass and hung on for twenty laps, then Allison, then Petty, again and again. The two swapped the lead eighteen times during the course of the race. David Pearson and Buddy Baker were the only others to get a sniff of clean non-carbureted air, but only for one lap each.

The last pass came on lap 392. Petty used his bumper on Allison coming off the third turn to take the lead, then Allison returned the favor going into turn three, turning the number 43 sideways. Allison backed off to let Petty straighten up, but Buddy Baker, who was running third, couldn't react

in time, collected Petty, and sent his car sliding up on top of the outside guardrail. "I figured whoever was running fourth was going to win the thing," said Petty, but miraculously, he was able to bring his car back down off the rail, keep it pointed in the right direction, and hang on to the lead. Buddy Baker's number 71 got the worst of the incident and he had to take the K&K Plymouth behind the wall. Allison suffered only minor damage in the exchange, but fell almost a lap behind the STP Charger. Good thing for Petty—he finished the last twenty laps with a tire going flat and needed the cushion to keep the lead and get the win.

Richmond and the Pettys

Richmond has actually been a good track for the entire Petty clan—it's the only track where three generations of racing Pettys have won a race. Lee took the opener in 1953, Richard scored thirteen wins there (the track record), and Kyle earned his first Winston Cup win there in 1986, despite running near the back of the pack with only a couple of laps left in the race. In that race, Darrell Waltrip's spin after contact with Dale Earnhardt gathered up all of the cars on the lead lap except Kyle's. Petty guided his number 42 through the carnage to take the caution flag as the leader. Petty got the victory and Earnhardt a hefty fine. Even Maurice Petty had a turn at the wheel at Richmond. The master mechanic got his first chance to drive the cars he prepared at the track in 1960, finishing a respectable ninth.

Richmond was also the track where Richard won his fifty-fourth race; the spring 1967 victory tied him with his father for the NASCAR record for most wins. Of course, Richard didn't stop there and no one since has come close to touching his record of 200 victories. Petty was so dominant at Richmond that he once won a race there without even being in the starting lineup. The twenty-five-car field for the March '71 race excluded several of the top drivers, including Petty, Bobby Allison, Benny Parsons, and James Hylton. Petty, Parsons, and Hylton had failed inspection, and Allison didn't make it to the track in time to qualify. Being a top name has its perks, though. Owner Paul Sawyer announced a last-minute expansion of the field to include the stray cats. It paid off for Petty, who cut into Bobby Isaac's points lead by winning the race. Fittingly, Richard went on to win that year's championship with a victory in the fall race at Richmond.

Richmond and Everyone Else

Of course, other drivers have made their way from the back of the field to victory circle at Richmond. Bobby Allison blew an engine in practice before the fall 1969 Capitol City 250

TOP: Flagman Harold Kinder was a long-time fixture on the NASCAR scene. Dale Earnhardt, in Bud Moore's number 15 Ford, takes Kinder's wave of the green here in the 1982 Wrangler 400. ABOVE: More so than in any other sport, NASCAR is a family affair. Three generations of Pettys (left to right: Lee, Richard, and Kyle) have been successful in NASCAR's top series. Kyle's son, Adam, carried on the family tradition into a fourth generation, until his life was tragically cut short in a crash early on during the 2000 season.

Richmond Raceway (seen here) was one of the first of today's tracks to add lights and a night race. Lighting a racetrack poses several challenges: the light must be bright, cover the whole track surface without shadows, and mustn't shine in the drivers' faces at any point around the course. Musco Lighting has met these challenges admirably at several tracks, including the 2.5-mile (4km) Daytona speedway.

and didn't get a replacement until just before the green flag, putting him last on the grid. The sub must have been a winner, though—he cut though the competition, then took and held on to the lead, despite twice making contact with LeeRoy Yarbrough on pit road and a late-race charge by Yarbrough that made up four laps on Allison's number 22 Mario Rossi Dodge.

Joe Weatherly's win in the '62 event didn't come until well after the race was over—at the checkered flag, he wasn't even shown in the top ten. A review of the data showed that his scorer had somehow missed twenty-three of his laps. When those were added in, he went from zero to hero.

Other drivers with a winning history at Richmond include David Pearson and Rusty Wallace. Though Pearson is remembered mostly as a superspeedway ace, he enjoyed quite a bit of success at Richmond, with six wins at the track. In typical Silver Fox style, he commented after his March 1968 win (by more than a lap), "I didn't use half the horsepower I had." Wallace has been the dominant driver at Richmond since the reconfiguration in '88, with six wins. Tony Stewart, who was the 1999 Rookie of the Year, converted winning potential into reality, earning the first of his record-setting three trophies that year at Richmond. Stewart dominated the race, leading 333 of the 400 laps in the fall race under the lights.

Change is again underway at the track, even at this writing. In January 2000, it was announced that International Speedway Corporation (ISC) acquired ownership of the Richmond International Speedway from the Sawyer family. Paul Sawyer will remain on as chief operating officer for the facility. A companion press release announced that Richmond would be part of the Winston "No Bull 5" program, with one of its races replacing the Darlington Southern 500, which had been a member of the Winston program since its inception in '85.

BOWMAN-GRAY STADIUM

LOCATION: *Winston-Salem, North Carolina*
RACE LENGTH: *37.5–62.5 miles (60–100km) on a ¼-mile (0.4km) paved oval*
NUMBER OF RACES RUN: *Twenty-nine Grand National, between May 24, 1958, and August 6, 1971*
SPEED RECORD (AVERAGE FOR AN ENTIRE RACE): *51.527 mph (82.4kph), set on August 28, 1970*

This flat ¼-mile track was built around the outside of the Bowman-Gray football field, used by Winston-Salem University. Alvin Hawkins, NASCAR's first flagman, established the paved oval for racing, in partnership with Bill France Sr. in 1949. Despite the diminutive size, the track has survived the years and still hosts Winston racing series events on Saturday nights, under the continued guidance of the Hawkins family.

The configuration of the track was quite unusual. The grandstands—tall concrete structures built in the shape of a horseshoe that extended from halfway down the backstretch to the start/finish line, around turns three and four—encircled half the track. The pits were on the outside of the track, beneath the stands, with the pit entrance on the back straight and the exit at the end of the front stretch, going into turn two. The track itself was a narrow asphalt ring. Lineups for the events there seldom exceeded twenty-five entries—any more and there would be gridlock. The races were also among the shortest (starting at 37.5 miles [60km] and topping out at 62 miles [99.2km]) and slowest (one race averaged only 39 mph [62.4kph]) ever to appear on the NASCAR schedule. As you might expect, there was plenty of exciting racing action in the tight quarters of Bowman-Gray over the years.

The 1966 Myers Brothers Memorial 250

One of the most intense battles ever waged at Bowman-Gray was between Bobby Allison and Curtis Turner in the 1966 "Myers Brothers Memorial." Curtis Turner, always known as a hard-charger, was back in NASCAR after an enforced hiatus following his attempt to unionize drivers. After the loss of some of the sport's biggest stars, Bill France was looking for something to peak fans' interest. At the beginning of the '66 season, he offered a reprieve to Turner, hoping he would bring some excitement back to the track. He got all that and more in the August 27 race at the Winston-Salem ¼-mile track.

It started early in the race when Turner, on his way to the lead, hooked the back bumper of Allison's number 2, spinning him around. It took him a while, but Turner finally grabbed the lead from David Pearson on lap ninety-eight. He was soon challenged by "Tiger" Tom Pistone, with Richard Petty and Pearson just behind. At one point, Pistone tried to get by Turner on the high side; Turner, in the Junior Johnson–owned number 26, juked up to block him. Allison, hoping to get back on the lead lap after the earlier spin, saw

Rex White had a knack for getting around Bowman-Gray's tight corners and holds the track record for wins, with six (1959 to '62). White burned up the Grand National circuit as a whole in the late '50s and early '60s, winning twenty-eight races during that time. In '60, he picked up six wins on the circuit (though not at any of the Bowman-Gray events) on his way to the championship.

an opportunity and dove to the inside of Turner to make it three-wide. There just isn't room for that at Bowman-Gray, and Turner was sent spinning, losing the lead.

After a stay on pit road, Turner returned to the track, but was running well off the pace—clearly lying in wait for Allison to come around. As Allison approached, he saw what was coming and just rear-ended Turner rather than try to pass him. The two commenced a heated exchange of heavy-metal blows, lap after lap, many of them under a subsequent yellow flag. When it got to the point that neither car was fit to run, NASCAR ejected them both from the race. The combatants stopped their cars on the front stretch to "talk things over" and were immediately joined by hundreds of fans pouring down from the stands. The police quickly settled the crowd, booted the two drivers, and let David Pearson recommence his run to the win.

The two headstrong racers seemed to have gotten it all out of their systems and didn't carry the battle beyond the 1/4-mile. Turner competed in twenty-one races in 1966, but then only a handful in '67 and '68 before he left the NASCAR scene for good. The flamboyant lumberman, entrepreneur, and ace racecar driver was killed in '70 when his private plane crashed.

Milestones at Winston-Salem

The races at Bowman-Gray Stadium often featured sports and foreign cars as well as the more typical stock fare, though the International 200 has never been won by any other than the usual cast of stock car models. Those cars were driven by the usual cast, too, whether it was Rex White racking up one of his six wins (the track record) or famed founder of the Wood Brothers team, Glenn Wood, coming out from under the car to climb behind the wheel and take four wins.

Richard Petty passed several milestones in his career at the track, including his first stadium win in 1962. Then the number 43 went to victory lane again in '63, but with Jim Paschal piloting that famous car while Richard drove the number 41. In '67, Petty took his nineteenth win of the year in the August race, breaking Tim Flock's record of eighteen wins in a single season. Just two years later, in the August '69 race, Petty earned his one-hundredth Grand National win, an unprecedented feat in the series at that time.

The 1/4-mile (0.4km) course at Bowman-Gray Stadium is shown here in 1954. The track was first used for auto races in the late '40s, though NASCAR didn't come calling until '58. The facility came ready-made with large stands and lights for night races, but the track was so narrow that the field sizes were severely limited. Despite, or perhaps because of, its idiosyncrasies, the track was popular with fans and still remains open for events today.

LOCATION: *Nashville, Tennessee*

RACE LENGTH: *100 to 250 miles (160–400km) on a ½-mile (0.8km) (rebuilt to 0.675 miles [1.1km] in 1970) paved oval*

NUMBER OF RACES RUN: *Forty-two Grand National and Winston Cup, between August 10, 1958, and July 14, 1984*

SPEED RECORD (AVERAGE FOR AN ENTIRE RACE): *98.419 mph (157.5kph), set on May 12, 1973*

The layout of the Nashville speedway has changed several times over the years. The Fairground Speedway had been built in 1907, originally as a one-mile (1.6km) horse track. In 1958, it was shortened and surfaced for auto racing. NASCAR first visited the track that year, when Joe Weatherly got his first "official" Grand National win (he had finished first twice before but had been stripped of both wins on technical grounds).

Nashville started out as a banked, paved ½-mile, ringed by wooden billboards outside the guardrail. It was a tough track, too—more than one competitor put the front end of his car through those placards over the years. The facility underwent a dramatic change at the end of the 1969 season, when it was extended to ⅝ mile (1km) and the banking was cranked up to an impressive 35 degrees. Drivers hated the new track—the banking and surface were hard on tires and there were lots of wrecks as a result. "Lil" Bud (Paul) Moore summed up the dangerous nature of the track, recalling that when he was introduced to the past track champions, "they were all in wheelchairs." In '73, management reconfigured the facility again, dropping it back down to a safer 18 degrees of banking and again resurfacing it.

Cale Yarborough was a victim of the banking at Nashville in 1963, though in an unexpected way. Tiny Lund had crashed head-on into the billboards, tearing up and setting fire to his number 32 Ford. Lund scrambled out of the car and took off away from it down the track. Lund (who despite his nickname was 6-foot-5 [195.6cm] and 270-plus pounds [122.3kg]) had built up quite a bit of momentum coming down the steep banking and ran smack into the side of Yarborough, pushing in the right side of his Herman Beam–owned Ford. Beam, known as "Turtle" for his slow but steady approach to racing, had been futilely scribbling for Cale (via pit board messaging) to take it "EZ" through most of the race. After the event he chastised the South Carolina driver: "If you would have driven slower he would have missed you!"

Scoring Squabbles

There were lots of confused scorings at the Nashville track over the years, in part due to the unique pit road setup there. Drivers entered pit road in the first turn, ran around an inner

Richard Petty won many races in the sleek Dodge Charger; indeed, if you had to pick the most famous car in NASCAR history, it would probably be this one. Petty was top gun at Nashville Speedway as he took this checkered flag in the 1974 Music City USA 420 (at that point he had won eight of the last ten events there). Interestingly, the race was run over two days—it had been halted due to rain on Saturday night and was resumed, where it had left off, on Sunday afternoon.

oval, and exited in the fourth turn. In 1982, James Hylton gave the scorers another headache with his unique paint scheme for the spring race that year. Hylton's number 48 was one color on the left side, a different color on the right, and two others on the top. NASCAR took the complaints of the scoring staff to heart and advised Hylton that his art experiment was not appreciated.

The biggest scoring hubbub, however, unfolded after the May 1984 race, and had nothing at all to do with pit road or the cars' colors. Neil Bonnett wheeled his number 12 Chevy around race leader Waltrip as a caution flag came out at the very end of the race, and was declared the winner. Well, Waltrip was waiting in victory lane as well, figuring he earned the trophy since Bonnett had passed him under a yellow caution flag. It took NASCAR two days to work out the intricacies of the ruling, but Waltrip was eventually awarded the victory. (Of course, team owner Junior Johnson was okay either way, as Bonnett and Waltrip happened to be teammates.)

TOP: Rookie Joe Millikan (number 72) lines up inside of Buddy Baker (number 26) for his first, and only, Winston Cup pole, in the 1979 Music City 420 at Nashville. Millikan beat stiff competition that season (Earnhardt, Labonte, Gant) for Rookie of the Year honors by claiming fifteen top-ten finishes, but this Nashville race wasn't one of them—the L.G. DeWitt number 72 lost its engine and finished in twenty-third place. ABOVE: Darrell Waltrip, no stranger to the winner's circle, thought he had the perfect name for his first daughter: Victoria Lane. His wife, Stevie, disagreed. Here, Darrell (right) and Stevie Waltrip enjoy a moment together in victory lane after Darrell's 1978 Southeastern 500 win at Bristol.

Driver Cale Yarborough (left) had his first steady ride with Herman Beam (right), though the two men had distinctly different philosophies on racing. "Turtle" Beam focused on taking care of his equipment and staying out of trouble, while Cale was a foot-to-the-floor racer who wasn't shy about making contact. Yarborough spent three seasons with Beam before moving on to greater success elsewhere.

Masters of Nashville

Yarborough was one of the drivers who dominated the track for a period, earning seven victories there. He had another in the bag in 1973 when, during a caution and for no apparent reason, he crashed into the pit wall along the front stretch. "I guess I just forgot what I was doing," he later lamented.

Waltrip was also a regular in the winner's circle at Nashville, his home track from his Sportsman series days. He earned his first Winston Cup win there in 1975, one of eight wins at the speedway. Richard Petty holds the record with nine wins, including a gift in the May '79 race, when he inherited the lead from a dominant Cale Yarborough as the result of a new tire rule. The rule, issued by NASCAR earlier that year and intended to lessen the tire costs borne by the teams, stated that drivers who changed tires under caution flags would be penalized. Yarborough had a tire going down late in the race, and was unable to change it during the last caution, so fell back, letting Petty by for the win.

Independent owner/driver J.D. McDuffie came close to capturing a NASCAR win, and ended up with one of his best finishes ever, at the track in 1979. McDuffie dueled (and spun) with Cale Yarborough near the beginning of the race, then came back to pass Richard Petty for the lead on lap 250. He was forced to pit for tires near the end, though, and ended up in fifth place.

The Now and Future Nashville

Since the events at Nashville were longer than the 250-mile (400km) Winston Cup cutoff, the track survived the schedule changes in 1972, and was part of the series until '84. The raceway property actually is part of the Nashville fairgrounds, and is leased and run by the speedway managers. In '83, Warren Hodgdon—also part-owner of Bristol, Richmond, and North Wilkesboro speedways—gained control of Nashville. Heavily leveraged through his personal business, these acquisitions were hit hard when his financial base dropped out from under him (his engineering firm was accused of bid rigging, and subsequently lost more than $30 million in lawsuits). Allegedly, Hodgdon had tried to use the Nashville events as financial collateral, which would have put NASCAR in a precarious position; as a result, the speedway's Winton Cup dates were dropped altogether in '84.

The last Winston Cup race at Nashville was held in 1984, won by Geoffrey Bodine. The track still sits on the fairgrounds and hosts numerous auto-racing events. NASCAR's Busch Grand National and Craftsman Truck series run there, as do events in the ASA and local racing divisions. Big changes are underway as a brand new facility is being planned for the 2001 season. The 3,100-acre (1,252.4ha) complex will include a 1.3-mile (2.1km) superspeedway as well as a ⅝-mile (1km) short track and drag strip.

BRISTOL MOTOR SPEEDWAY

LOCATION: *Bristol, Tennessee*

RACE LENGTH: *266.5 miles (426.4km)(500 laps) on a 0.533-mile (0.9km) paved oval*

NUMBER OF RACES RUN: *Eighty Grand National and Winston Cup, between July 30, 1961, and August 26, 2000*

SPEED RECORD (AVERAGE FOR AN ENTIRE RACE): *101.074 mph (161.7kph), set on July 11, 1971*

According to Darrell Waltrip's colorful simile, driving a fast car around Bristol Motor Speedway is akin to "flying a jet airplane around inside a gymnasium." Combine a ½-mile oval with the highest banking in NASCAR (36 degrees in the turns, 18 degrees on the straights) and ring it all around with seating for 130,000-plus people, and you have the world's fastest and most treacherous short track. Thunder Valley is a high-speed "bowl" that keeps drivers on the edge of their seats, so to speak, from the drop of the green flag to the drop of the checkered.

The record qualifying speed at Bristol is more than 125 mph (200kph), 30 mph (48kph) faster than at Martinsville, the other ½-mile track on the circuit. At that speed, the G-force on the racers as they dive into the turns is brutal. Because of the steep banking, visibility out the front windshield is limited to the short section of track just in front of the car. On top of that, the track is only forty feet (12.1m) wide and self-scrubbing (that is, steep enough so that slowed or stopped cars roll down to the inside of the track). And with laps in the neighborhood of 15.5 seconds, there's no time for a driver to react to problems on the track.

Speed, action, and not one bad seat in the house—no wonder NASCAR fans love Bristol, perhaps the toughest ticket to find on the circuit. Of course, the racers don't necessarily share the fans' enthusiasm. In fact, championship contenders fear the races there because (as in 1999, for instance, when points leader Dale Jarrett fell victim to someone else's wreck) you have little control over your fate once the race commences. With traffic all the way around the track, drivers at the front of the field are as likely to be caught up in accidents as the back markers.

ABOVE: Neil "Soapy" Castles (number 88) runs along the bottom lane at Bristol in 1964. Fred Lorenzen was on top of his game that year, winning half of the races he ran, including both Bristol events. Bristol was a more forgiving track back then—there were only five cautions over the two races (the average for roughly twenty laps of racing there today). OPPOSITE: Johnny Allen (right) took the checkered flag and Jack Smith got the trophy during this 1961 race at Bristol. The floorboard in Smith's number 48 was perforated, and the heat from the engine burned the veteran driver's foot partway through the race, preventing him from continuing. Allen, who had dropped out earlier, took over in the cockpit at a point when Smith had a three-lap cushion over the second-place car, so the switch was made without losing the lead. It was Allen's first victory, but not his last; he would get one on his own the next year.

Short Tracks and Bullrings

The Road to Bristol

The original site for the speedway, opened in 1961, was not in Bristol. Larry Carrier and Carl Moore had attended a race at the Charlotte Motor Speedway in '60 and were so impressed that they decided to build a speedway of their own in Tennessee. The locale that they and co-founder R.G. Pope selected was in Piney Flats. Unable to convince the locals of the benefits of hosting a motorsports event, however, they moved down the road a few miles and bought a dairy farm in Bristol, where they built an intimate ½-mile paved oval. The original track was more forgiving than it is now: it was sixty feet (18.2m) wide on the straights, seventy-five feet (22.8m) wide in the turns, and banked at 22 degrees.

The first race was the inaugural Volunteer 500, held in July 1961. Forty-one cars fired up behind pole-sitter Fred Lorenzen after seventeen-year-old Brenda Lee finished singing the national anthem. Jack Smith won the race, but had to share the purse with Johnny Allen, who subbed for him in relief partway through the event.

David Pearson, Joe Weatherly, Fred Lorenzen, and Paul Goldsmith were among the drivers who won on the old track. Bristol was one place where Richard Petty did not dominate, scoring only three wins there in his career. Pearson took five trophies from the track, including one that pretty much fell into his lap in 1967. With only nine miles (14.4km) remaining in the Southeastern 500, Pearson's number 6 Dodge was two laps behind leader Dick Hutcherson and one behind second-place Cale Yarborough. On lap 482, the engine in Hutcherson's Ford expired, sending him into the guardrail. As the caution came out, Pearson ducked around Yarborough to get back on the lead lap. Shortly after the green flag waved again, debris cut a tire on the Wood Brothers Ford. Yarborough hung on, running on the inner liner, and kept the lead until lap 494, when Pearson made the pass. Pearson took the win and Cale, who was looking for his second GN win, limped home as runner-up.

Bristol underwent a drastic change in July 1969, when the course was redesigned to its current form. Drivers' reac-

LEFT: In 1984, Junior Johnson brought on Warner Hodgdon as a business partner. Hodgdon had sponsored Neil Bonnett at the number 75 team the previous year, and brought him along to a second Johnson team. Bonnett earned his keep, with three wins from '84 to '86, but Waltrip (seen here in victory lane after the April '78 Bristol race) remained the star of the teams, racking up thirteen wins and a championship during the same period. RIGHT: The first of Dale Earnardt's many wins occurred at this race in Bristol in 1979, his rookie year. He won in only his sixteenth Winston Cup start.

Before the days of concrete retaining walls, the flimsy guardrails around the outside of many tracks served more as a marker for the edge of the racing surface than any real barrier. Cars went over, or through, them with regularity. "Fireball" Roberts (number 22) stayed on the track in this 1963 Volunteer 500 crash, but injured his back as the car tumbled just inside the rail.

tions were pretty unequivocal. "They ruined a good race track," complained Richard Petty. Rookie Dick Brooks summed up many drivers' feelings when he said, "This is a dangerous place and it's going to be rough on equipment." Indeed, only ten out of the thirty-two-car field finished the first race, and no two of the survivors were on the same lap when it was over.

Most races at Bristol see multiple caution flags for accidents (the 1989 Valleydale Meats 500, in an extreme instance, had twenty). As a result, victory often comes to the best car left on the track after the wrecks (as was the case in Terry Labonte's '84 Busch 500 win, which he pulled off in spite of two crashes). Or maybe by the judicious application of a fender to the leader, as in Cale Yarborough's last-lap duel with Buddy Baker in '74. The hard contact between the two prompted Junior Johnson, Yarborough's car owner, to reminisce, "This is what it used to be like when I was driving."

The toughness of the track seems to bring out the scrappiness in racers. Dale Earnhardt found himself at the center

of controversy in 1999 when he gave Terry Labonte a last-lap tap that sent Labonte into the wall, while the number 3 went on to the win. Earnhardt protested that he didn't mean to spin Labonte (who, to be fair, had given the Goodwrench Chevy a nudge a few laps earlier)—he just wanted to "rattle his cage." Not long afterwards, Labonte invited Dale to go hunting with him....

The 1990 Valleydale Meats 500

Tempers often flare when the stress of driving 500 circuits climaxes in a crunched racecar, and there was plenty of opportunity for that during the April 8, 1990, Valleydale race. Ernie Irvan and Geoffrey Bodine, the first two of ten leaders that day, were on the front row for the start. But they were both caught up in crashes (there were twelve caution periods that day) and dropped out of contention. Sterling Marlin, Dave Marcis, and Darrell Waltrip all took turns running in front, but in the late stages of the race, Davey Allison was the man to beat.

Through the first half of NASCAR's history, the Grand National circuit made use of a host of short tracks throughout the Southeast. Many of those tracks had previously hosted local racing, and some continue to do so fifty years later.

Greenville-Pickens Speedway

Bill France first promoted races at the dirt oval at Greenville, SC, as far back as 1946. Home track to many luminaries through the last several years, the speedway still hosts weekly races today, though it was dropped from the Grand National schedule in '70 with the change to the Winston Cup. The last GN race, in '71, was televised by ABC for its *Wide World of Sports* television show. Past track champs include David Pearson, Ralph Earnhardt, Butch Lindley, and Robert Pressley.

Hickory Speedway

Located in Hickory, NC, this was another ½-mile site that hosted the series, from 1953 through '71. Harry Gant, Bob Pressley, Ralph Earnhardt, Junior Johnson, Jack Ingram—all were champions at the facility before (or in some cases, after) moving up to the premier series. Hickory was paved in '67 and is still open for exciting Saturday night racing as part of the Busch Grand National schedule.

South Boston Speedway

South Boston opened in 1957 as a ¼-mile dirt track. Junior Johnson won the first Grand National race held there, in '60. The series visited SBS, in South Boston, VA, ten times through '71. Benny Parsons earned his first Grand National win in the last GN event held there. Since then, South Boston has continued to thrive as a local racing site and with a date on the NASCAR Busch Grand National circuit.

Savannah Speedway

The first St. Patrick's Day 200 at Savannah, GA, was plagued with problems as the new track surface came apart, reducing driver visibility to zero and requiring a

Brothers Herb and Donald Thomas pace the field in matching Hudson Hornets at the start of the 1954 race at Oglethorpe Speedway in Georgia. Al Keller, starting third, won the event. NASCAR visited the track only once more, the following year, but later returned to the general area in '62, at the Savannah Speedway.

caution to hose down the dust. Black driver Wendell Scott got his only NASCAR pole in the July 1962 race. Several drivers, including Richard Petty, crashed through the fence over the years and ended up in the adjacent mud swamp (reputedly home to a large alligator). LeeRoy Yarbrough got his first GN win at Savannah in May '64 and Bobby Allison won his first dirt-track race there (having won four previous races on asphalt).

Smokey Mountain Raceway

Located at Maryville, TN, this is a tough ½-mile track. Buddy Baker got a taste of that in the June 1968 race. Baker had injured his ribs in a crash and was placed in the ambulance to make a trip to the local hospital. As the ambulance pulled up to the exit gate, Baker's gurney rolled out the back doors and down across the track. The race was under caution, but the cars were speeding around to catch the pace car after pit stops; Baker, strapped to the runaway stretcher, was nearly run over. He made it down to the bottom of the track without being hit, but the gurney flipped end over end in the mud there, with Baker still strapped down. The track is still open today.

Allison came back from a crash with Rob Moroso and overcame the disadvantage of pitting on the backstretch (a particular handicap in a race with so many yellow flags). When the last caution flew on lap 391, the Havoline team decided that track position was more important than new tires and didn't pit. Allison restarted at the front and stayed there, but with old tires he wasn't able to motor away from the competition and beat Mark Martin to the checkered by only eight inches (20.3cm).

Just behind the number 28 and number 6, Marlin and Ricky Rudd were running third and fourth, respectively, going into the last lap. Rudd tapped the number 94 Olds on the final go-round, sending him spinning into the inside wall and dropping him to seventh place while Rudd took third. On the "cool down" lap after the race, an irate Marlin stopped his car on the track and waited for Rudd to come around. Spotting the Sunoco car, Rudd stopped his car a distance behind Sterling, who then started to back up to Rudd. Rudd backed away from him and the two conducted a slow-motion race in reverse until Sterling gave up and took his argument directly to the number 26 trailer.

Into the Present

In 1973, Cale Yarborough proved that drivers do occasionally have a smooth time of it at Bristol. In the '73 Southeastern 500, Cale started on the pole and lead all 500 laps. "I've never had an easier ride," the South Carolinian exclaimed with a smile. His Richard Howard number 11 Chevy was quick enough to lap the entire field within 100 circuits and was unfazed by the seven cautions.

Yarborough had a lock on the track through most of the 1970s, with nine wins in sixteen races, but Darrell Waltrip is the master of the Bristol ½-mile, with a record-setting twelve wins. Through the '80s, he and Dale Earnhardt alternated wins (Dale has eight at the track) or wrecked going for them. Waltrip's '84 Valleydale Meats 500 win was his seventh straight victory at the track (and the eighth in a row for owner Junior Johnson).

Lights were added to the track in 1978, and since then one of the two races each year is run on Saturday night. Bristol was bought by Warren Hodgdon in '83, but returned to the stewardship of Larry Carrier in '85 when Hodgdon filed for bankruptcy. The facility was sold to Bruton Smith in '96 and has since seen a significant investment of capital. The facility's popularity has required repeated additions of grandstands, with seating capacity now exceeding 130,000. Bristol is the largest sports arena (by seating) in Tennessee, and one of the largest in the country. The continued improvements, along with the track's immense popularity with fans, should guarantee BMS a place in NASCAR's Winston Cup schedule for many years to come.

T here was a pretty good gap between the opening of NASCAR's first superspeedway, Darlington, and its next, but once the building trend caught on it became an avalanche.

The series was still in its baby shoes in 1950 and had yet to prove its long-term viability. The opening of Daytona International Speedway in 1959 caught everyone's attention, though, and put NASCAR at the center of every race promoter's focus. Developers soon began investing in NASCAR, and large, expensive facilities for stock car racing popped up one after another over the next decade. Charlotte and Atlanta were built in '60; Rockingham in '65; Talladega, Dover, and Michigan in '69. The Grand National schedule quickly changed complexion as asphalt replaced dirt and race lengths and speeds increased dramatically. Many of these tracks are still on the Winston Cup circuit and host some of the most exciting racing in the world.

To be sure, the bullrings hadn't gone away. The superspeedways usually added two dates apiece to the schedule, but the series continued to visit new or different short tracks as well. In 1964, race teams made sixty-two stops in a season that spanned a full year, with forty-eight of those stops still on short tracks. It wasn't until the start of the modern era, in '72, that the preponderance of races shifted from short tracks to superspeedways.

Though there were still new short tracks being built in the 1960s, most were paved and more and more were longer than ½ mile (0.8km). In 1971, the last new short track was added to the schedule. More telling, it was the superspeedways that were getting the biggest attention and capturing the public's imagination. The image of stock car racing began to change from backwoodsmen racing on Saturday nights to high-profile daredevil speedsters rocketing around high-banked speedways. Auto manufacturers began to see NASCAR as a testing ground for their products, and as the engineering improved, the speeds went up.

A pack of sleek, colorful Impalas, Galaxies, and Belvederes racing in close formation on a high-banked track was an appealing sight to television broadcasters as well as car manufacturers and fans. Racing at Daytona and Talladega was the type of on-the-edge sport that was deemed worthy of coverage on the Sunday specials and news highlights segments. It was this coverage, much more than the fact that the series visited most states to race each year, that broadened NASCAR's exposure and image beyond the Southeast.

Then in 1971 everything changed. The R.J. Reynolds Tobacco Company adopted NASCAR as a medium for advertising its products, and instituted the Winston Cup (named after RJR's

top brand of cigarette). The sponsorship brought immense benefits to the series (as well as the company), but also brought about some drastic changes. RJR wanted to make sure it got the most bang for its buck, and realized that it was the big races that got the most attention and thus had the most advertising potential. Accordingly, they would sponsor only races greater than 250 miles (400km) in length. In '71, the Winston Cup existed as a subset within the overall forty-eight-race Grand National schedule, but in '72 the schedule itself was trimmed so that NASCAR would only run Winston Cup races. The schedule dropped to thirty-one events and has remained in that ballpark ever since. Bowman-Gray, Columbia, Middle Georgia Raceway, Smoky Mountain, and other small tracks disappeared from the premier series, while Martinsville, Richmond, Bristol, North Wilkesboro, and Nashville upped their races to 250 miles and kept short-track racing alive.

The tide had irrevocably turned, though, and NASCAR became more and more associated with superspeedway racing. That's where the big money and prestige was, and teams that ran partial seasons inevitably picked the superspeedway events to run. It's telling that when a driver's wins are listed, the total number is usually followed by "number of wins on a superspeedway," as though those victories are somehow more valuable or difficult to earn.

DARLINGTON RACEWAY

LOCATION: *Darlington, South Carolina*
RACE LENGTH: *Various, on a 1.25-mile (2km)—reconfigured in 1953 to a 1.366-mile (2.2km)—paved oval*
NUMBER OF RACES RUN: *Ninety-five Grand National and Winston Cup, between September 4, 1950, and September 3, 2000*
SPEED RECORD (AVERAGE FOR AN ENTIRE RACE): *139.958 mph (223.9kph), set on March 28, 1993*

Daytona Beach is without question the birthplace of NASCAR, and the bullrings of the Southeast nurtured the sport. But the heart and soul of NASCAR is in the small South Carolina city of Darlington, home to the legendary Darlington Raceway.

Local businessman Harold Brasington was no stranger to auto racing. He'd raced on the beach at Daytona and even finished in the top five there, in 1938. When he visited the Indianapolis Motor Speedway, he was smitten by the grandeur of the Brickyard and carried the idea of building his own version of a big track

PAGES 58–59: The talent of the future. Tony Stewart (car 20) and Dale Earnhardt Jr. (car 8), seen here in the 1999 season finale at Atlanta, are two of the up-and-coming young stars of the sport. PAGE 59: Rusty Wallace is a talented and driven competitor. The 1989 Winston Cup champion has dedicated himself to earning a second title, but despite subsequent seasons with as many as twelve wins, he has yet to find the way to a second championship.

back to the Palmetto State. Between business concerns and WWII, Brasington's dream remained a dream until the end of the '40s. In '49, at their weekly poker game, Brasington made a deal with another Darlington resident, Sherman Ramsey, for about 100 acres (40.5ha) of land. With the locale secured, Brasington sold shares to raise money for construction, jumped up onto the bulldozer himself, and started to build a speedway.

Brasington's engineering was largely seat-of-the-pants, and the track had some interesting characteristics as a result. It was sized to fit the property—1.25 miles (2km) around in its first incarnation. Like Indy, it was paved. Unlike most tracks, though, it was asymmetrical. The track was egg-shaped, with turns three and four broader than turns one and two. This was due to a precondition placed on the builders by Ramsey—that the track not interfere with the minnow pond at one end of the property. To skirt the popular fishing spot, they narrowed one end of the track. The banking at the two ends of the track was different as well. These qualities make Darlington a distinctive racetrack.

The Lady in Black

The toughest spot on the track is just after turn four, at the wide end of the "egg." Instead of sweeping out of the corner to the straightaway, there is a bit more turn there, as the front stretch angles to the left toward the narrower end. Originally, drivers earned their "Darlington stripe" by running right up against the guardrail (and leaving behind a paint sample) in order to get the most momentum going into the front stretch. Nowadays, with a concrete barrier, the stripe has come to denote the nasty surprise the track has in store for careless or inexperienced drivers taking that turn too fast. Many drivers feel this is the trickiest set of turns on the course. Drivers who run well at the track, like Dale Earnhardt, use it to their advantage and are awfully tough to pass there. Otherwise, the afternoon of the race is going to feel like an eternity. (Kyle Petty, not a fan of the track, said he'd like to see them fill the infield with water and turn the whole place into a bass-fishing lake.)

The track is tough on tires, as well as sheet metal and drivers' nerves. The locale is in the sand hills of the Carolinas and the surface of the track is like sandpaper. Tire management is a skill any driver who hopes to win there must learn right away.

All in all, its peculiarities have made Darlington a track that takes skill and experience to drive well. Its nicknames—The Track Too Tough to Tame, The Lady in Black (which initially referred to the black asphalt used on its surface)—reflect the challenges of racing there. Darlington's not the fastest track on the circuit and it sure doesn't have the most state-of-the-art facilities, but more than any other speedway it's a racer's racetrack. As 1970 champion Bobby Isaac said, "I'd rather race on any other track than Darlington, but I'd rather win at Darlington that at any other track."

Harold Brasington (left) and Big Bill France (center, pointing) look over the plans for the Darlington Raceway in 1950. Initially, France wasn't keen on running a 500-mile (800km) event, fearing that the stock cars wouldn't hold up well over that distance, but his hand was forced when Lakewood Speedway owner Sam Nunis announced a 500-miler at that track. Rather than support a long race at Nunis' more difficult track, France threw in with Brasington.

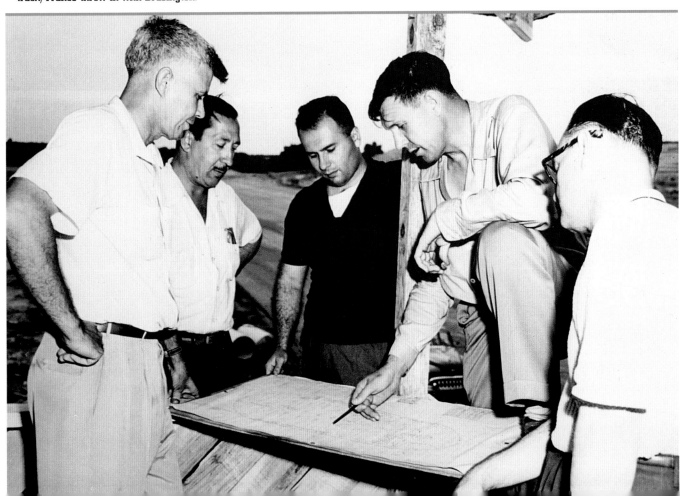

"Madman" Johnny Mantz only ran in three events in 1950, scoring a win and another top-ten. According to the points scheme of the times, however, the win was enough to catapult him to sixth place in the standings (well ahead of Dick Linder, for instance, who had run thirteen events and won three). That Southern 500 at Darlington was Mantz's only win, and he left the sport in '56. Sadly, Mantz died in an auto accident in '72.

The 1950 Southern 500

The Southern 500, long one of the gems of the NASCAR season, was not originally planned as a NASCAR event. The Central States Racing Association (CSRA) was slated to run the race, but could not guarantee a full field of cars. Meanwhile, Bill France wanted NASCAR to be involved in the first 500-mile (800km) stock car race, so offered to co-sanction the event with the CSRA. The deal was signed, and Harold Brasington quickly had a starting grid of seventy-five cars for the September 4, 1950, race.

Starting positions were determined by time trials held over a period of two weeks starting in mid-August. The first five positions were set on day one, by the cars with the fastest speed that day. The rest came back the next day to run for positions six through ten (with the fastest five that day winning the spots), and so on. The overall fastest speed was Wally Campbell's 82.400 mph (131.8kph). Wally didn't make that lap until late in the process, though, so ended up sixtieth on the grid. Curtis Turner had the first day's fastest speed, at 82.034 mph (131.3kph), and thus the pole. The slowest qualifier was former Indy racer "Madman" Johnny Mantz, at just more than 73 mph (116.8kph).

More than 25,000 spectators showed up for the race. The accommodations were rough, and wholly inadequate for a crowd that size, but the fans didn't seem to mind. If you think it's tough booking a motel room for a Winston Cup race today, there was only one hotel anywhere near Darlington in 1950. Overnighters either slept in their vehicles or enjoyed the hospitality of the local citizenry.

That first race—500 miles in 400 laps—was not about close competition among top-notch drivers. It was more of a hard lesson taught to drivers who, for the most part, had never run on a paved track before, and certainly not at those speeds or for anywhere near that long. The starting field, twenty-five rows of cars three abreast (Indy style), nearly filled the front stretch. They took the green flag at about 11 A.M., and the race was underway.

From his starting spot on the outside of the front row, Gober Sosebee had the best run into the first turn and immediately took the lead. Sosebee led the first four laps, then pole-sitter Curtis Turner worked past him to pace the field for the next twenty-two laps. By that point, it had become clear to the teams that Darlington was a different sort of beast—one with a voracious appetite for tires. Cotton Owens picked up the lead from Turner. His Plymouth was fast—he had quickly moved up from the thirty-ninth starting spot—but like the other speedsters that day, Owens was handicapped by the need for frequent pit stops for fresh tires.

So while the quickest racers "rabbited" around the track, chewing up their rubber on the abrasive surface (one team went through twenty-four tires), the "tortoises" were steadily gaining ground.

The slow but steady approach turned out to be the right one that Labor Day, particularly for one driver. Johnny Mantz had barely made the field and certainly wasn't racing anywhere near as fast as the early front-runners, but he had one thing going for him. While most teams made ten or twenty pit stops for tires, Mantz pitted only three times. Mantz's experience in AAA racing paid off—he knew what high speeds on asphalt were going to do to the tires and had his team mount special hard compound rubber on the car. So while everyone else was in the pits, he was making laps. When the challengers roared out of the pits, they could pull away from him like he was standing still, but only for a couple of laps. Then they were hanging on for dear life until the tires let go and they were stopped again.

At just more than 75 mph (120kph), Mantz lead the race from lap fifty to the end, winning the first Southern 500 by more than nine laps. Fireball Roberts came in second and the previous year's champion, Red Byron, took third. Surprisingly, there were only two cautions. Buck Baker was involved in one of the wrecks, and seemed to be the track's first casualty. When track workers approached the damaged car, they saw

Baker covered in blood, and frantically called for the ambulance. What the driver needed, however, was a shower rather than a doctor. Concerned that he might become dehydrated during the long race, Baker had wedged a glass bottle of tomato juice in the seat. When he crashed, the bottle broke and he was covered in the red fluid.

Even with just two yellow flags, the race took more than 6½ hours to finish (victory circle photos clearly show the darkening sky). Mantz's victory was not without controversy. Witnesses, NASCAR officials among them, felt that Mantz's number 98 had illegal springs and shocks and possibly engine modifications. For some reason, the car never went through postrace inspection, though, so the victory, Mantz's one and only in NASCAR, stood.

A Palpable Hit

The new track was a success. Attendance surged each year and the Southern 500 became the premier NASCAR race. It was also the longest race: the 1952 event took 6 hours, 42 minutes (the longest uninterrupted event in NASCAR history). Fonty Flock took that interminable race, Buck Baker won the '53 iteration, and Herb Thomas proved that he was a superspeedway ace as well as a short-track star, winning in '51, '54, and '55. The latter win was accomplished without a single tire change, using a new, specially formulated

Completed in 1950, Darlington Raceway was the first stock car superspeedway, and there was nothing else like it for the next decade. In this view, the fishing pond that helped shape the asymmetrical track can be seen at the top left, outside of turn two. In the '50s, the track also featured a pedestrian walkway that spanned the backstretch, where spectators would stand to watch the races. It was torn down and replaced with tunnels in 1956.

Joe Weatherly (number 12) and Tiny Lund (number 45) were among the many casualties of the 1960 Southern 500, a race marred by tragedy and confusion. Three pit road workers were killed when Bobby Johns' Pontiac flipped into the open pit area. Another track worker was injured by flying concrete from a backstretch crash. Buddy Baker got the win, but second-place finisher Rex White insisted he received the white flag twice and should have therefore taken the trophy.

Firestone compound. The Convertible Division of NASCAR had its first superspeedway audition in the Rebel 300, a May race at the track, starting in '57. Those races were green-flagged from a standing start, like Indy car events, for more excitement.

In 1953, the track was resurfaced and turns one and two were rebuilt, which extended its length to 1.375 miles (2.2km). Unfortunately, track founder Harold Brasington wasn't there to enjoy the venue's success. A combination of tax concerns (which resulted in the sale of his shares of stock) and a shift in power on the board put Brasington on the outside. Bob Colvin was the new track president.

As speeds increased on the superspeedway, so did the danger. Speedy Thompson's 1957 win was marred by the death of Bobby Myers, father of the then nine-year-old "Chocolate" Myers (later a well-known gasman for Dale Earnhardt's number 3 team). Myers ran at full speed into Fonty Flock, who was sitting still on the track after a spin. Myers' car flipped end over end, destroying the vehicle and ending the thirty-three-year-old's promising career.

More than once, race cars have been filmed vaulting over or tearing down the inadequate metal guardrails in the turns. When Eddie Pagan tore down a section of the rail in the 1958 race, it was deemed irreparable. Rather than red-flag the event, though, the officials just warned drivers to stay away from the high groove on that part of the track. Needless to say, several cars shot right through the gap and over the embankment. In the '60 race, Johnny Allen took out not only the rail, but also the left side of (and the stairs to) the scorer's stand. Luckily, the structure stayed up and scorers were able to exit safely via fire truck ladder.

The 1961 Rebel 300

By 1961, the only race convertibles still ran was the May race at Darlington. There was no longer a separate division for the cars, so the points were rolled into the Grand National standings. The hotshots of the day—Curtis Turner, Joe Weatherly, and Fireball Roberts—had won all the Rebel 300 races among them and Roberts was favored to take his third win in the May 6, 1961, event. Fireball started on the outside of the front row that year (Darlington had just switched from three- to two-abreast starting grids); the fellow on the pole, a relative newcomer to NASCAR, was Fred Lorenzen.

Lorenzen had been collecting trophies around the Midwest on the USAC circuit (he was from Elmhurst, Illinois) and had decided to give NASCAR a shot. He ran seven races in 1956 without success and soon went back north. He made a second go at it in '60, with pretty much the same results. As he was about to call it quits, he was approached by Ralph Moody, partner in the Ford factory Holman-Moody team. They were looking for a driver for the '61 season, and Lorenzen had attracted their attention. They swung the deal and Lorenzen had a seat behind the wheel of the white and blue number 28 Ford for the next year.

Lorenzen got his first NASCAR win with the team in the rain-shortened April race at Martinsville. That was the only high point of the first part of the season, however, so heading to the May ragtop race he was not favored to win at the circuit's toughest track.

Lorenzen quickly demonstrated that he'd come to race, though, taking the pole position and leading the first five laps. Fireball took over for a handful of laps, then Lorenzen recaptured the lead and hung onto it through lap seventy-one. Weatherly, Ralph Earnhardt, Curtis Turner, and Johnny Allen also took turns at the front. Roberts looked strong late in the race, but lost a tire and fell back several laps as he pitted. With twenty to go, it was the tough old veteran Curtis Turner in the lead in the Wood Brothers number 21.

Lorenzen had also lost time on pit stops and was running a distant second, but over those last twenty laps, the number 28 was handling flawlessly and "Fast Freddie" charged forward to catch the leader. Over the last ten laps, Lorenzen tried again and again to get by Turner and each time was blocked by the wily veteran. Lorenzen had been working the high side of the track, and Turner repeatedly slid up, pinching him into the guardrail to hold him off. With two laps left, Lorenzen went high again and Turner again drifted up to slam the door. But the move was a feint and the number 28 shot to the inside instead, pulling up before Turner could cut him off. The cars went through the first and second turns welded together, side-by-side. As they shot onto the backstretch, Lorenzen skittered ahead, just keeping control as Turner gave him a final shot, and moved to a five-car-length lead. This time, "Fearless" Fred Lorenzen held on to take his second win in what was then called the most competitive race in NASCAR history.

Turner was unhappy, to say the least, about losing the first-place prize. He was a partner in the new Charlotte Motor Speedway and needed that $8,400 winner's share for construction costs. He let the youngster know how he felt about being outfoxed by giving him a small pop on the cool-down lap.

Fred Lorenzen went on to win twenty-six races in his career. With his boyish good looks and squeaky-clean lifestyle, he provided a much-needed counterpoint to the rough-and-ready crowd, and helped enhance NASCAR's backwoods image. Lorenzen retired early, while still at the peak of his career, in 1972.

Writing the Record Book

Underdogs Nelson Stacy and Larry Frank added their names to the winners' list in the 1961 races, though Frank wasn't awarded the trophy until the day after his race. As the result of a scoring error, Junior Johnson stood in victory lane that Labor Day. Press photos later had to be doctored to show Frank with the trophy and girls instead of Johnson.

The last convertible race was held in 1963, using a different format. The 300-mile (480km) event was split into two 150-mile (240km) races with a mandatory pit window between them. The overall winner was the driver who had the best average finish. Joe Weatherly earned the win, but the scoring further down the field was so confused that NASCAR suggested that the format never be repeated.

Surprisingly, Richard Petty won only one Southern 500 in his amazing career, during his dominant 1967 season. Cale Yarborough, however, holds the track record, with five

The McDonald's Ford, seen here in Darlington in March 2000, is one of the most popular and recognizable cars in the Winston Cup garage, but owner/driver Bill Elliott has not enjoyed much success with the sponsor since they came on board in '95. When McDonald's announced that it would leave the number 94 team after '00, Elliott pulled up stakes and decided to close down the team. Elliott planned to return to the familiar number 9 in '01, driving a Dodge for Ray Evernham.

The 1984 Southern 500. Cars race three abreast down the front stretch, but the drivers will be very careful to thin down to single file before diving into the treacherous turns at Darlington. Lake Speed (in the number 1) leads the pack in this photograph, but pole-sitter Harry Gant took the win, the biggest of his career.

Southern 500 wins. The first occurred in '68 while driving for the Wood Brothers. David Pearson had the faster car at the end of that race, but Yarborough was able to hold him back on the one-groove track. When Pearson tried to dive under him their cars touched; Pearson spun to the infield, but Cale skidded along the rail and kept going.

In 1969, LeeRoy Yarbrough (no relation) was the victor on a new Darlington track. Turns three and four had been rebuilt up to 25 degrees of banking, giving it a wider racing groove. The entire track was resurfaced as well. That year, Yarbrough was also the first winner of the "triple crown" of NASCAR, which means he won the three biggest events—the Daytona 500, the World 600, and the Southern 500.

Between them, David Pearson and Cale Yarborough had Darlington pretty well sewn up during the 1970s. Yarborough earned four more Southern 500 victories, in '73, '74, '78, and later in '82. He took the '74 event almost by default—his was one of only twelve cars left running at the end. Mechanical problems and eleven crashes sent a total of twenty-eight cars to the garage, including all of the other top contenders.

Pearson, first with Holman-Moody then with the Wood Brothers, was practically unbeatable at Darlington. His smooth driving style was especially effective on the tough track, so it is no surprise that the "Silver Fox," as he was known, holds the record there with ten wins. The number 21 team was so dominant, in fact, that Pearson won the '73 Rebel 500 (the race length had increased to 400, then 500,

miles [640km, then 800km]) by thirteen laps. He also repeated Yarborough's triple crown performance in '76. The '79 Rebel 500 was Pearson's last race with the Wood Brothers. Tensions in the team exploded when miscommunication during a pit stop resulted in Pearson's wheel falling off as he drove off pit road. Perhaps the most successful team in NASCAR history called it quits. Pearson wasn't done with Darlington, though. His last two wins were the '79 Southern 500, with Rod Osterlund's team, and the '80 Rebel 500, with Hoss Ellington.

A Changing of the Guard

In the 1980s, a new generation of stars moved to the forefront at Darlington. Sophomore driver Terry Labonte snaked through a late-race pileup to get his first Winston Cup win in the prestigious Labor Day classic in '80. Neil Bonnett took over the number 21 ride and cashed in on the Wood Brothers' Darlington savvy with a win in '81. Harry Gant, the "Skoal Bandit," won the '83 TranSouth 500, then followed it with the biggest win of his career, the '84 Southern 500. Tim Richmond and the Rick Hendricks number 25 team were on fire the second half of the '86 season; one of their wins was at Darlington in September.

A young redhead from Georgia made an indelible impression on sports history with his 1985 Southern 500 win. That was the year that the R.J. Reynolds Tobacco Company started the Winston Million program. The tobacco giant promised a cool million dollars to any driver who could win three out of four prestige WC events: the Daytona 500 (most famous), Winston 500 (fastest), World 600 (longest), and Southern 500 (oldest). Bill Elliott, in his red and white Coors Ford, had won the Daytona and Talladega races but fell short at Charlotte. The Darlington race was his last chance. The number 9 team and the track were under a media microscope as the haulers rolled into South Carolina in September. Elliott took the pole and led on and off throughout the race, but was running behind Cale Yarborough toward the end. On lap 324 of 367, Yarb's car began smoking, forcing him to pit. Elliott went on to the win and instant fame. The $1,053,725 payday was by far the largest ever for NASCAR and earned Elliott the nickname "Million Dollar Bill."

Elliott may have made a huge splash, but throughout the 1980s and early '90s, it was clear that Dale Earnhardt was the modern master of the Lady in Black. With nine wins at the track to date, Earnhardt is second only to Pearson. Then there's the patented "Earnhardt move" that delights fans and frustrates unwary opponents: The new guy at the track decides to pass Earnhardt and dives under him going into the turn. Earnhardt pressures him, but gives him the bottom, so the contender shoots by, barely braking. But the challenger has overcommitted, and has to slide up the track through the center of the turn. Earnhardt, meanwhile, is waiting for that, and with a smoother entry into the turn,

is able to turn left and get back under the other car, recapturing the lead as they exit the turn. There have been races where a driver has tried this approach ten laps in a row, wearing out his tires in the process, and each time Earnhardt comes out in front.

Earnhardt's first Darlington win was in 1982, the year the track was purchased by the International Speedway Corporation. His '87 TransSouth 500 was a particularly convincing performance—he lapped everyone but the second-place car and led every lap he was on the track; he followed that with his first Southern 500 win that year. In '89, when the Southern 500 first ran under corporate sponsorship, Ralph Earnhardt was inducted into the NMPA Hall of Fame. His son continued the legacy with a victory that day, making the '89 Heinz Southern 500 weekend an Earnhardt family celebration.

Darrell Waltrip had won the spring race four times, but when Labor Day rolled around, 'ol DW always seemed to have hard luck. He expressed his frustrations in true Waltrip style after kissing the wall several times in the '89 race: "I love Darlington in the spring, and I love Darlington in the fall. I love Darlington in victory lane, but I HATE Darlington in the wall!" His turn finally came in '92, his twentieth attempt. Davey Allison was going for the Winston Million and had a strong car, but when the race was red-flagged for

NASCAR's first million-dollar paycheck—and giving it away was worth every penny. The publicity for R.J. Reynolds from Bill Elliott's 1985 Southern 500 win at Darlington (which made him the inaugural recipient of the Winston Million) was incalculable. And despite his shyness and "Aw, shucks" persona, "Awesome" Bill became an overnight media sensation. His historic achievement no doubt played a big part in his being elected "Most Popular Driver" virtually every year since then.

The Lady in Black hasn't lost her bite. Mike Skinner makes a rapid exit from his smoking car after a crash early in the 1999 Southern 500. The number 31 team was able to put the car back on the track, but Skinner finished in thirty-fifth place. Skinner wasn't the only one to have a tough weekend: veteran driver Ernie Irvan announced his retirement from racing, due to repeated injuries, just prior to the event.

rain, Waltrip—who was off-sequence and hadn't pitted yet—was in the lead. It never went green again and he got the win, adding, "You take 'em whenever you can get 'em, however you can get 'em."

In the mid-1990s a new rising star showed NASCAR fans that raw talent can sometimes make up for age and experience—even at Darlington. Jeff Gordon seemingly "tamed" the untamable track with three consecutive wins in '95 and '96. And he wasn't finished.

The 1997 Mountain Dew Southern 500

Since RJR had instituted the Winston Million, only Bill Elliott had won the big prize, though several drivers had earned the consolation award ($100,000 for winning two of the relevant races). Coming into the Southern 500 on August 31, 1997, Jeff Gordon had won at Daytona and Charlotte, and so was in position to go for the mil.

The odds makers in the garage gave him a slim chance to win, based on previous history as much as anything. Gordon had the 1995 and '96 trophies on his shelf and no one had ever before won three Southern 500s in a row. Combined with the Damocles sword that seems to hang over the head of every candidate for the prize—well, he'd be lucky to finish the race in one piece. On top of that, this was a brand-new Darlington. To accommodate the addition of grandstands, the front and back straights were switched. The start/finish line was now on the old backstretch and treacherous turn four was now turn two. While the track itself was the same, the novel arrangement gave the place a different feel, and teams were working hard to adjust.

The usual cast of characters qualified up front. Bobby Labonte started on the pole, just topping a fast lap from old favorite Bill Elliott. Gordon managed only seventh, and the skeptics nodded their heads knowingly.

The first crash came on just the second lap in an incident that left everyone shaking his or her head. Dale Earnhardt had qualified poorly and started at the back of the pack. On the second lap, the number 3 slapped the wall coming off turn two and then coasted onto pit road; there was no caution. The normally tough-as-steel Earnhardt had to be helped form his car and was taken to the infield care center in a daze while Mike Dillon jumped in the car as a sub. It was later revealed that Earnhardt had briefly lost consciousness—before he'd hit the wall. Over the next week, he underwent a battery of medical tests, but no cause for the episode was discovered and no further symptoms developed.

Labonte led the first few laps, but Bill Elliott soon took charge. The number 94 Ford led three times for a total of 181 laps, and Awesome Bill's legion of fans had hopes that he'd end his long winless streak. Ted Musgrave and Jeff Burton took turns up front, and Michael Waltrip, whose ride showed the Wood Brothers touch of old, led several laps in the number 21. Jeff Gordon? He led forty laps, but certainly didn't appear to have anything on Elliott.

The afternoon had started out under sunny skies but around the 250-lap mark, clouds covered the track and the complexion of the race changed. Elliott's car didn't handle as well as the track cooled and he soon lost the lead to a charging Dale Jarrett. The clouds opened up on lap 295 and the race was yellow-flagged for rain. After a brief sprinkle, it looked like the race would go back to green so Jarrett hit pit road for fresh rubber. When he came back out, Gordon's number 24 car was in the lead. The DuPont team took a chance and stayed on the track when the leaders pitted. Everyone knew that was the kiss of death—you just can't outrun fresh tires at Darlington.

The green flag flew again on lap 303, and Jarrett clearly had the better car. But there's much more to racing than having a fast car. Lap after lap, Gordon hung onto his ill-handling Chevy, shutting down every opportunity Jarrett had to pass. If he'd had a less patient stalker behind him, the number 24 would have gone spinning but Jarrett played it straight. The number 88 had not only the lead to worry about: soon, Jeff Burton's Exide Ford was filling Jarrett's rearview mirror. Jarrett eventually used up his tires trying to get past Gordon and lost second place to Burton.

With only a couple of laps left, Burton knew he had to make his move, and immediately pressured Gordon. As the two came across for the white flag, Burton dove low under the number 24 into turn one. This was the moment. Gordon could back out, keeping the car under him and losing the lead or he could go for broke, "checkers or wreckers." Gordon cut down hard on Burton and they came together. Burton laid his right front wheel into Gordon's quarter panel, but the number 24's move limited Burton's angle of entry into the corner, and he couldn't get the purchase to push

his way past. Gordon stood on the gas to keep his rear end behind him and came out of the turn a car length ahead. Burton had no time to attempt another pass, and Gordon took the win by half a car length. Against all odds, Gordon had won an unprecedented third straight Southern 500, and the Winston Million.

The postrace interviews were studies in contrast. Jarrett was calm and philosophical. Gordon was ecstatic, and looked for magnanimity from Burton: "Jeff, buddy, it was for a million bucks!" But Burton was just plain ticked off and was having none of Gordon's bonhomie, claiming he had tried to punt Gordon out of the way when he cut down on him, but hadn't been able to manage it. In the end it didn't matter: Gordon got the million, and every fan in the stands got his money's worth from that race.

Starting in 1998, the Winston Million program was replaced by the "No Bull 5," which worked a little differently: each of the top five finishers in select races become eligible to win a million dollars if they win the next select race.

Gordon went on to win an incredible fourth consecutive Southern 500 in 1998, but Burton really got his in '99. Not only did he win $2 million in the No Bull 5, he also swept the '99 races at Darlington. Another Burton was in victory lane, in March 2000, this time older brother Ward, with his second Winston Cup win.

Seen through a storm of confetti, Jeff and Brooke Gordon celebrate (over a crouching NASCAR official) after Jeff's 1997 Southern 500 win, which also gave him the Winston Million. It took twelve years for Bill Elliott's '85 Winston Million performance to be repeated—and Gordon would be the last. Several drivers have since won the "No Bull 5" payoffs, but even though the cash award is higher, the achievement just isn't quite the same.

DAYTONA INTERNATIONAL SPEEDWAY

LOCATION: *Daytona Beach, Florida*

RACE LENGTH: *100–500 miles (160–800km) on a 2.5-mile (4km) paved tri-oval*

NUMBER OF RACES RUN: *108 Grand National and Winston Cup, between February 20, 1959, and February 18, 2001*

SPEED RECORD (AVERAGE FOR AN ENTIRE RACE): *183.295 mph (293.3kph), set on February 19, 1970*

Bill France had been running beach races at Daytona since 1937. He foresaw the day when he'd no longer be able to use highway A-1-A and the parallel stretch of beach for that purpose, and lobbied the local commissioners for a permanent race facility. It looked like he had sufficient commitment by the mid-'50s to build a track, and it was announced that the '55 Daytona race would be at a new location. Politics and red tape put the brakes on the project, however, and it wasn't until '58 that construction on the Daytona International Speedway began.

At twice the size of Darlington, the only other superspeedway the circuit visited, the new Daytona track was unbelievable. To build it, 480 acres (194.2ha) of cypress swamp west of the city near an old airbase was cleared. It was designed as a tri-oval, with a rounded front straight that gave fans situated along the bow a panoramic view of the action. There was even a 180-acre (72.8ha) lake, Lake Lloyd, located inside the track along the backstretch. With the broad sweeping turns and high banks (31 degrees), the track would support speeds 30 to 40 mph (48–64kph) higher than what the Grand National boys were used to.

The facility was completed and ready for the first race in February 1959. Most sports position their biggest game at the end of the season, but the Daytona 500—the "Super Bowl of Stock Car Racing"—is instead the very first race in the NASCAR season. Winning that trophy is every Winston Cup racer's dream and the focus of team efforts from the time the checkered flag falls at Atlanta the previous November until the cars are unloaded from the hauler for Daytona's Speedweek events in the second week of February. The outcome of the opening Daytona race can inordinately affect a team's year. A good finish provides momentum that can buoy a team through the first quarter of the season—just as a loss can bog the a team's season down.

The Daytona 500 has a different qualifying format than any other event in the series. Teams make qualifying speed runs, but only the first two spots on the grid are determined

Daytona before: the newest and biggest superspeedway of its day was carefully laid out and designed. Besides the big oval, short-track and road courses are clearly visible. This versatility allowed the venue to host a variety of racing series and events. Unlike Darlington, where the fishing pond dictated the track layout, Lake Lloyd was manmade as part of the attraction. The lakebed was still being excavated in this 1958 photo.

this way. Positions three through thirty-two are decided by the finishing order in two "heat races," the Twin 125s. The first fifteen finishers in each of those races (each team runs in one or the other of the two sprints) get the remaining starting spots for the 500. Positions thirty-three through thirty-seven fall back to qualifying speeds again, with the fastest five cars not yet in the field getting a spot. The remainder of the field is open for provisionals—starting spots reserved for teams that don't make the field, prioritized by their place in the point standings.

The Firecracker 400 (now the Pepsi 400), the second Daytona race of the year, follows the usual qualifying format and is always run on the Fourth of July.

The 1959 Daytona 500

The first Daytona 500 set quite a precedent for the new track. The initial reaction of drivers and fans alike on first seeing the 2.5-mile (4km) expanse of asphalt was that the speeds possible on the big banked track would lead to certain disaster. A mixed field of Grand National and Convertible Division drivers proved that impression wrong on February 22, 1959, a sunny Sunday.

Qualifying for the race began a week ahead of time, but few cars actually ran qualifying laps. Most of the spots were determined by the tried-and-true method of a "heat race."

To ensure a full field and bolster the struggling Convertible Division, the first 500 included cars from that series as well as the Grand National entries. The plan was to position the GN cars in the inside lane and the convertibles beside them.

In the convertible qualifying race, which took place on Thursday, Shorty Rollins beat Marvin Panch, Richard Petty, and Glen Wood. These and the other top-finishing convertibles would start the 500 in second, fourth, and sixth, and so on down the line. The GN hardtops qualified on Friday. The race averaged a speed of 143.198 mph (229.1kph) and was won by Bob Welborn, who earned the pole for Sunday's big event; Fritz Wilson would start in third, Tom Piston in fifth, and Joe Weatherly in seventh, and so on.

The field of fifty-nine cars took to the track on Sunday. The flagman waved the green, standing on the track just to one side of the speeding behemoth, and the pack was off.

It was quickly evident was that the convertibles couldn't run at the same pace as the GN cars. At race speeds, wind currents created tremendous drag and compromised the handling of the convertibles, while the more streamlined hardtops were able to run about 10 mph (16kph) faster.

Bob Welborn led the first lap, then swapped the lead back and forth with "Tiger" Tom Pistone over the next twenty. Thirty-ninth-place starter Fireball Roberts hooked up with Tim Flock and Jack Smith and drafted together to the front

Daytona after: today, Daytona is one of the old-timers of the NASCAR circuit. The track itself has remained basically unchanged over the years and has hosted more NASCAR races than any other track to date. As this photograph shows, the surrounding area has been substantially developed over the years.

(though at that time no one knew about drafting per se). Roberts led for twenty laps, until he was sidelined with a bad fuel pump.

Midwesterner Johnny Beauchamp was in only his second NASCAR race. He'd started his number 73 T-Bird in twenty-first but worked through traffic and took the lead after Roberts was forced to pit. At the halfway point of the race, teams began experiencing engine problems and shredding tires. The race had run green since the flag and the long run at high speed was wearing down the hardware. Jack Smith led fifty laps, until blistered rubber sent him to the pits for an unscheduled stop.

Richard Petty actually started the first Daytona 500 in a better spot than his father, Lee, but Richard ran in the Convertible series (in a number 43 similar to this car, photographed at Columbia Speedway), which ran alongside the hardtops. The convertibles were no match for the hardtops at Daytona's speeds, however, and dad won the race; Richard blew up his engine and finished in fifty-seventh place.

The Superspeedways

By lap 150 there were only two cars left on the lead lap: Johnny Beauchamp's number 73 and Lee Petty's number 42. Over the last fifty laps the two dueled back and forth, exchanging the lead eleven times. As the laps wore down they ran up on the lapped Chevy of Joe Weatherly and the three cars rocketed past the white flag side-by-side. And they stayed that way. As 42,000 fans watched intently, the trio crossed the finish line three abreast, neck and neck. It was so close that no one knew who'd won.

Flagman Johnny Bruner and Bill France, who was at the line with him, called Beauchamp the winner. Petty's crew, sure they'd won, headed to victory lane as well, to be told there that they'd finished second. The winner's circle celebration proceeded with Beauchamp, but over the course of the day doubts about the finish accumulated until France announced that the outcome was not yet official.

There was no photo-finish equipment at the track to resolve the issue so NASCAR solicited photos and movies from fans and news agencies to help make the call. Three days went by before a New York newspaper sent a film reel that clearly showed Weatherly's (lapped) car a fender ahead of Petty, who was a fender ahead of Beauchamp. Lee Petty was declared the official winner of the first Daytona 500.

A photo finish, thirty-three lead changes, and no cautions—what a race! The average speed was 135.521 mph (216.8kph). The cars held up under the strain (for the most part) and the drivers handled the high banks expertly. The Daytona race had clearly opened the door on NASCAR's superspeedway era.

Daytona in the Grand National Era

The 1959 Firecracker 250 also featured convertible cars. Joe Weatherly, one of the drivers that day, made a fundamental discovery about racing at Daytona. Though the convertibles by themselves couldn't really compete with the GN cars, Weatherly found that if he tucked right up under the tail of one of the hardtops, his car ran much faster than it would running alone. In that manner Weatherly followed Fireball Roberts around the track and to the front, pulling off an improbable second-place finish. The trick (which, in the hands of the masters, became an art) would come to be called "drafting" and it would become a huge factor in how races were run at the biggest superspeedways.

Richard Petty is the king of Daytona, with ten wins, including an incredible seven Daytona 500s. If you look at race teams, the Wood Brothers are on top, with more victories at the track (fourteen, with four 500s) than any other owners. Cale Yarborough is the only driver to come close to Petty, with four Daytona 500 wins and four July victories. The big track seemed to suit the style of Indy drivers who tried their hands at NASCAR over the years. American racing legends Mario Andretti and A.J. Foyt both have Daytona 500 wins, in 1967 and '72, respectively.

Not surprisingly, the list of Daytona victors is a *Who's Who* of the elite of NASCAR: Petty, Pearson, Yarborough, Yarbrough, Johnson, Roberts, Lorenzen, Allison (Bobby and Davey), Baker, and so on. Bill Elliott used the high banks set a lap record of more than 210 mph (336kph), and Buddy Baker set the speed record for a Daytona race: 177.602 mph (284.2kph) in 1980. Sterling Marlin, Jeff Gordon, and Dale Jarrett are also multirace winners at Daytona.

Lee Petty, one of the true pioneers of NASCAR, died in April 2000 at age eighty-six. He had fifty-four wins and three championships to his credit, and might have won more if his career hadn't prematurely ended at Daytona in 1961. On the last lap of his qualifying race, he and Johnny Beauchamp tangled in turn three. Both cars vaulted over the guardrail at full speed and flew out of the track. Both drivers were injured, Petty critically. Both men recovered, but their racing days were over.

Tiny Lund's big break, and first win, came in the 1963 Daytona 500. Lund had rescued Marvin Panch, the driver of the Wood Brothers number 21, from a flaming crash a week earlier. The Wood Brothers offered Lund the ride in their Ford for the 500. Lund moved up from twelfth place at the start to take the lead with eight laps left thanks both to crafty pit work (one fewer pit stop than the competitors) and Lund's hard-charging style. Lund won without a single tire change.

If good fuel mileage alone could win a Daytona 500, Gordon Johncock, in Smokey Yunick's car, might have taken the 1968 event without a contest. Yunick, widely known as a "creative" car builder, ran into trouble in the prerace inspection. Looking for irregularities, the officials went over the car with a fine-toothed comb, even going so far as to remove the gas tank to carefully measure its contents. They gave Yunick a list of nine items to fix. He insisted there was nothing wrong with the car. When they couldn't come to terms, Yunick told them, "Better make that ten," jumped in the car, and drove it away—without its regulation gas tank.

The 1976 Daytona 500 was one of the most important races in the sport's history. NASCAR had inked a deal with ABC to broadcast the end of the race on national television. As it turned out, the finish couldn't have been scripted any better. Richard Petty and David Pearson swapped the lead back and forth through the last laps, culminating in contact that sent both cars spinning. Petty came to a stop just short of the start/finish line, but his engine was stalled and wouldn't restart. Pearson, whose car had sustained more damage and was farther back, had kept his engine running and so was able to limp past the motionless number 43 to take the checkered flag at a roaring 20 mph (32kph). Best of all, much of the East Coast was snowbound that day, so the television-watching audience (most of whom saw the close action and excitement of NASCAR racing that day) was at a record high.

Lots of exciting things have happened at Daytona. Here, Johnny Roberts becomes airborne during a 1967 Sportsman series race. Window nets weren't in use then and you can see Robert's helmet sticking out of the window of his disintegrating car—not a good sign.

The 1979 Daytona 500

The February 18, 1979, Daytona 500 featured the most exciting stock car finish of all time. Not because it was close, though Richard Petty only just held off an eager Darrell Waltrip to win by a mere car length. Not because a first-time or surprise winner made it to victory lane (Petty's win was his sixth there). No, it was because of "The Fight." While other races had ended with bigger and badder brawls, this fight was broadcast via network television into millions of homes across the country. No Madison Avenue firm could have sold NASCAR a more effective advertisement. Uncouth as it made the sport appear, the event galvanized interest level in stock car racing on the national level.

Buddy Baker had the pole for the race with Donnie Allison's number 1 Olds beside him. Cale Yarborough was third in the number 11 and Donnie's brother Bobby was not far behind in seventh. Those four men battled at the front until a wreck on lap thirty-two sent Yarborough and both Allisons spinning into the muddy infield. Donnie lost a lap trying to extricate himself, Bobby lost two, and Cale three. The number 1 and number 11 were still strong runners, and by working the seven caution flags, were able to climb back into the lead lap. When pole-sitter Baker dropped out, they proved to be the fastest cars. At lap 108 Allison was back up front, with Yarborough coming on strong.

By the last lap, the two were nose-to-tail, with Allison showing the way. As they rode down the backstretch, Yarborough made his move, cutting to the left to dive under Donnie. Allison later said that he was determined that if Cale

was going to pass him, it would have to be on the outside, so he cut hard left to block the lane. Neither driver yielded an inch, and their cars touched. Both cars bobbled then straightened. Again they touched and slid, as though joined, together across the track. Out of control now, they hit the wall and spun back across the asphalt, coming to a stop not far from each other in the grass.

Petty, a distant third, got the word over the radio and raced Waltrip back to the checkered. While one broadcaster was cheering on the number 43, Ken Squier broke in yelling that there was a fight in turn three. Cameras shifted and caught Bobby and Donnie Allison and Cale Yarbrough punching and wrestling in the mud amid a crowd of rescue crewmen. Cale got out of his car to give Donnie hell for blocking him, and Bobby, who was a lap down and had stopped to check on his brother, intervened. The argument escalated into a fistfight, which CBS captured and relayed to the viewers.

A large part of the East Coast was snowbound that weekend and had tuned in to the show, so the ratings were a record high. The combatants were all fined by NASCAR for unsportsmanlike conduct, but the racing organization might just as well have rewarded them—suddenly NASCAR was big news. A couple of good ol' boys duking it out had accomplished in a heartbeat what years of careful planning and grooming couldn't.

P.S. Donnie and Cale wrecked each other the very next week at Rockingham also. They both claimed it was "just a racing thing" and had nothing to do with the incident that had occurred a week earlier.

Daytona in the 1980s

One of the best-known stock car finishes was Richard Petty's 1984 Firecracker 400 win. A staunch Republican, Petty was especially happy to have President Ronald Reagan in the stands (well, the executive suite, to be exact) as he and Cale Yarborough battled back and forth over the last laps. Petty beat Yarborough back to a race-ending caution flag by just inches. The win was also special because it was Petty's 200th NASCAR win, and was to be his last. Incidentally, Yarborough didn't finish second in the race. His "brain blew up" (according to him) and he pulled into the pits a lap too early, relinquishing second place to Harry Gant.

Daytona was the site of another emotional ending, in 1988. Davey Allison had two wins the previous year, his rookie season, and was running second as the '88 opener was on the last lap. He couldn't have been happier if he had won because the driver ahead of him was his father, Bobby. The elder Allison won his third 500, and the two engineered the first father/son, first/second finish since Lee and Richard Petty had stormed Heidelberg raceway in '60. Davey got his own Daytona 500 win in '92.

Though Daytona is among the toughest tracks to win at, a number of drivers earned their first victories there. Sam McGuagg's sole win was in the 1966 Firecracker 400. Likewise, Greg Sacks' only win was in the '85 Fourth of July race, driving an experimental car for the DiGard team.

Derrike Cope scored a surprise 500 win in the 1990 race when leader Dale Earnhardt blew a tire in the last lap. Ernie Irvan had success in the Morgan-McClure Kodak number 4, with a 500 win in '91, and Sterling Marlin—in the same car—notched his long-awaited first win in the '94 Daytona 500.

More excitement at Daytona: for better or worse, this ugly fracas was a defining moment in NASCAR's history. Bobby Allison (on the ground) and Cale Yarborough (helmet in hand) disagreed over who had been responsible for the events leading up to a last-lap crash that had taken Yarborough and Allison's brother, Donnie, out of the race.

Marlin won again in '95, and then again in the July '96 race. More recently, John Andretti earned his first (and the first for Cale Yarborough as a car owner) when he wheeled the number 98 to the winner's circle in the '97 Pepsi 400.

The list of drivers who never won the Daytona 500 is perhaps more of a surprise than the list of Daytona champions. It took three-time champ Darrell Waltrip seventeen tries before he got a 500 win. "Please tell me, this is the Daytona 500?" he mugged for reporters in victory lane. Among today's top drivers, Rusty Wallace, Terry Labonte, and Mark Martin have yet to score a Daytona victory in either event. And Dale Earnhardt's struggles to win stock car racing's premier event were the stuff of legend.

The 1998 Daytona 500

It was a familiar scenario: the Daytona 500 has just finished and some team other than the RCR number 3 is celebrating in victory lane. A frustrated Dale Earnhardt walks to his trailer, having lost yet another February classic. A reporter (either naive or very brave) sticks a microphone in his face and asks The Question: "Dale, when are you going to win the Daytona 500?" Everyone groans. "Who knows?" is the tired answer.

By 1998, Earnhardt had done it all—almost. He had seven championships, tying the King, and more than seventy wins (sixth all-time). He'd won on short tracks, road courses, and superspeedways and had twenty-two poles to his credit. As the winningest speedway driver at the speedway, with thirty victories in total, he seemed the perfect candidate to conquer the Daytona 500. He had two Pepsi 400 wins, he'd won the Busch Clash six times, and as of '98 he'd won the last nine of the 125 qualifying races he'd been in. Toss in seven Busch Grand National wins at the track for good measure, and The Question takes on new meaning.

He came close to winning on several occasions. Every year he was strong, many years clearly outclassing the field, but before he could catch the checkered flag something always happened. Blown engines plagued him throughout the 1980s. In '86, he was running second with three laps left and had the strength to make the pass when he ran out of gas. He lost the '89 race on fuel mileage to gas miser Darrell Waltrip. In '90 he was leading going into turn three on the last lap and blew a tire in turn four. The '93 and '96 races were the "Dale & Dale" shows, except that it was Dale Jarrett who stole the lead on the last lap both times to take the win.

By February 15, 1998, the date of the Intimidator's twentieth attempt to win the Daytona 500, Earnhardt was answering The Question with: "Maybe I'm not supposed to win the darn thing." He hadn't won a single pole the previous year, so missed the Bud Shootout. He'd stopped running BGN races, and didn't compete in the Busch 300. So his first shot at Daytona that February was in his 125-mile (200km) qualifier. He won it, hands down, no contest. It was the first

win the team had had in quite a while. They'd gone fifty-nine races without a victory. Earnhardt, Childress, and crew chief McReynolds were all focused on breaking that streak and they wanted to do it at Daytona. Ultimately, Earnhardt wound up in the fourth starting spot for the race.

When the green flag flew, the number 3 went right to the front and stayed there. He led for more than half the race, 107 laps total on five occasions. He last took the lead from teammate Mike Skinner and was up front when the yellow flag flew on lap 174. Two tires, gas, and 8.5 seconds later the number 3 peeled out of its pit stall and resumed the lead, beating Skinner, Rusty Wallace, and Jeremy Mayfield to the line.

After the restart the two RCR Monte Carlos worked together to try and separate themselves from the Penske team entries of Mayfield and Wallace. But the blue and white Fords cashiered Mike Skinner, putting him out of the running, and drafting Jeff Gordon along for good measure, set their sights on the Goodwrench Chevy. Before they could mount a charge, Gordon pulled out alongside Wallace, breaking him out of the draft with his teammate Mayfield. Earnhardt used the breather to gain a bit of space. There were only a handful of laps to go. The next time Dale looked in his mirror, it wasn't the Mobil 1 Ford he saw, but the green Interstate Batteries

Pontiac of Bobby Labonte. Labonte had restarted in sixth but shot past the whole pack of contenders and moved into second behind Earnhardt. Labonte had started on the pole for the race so he clearly had a fast car.

With two laps left, Childress' crew chief, Larry McReynolds, was starting to get excited, sure they had the win. Childress quieted him. "We've been here before," he cautioned. On lap 199, three cars spun on the backstretch and the yellow flag waved. If Earnhardt could hold off the pack until he reached the caution, it would be all over. As Dale came out of the fourth turn, everyone held his or her breath, waiting for the lightning bolt that would rob him of the win.

But this time Earnhardt, who had taken the yellow and white flags, completed the last lap without incident and won the Daytona 500. Pandemonium erupted. Even the "anyone but Earnhardt" contingent had to admit that it was a proud moment for the sport. As he drove onto pit road, Dale was greeted by a long line of pit crews, each waiting to high-five him as he drove by. It was an unprecedented show of support from the whole community. This time the postrace interview was different, with Earnhardt laughing and joking. The Intimidator would never have to answer that particular question again.

PAGES 76–77: Each year more than 100,000 spectators and millions of television viewers watch the Daytona 500, which marks the opening of the NASCAR Winston Cup season. The 500-miler is the exclamation point at the end of a full week of racing events that includes the Bud Shootout and Busch Grand National and ARCA races, not to mention the 125-mile (200km) qualifying runs.
ABOVE: Richard Petty is congratulated by four clearly impressed young women for winning his 200th race, at the Firecracker 400 in July 1984 at Daytona. It was an unprecedented feat and one likely never to be repeated, though the last two wins were in a number 43 car owned by another team. Petty had taken his car, sponsor, and talents to Mike Curb Motorsports to allow Petty Enterprises to focus on son Kyle's fledgling number 7 team.

Dale Earnhardt begins a long and well-deserved victory celebration following his 1998 Daytona 500 win, the first in the Intimidator's long career. Here, the crews of the other teams line up to congratulate Dale on his long-awaited victory. The win broke not only his Daytona curse, but also the longest winless streak he'd had since the start of his career: fifty-nine races. It would be the only win for the number 3 team with crew chief Larry McReynolds, who moved over to Richard Childress' other team (Mike Skinner's number 31) in '99.

The 2001 Daytona 500

The forty-third annual running of the Great American Race had more backstory than there had been for years.

First, after a seventeen-year hiatus, Mopar was back in the Winston Cup, with the Dodge Intrepid. Several big name teams—Petty Enterprises, Bill Davis Racing, and Chip Ganassi Racing (formerly Sabco)—joined Dodge's flagship effort with the new model. Second, there was NASCAR's new television deal with Fox and NBC. The sport had grown by leaps and bounds, and now it had the extra boost it needed to compete with the "big three," the NFL, NBA, and MLB. Finally, to transform the (slightly dull) nine-lead-change 2000 Daytona 500 into the competitive race the new networks wanted, NASCAR made some significant rules changes for the 2001 Daytona. Aerodynamic changes would lower car speeds, but bigger openings in the restrictor plates would give the drivers more horsepower to work with and the ability to maneuver without a twenty-car-long draft developing.

Everyone expected the new Dodge teams to be fast, but there was still quite a bit of excitement when Bill Elliott put his number 9 Intrepid (sponsored by Dodge, the first direct factory sponsorship of a team in years) on the pole. Stacy Compton was in second in the Melling number 92 Dodge, while Sterling Marlin had won his qualifier in the number 40 Dodge.

When the teams lined up on Sunday there were some familiar faces near the front—Dale Earnhardt, Dale Earnhardt Jr., and Mike Skinner—while at the back of the pack there were some unexpected faces, including three-time Daytona winner Dale Jarrett and reigning champion Bobby Labonte.

Marlin and Ward Burton were among the fastest cars through the first half of the race, with Burton leading the most laps, though Earnhardt made his way to the front and took the lead on lap 27, making it the twenty-third Daytona 500 he'd led. Overall, the action was fast and furious. The familiar bunch of drafting cars was still there, but individuals and small groups of cars were pulling out and passing successfully. Through the first 160 laps there were only two cautions.

Then the "big one," as announcer Darrell Waltrip called the crash on lap 175, brought the race to a halt. Robby Gordon had touched the back of Ward Burton, who had spun into Tony Stewart. Stewart's number 20 Pontiac became airborne and the resulting scramble sidelined eighteen cars, including contenders Burton, Jeff Gordon, and Mark Martin.

When the race resumed, the front of the field looked like an advertisement for Dale Earnhardt, Inc. Michael Waltrip, with Earnardt's new number 15 team, was on the point, followed by Dale Jr., with Dale Sr. in third. Marlin, who'd lost a lap earlier, had charged back to contend with the front pack as well.

The last 20 laps were among the best ever in a Daytona race. As big brother Darrell coached from the announcer's booth, Michael Waltrip battled to keep the Earnhardts behind him. Lap after lap, everyone waited for the Intimidator to take the lead, but Waltrip hung on. With just a few laps left, the number 15 and number 8 extended their lead and had only each other to contend with for the victory. "You got 'em," hollered a teary-eyed Darrell Waltrip as little brother Michael took the checkered and earned his first Winston Cup victory.

But the story wasn't over. The footage of Waltrip crossing the line showed a small cloud of smoke in the background where several cars crashed coming out of turn four. Earnhardt Sr. had fallen back from the front two and was dueling for third with Marlin, Ken Schrader, and Rusty Wallace. As they came around the final turn, the four cars were glued together when Marlin just touched the back end of the number 3. Earnhardt drifted toward the apron, then jerked back to the right and drove across the track, head on into the outside wall at full speed. Schrader had nowhere to go and smashed into the right side of the number 3. The two wrecked vehicles slid down to the infield as the rest of the field roared by.

While the number 15 team hooted and danced in victory lane, waiting for Earnhardt to rush up and congratulate Waltrip, emergency crews rushed to the number 3. The Man in Black was removed from his car and rushed to the local trauma center, but to no avail. Dale Earnhardt, a racing legend and hero to millions of fans, had died on impact from massive head injuries.

The racing world was stunned. Thousands of fans camped outside of the raceway to commemorate the fallen champion. Newspapers and TV stations nationwide featured the story and the country mourned the loss of an American hero.

Daytona—NASCAR MVP

Many of NASCAR's most memorable and most important races have been run on the 2.5 miles (4km) at Daytona—a word that by now is synonymous with speed, excitement, and glamor—and today the Daytona 500 is the world's biggest motorsport event. Appropriately, the facilities for fans and race teams at this most famous of superspeedways are constantly growing and improving. Daytona is, hands down, the MVP in an all-star lineup of NASCAR speedways.

ATLANTA MOTOR SPEEDWAY

LOCATION: *Atlanta, Georgia*
RACE LENGTH: *300–500 miles (480–800km) on a 1.54-mile (2.5km) paved oval*
NUMBER OF RACES RUN: *Eighty-three Grand National and Winston Cup, between July 31, 1960, and November 20, 2000*
SPEED RECORD (AVERAGE FOR AN ENTIRE RACE): *163.633 mph (261.8kph), set on November 12, 1995*

The Atlanta International Raceway opened in 1960, with its first race date in June that year. Construction on the speedway had actually started much earlier and the track had been scheduled to open in '59, but various problems delayed its completion. At 1.5 miles (2.4km) around, the track was the

With wins the previous two weeks, rookie Tony Stewart (in the number 20 Home Depot car) was hoping for a strong Atlanta run as well in 1999. The car wasn't on the mark, though. He started thirtieth and finished fifteenth, leading only one lap.

In 1977, for the first time since NASCAR's very first season, three women raced in the same event, the Firecracker 400. Richard Petty beat Darrell Waltrip, but on a more socially relevant note, the race featured Janet Guthrie, Christine Beckers, and Lella Lombardi. Guthrie planned on racing most of the year, her second in NASCAR, in the Kelly Girl number 68, and started twentieth in the July race. Junie Donlavey put Belgian Christine Beckers in his number 93 Ford for that race, and Italy's Lombardi made her only Winston Cup start in Charles Dean's number 5. Mechanical problems sidelined all three before the halfway point, but the tradition of women behind the wheel was kept alive.

Janet Guthrie (RIGHT), Christine Beckers (BELOW LEFT), and Lella Lombardi (BELOW RIGHT), all of whom had experience in open-wheel series, were initially tapped for a tour of NASCAR racing by Charlotte's general manager, Humpy Wheeler, as a way to generate publicity for the series. For the Europeans it was a one-time deal, but Guthrie raced in thirty-three Winston Cup events, from 1976 to '80, racking up five top-ten finishes along the way.

Grant Adcox (in the number 22 car owned by his father, Herb), who had five top-ten finishes in his career (from 1974 through '89), was killed in this crash in the '89 season finale at Atlanta. Adcox slid hard into the wall on lap 202 and his car erupted into flames. He died from head and chest injuries, becoming the twenty-third Grand National/Winston Cup racer to perish in a racing crash.

biggest true oval on the circuit at the time. NASCAR had been racing at nearby Lakewood Speedway, a 1-mile (1.6km) dirt track, but shifted to the new track when it opened.

The first decade at the superspeedway pretty much belonged to Fearless Fred Lorenzen. Though Fireball Roberts won the first event, Lorenzen, driving the number 28 Holman-Moody Ford, won four races and had several second-place finishes through the mid-1960s.

The top NASCAR team owners apparently mistook the 1966 Dixie 400 for a custom car show. Junior Johnson unveiled his infamous "Yellow Banana" at the race. The number 26 Ford was clearly not stock: the hood and windshield were sloped for better aerodynamics, the roofline was lowered so the car sat closer to the ground and had a better center of gravity, and the rear deck was angled up to catch the air. Cotton Owens also entered a trick car: his number 6 had a cable in the cockpit that, when pulled by the driver, lowered the car closer to the ground. Other teams were equally creative and by rights they all should have been sent packing, but NASCAR's rulings after inspection were inconsistent to say the least. Ned Jarrett's Ford was a brand new model, but not obviously tricked up. Even so the team was slapped with a long list of "must fixes"; with no way to comply in time for the race, Jarrett's team went home. Owen's "cable ready" Dodge was nabbed and David Pearson had to sit out the race, but Johnson's Ford passed with flying colors. In the face of all this hoopla, Richard Petty's win was almost an afterthought.

Despite solid racing at the track, the facility experienced financial difficulties through much of its history. The track was acquired by Larry LoPatin's American Raceways, Inc. (ARI) in the late 1960s and struggled as the company experienced severe cash shortages. LoPatin exacerbated the track's problems by openly criticizing a number of NASCAR's rulings. Subsequently citing inadequate purses at the tracks as the reason, NASCAR officials conspicuously left ARI's speedways out of the big television deals that had been negotiated for the '70 season. Atlanta was one of the tracks affected, and the crisis came to a head when ARI was unable to post the promised purse for the '70 Dixie 500. At the last minute, Charlotte Motor Speedway General Manager Richard Howard came up with the funds and the race was held. LoPatin and his top aides resigned from the speedway corporation shortly thereafter.

The track continued operations for many years under new leadership, but by 1990 was once again on the verge of insolvency. This time, Speedway Motorsports, Inc. (SMI) owner O. Bruton Smith came to the rescue. At Smith's urging, SMI bought the track, changed its name to Atlanta Motor Speedway, and sank significant capital into improvements.

Atlanta's Highlights

Dave Marcis enjoyed success at the Georgia track through the 1970s. Driving the K&K Insurance Dodge for temperamental owner Nord Krauskopf, Marcis earned one of his five career wins in '76 and had several other top-five finishes there. He treated fans to a ride-along in '81, when he carried the first in-car camera for ABC Sports. Television viewers got to watch Dave race, then scramble as rookie Tim Richmond spun in front of him, then tumble along the front stretch. Dave survived uninjured, but the camera did not.

The Wood Brothers have been among the dominant teams at Atlanta since the track first opened. Marvin Panch took the team's number 21 to victory lane in 1965 and Cale Yarborough earned three consecutive Atlanta 500 wins for them from '67 to '69. The team didn't contend in the spring '71 race (they had pulled out in disgust over the apparent concessions given to Mopar, specifically the number 43), but A.J. Foyt kept the winning tradition alive in the late-season race. With David Pearson in the maroon and white Mercury, the Wood Brothers won three more. Proving the versatility of Glen and Leonard Wood's operation, Neil Bonnett, who replaced Pearson in '79, captured two November races. Morgan Shepherd's greatest success in Winston Cup has been at Atlanta: three of his four career victories happened there, the last of those in the Citgo number 21 in '93 (the Wood Brothers' last win to date). In '93, the "Great Blizzard" blanketed even the Southern states with snow and freezing sleet. The March race had to be postponed a week as temperatures in the Atlanta area dipped to –11 degrees Fahrenheit (–6.1°C) and local power grids succumbed to the storm.

The Man in Black, Dale Earnhardt, is the track record holder, with nine Atlanta trophies on his shelves, the first of which he won in 1980 (en route to the championship). The runner-up that day was a young kid in his very first big league race. Roger Penske prepped the number 16 Chevy for the young ARCA racer, Rusty Wallace, and was no doubt pleased with the second-place finish. The two hooked up again in '91 on the Miller Beer number 2 team that continues to be a familiar sight in victory lane today.

Earnhardt's most recent victory at this writing, in the 2000 Cracker Barrel Old Country Store 500, was perhaps the closest finish in NASCAR history. Mike Skinner, in the number 31, led much of the event, and looked like he might earn his first win. With twenty laps left, though, his engine blew, leaving the number 3 (Earnhardt) and the number 18 (Bobby Labonte) to contest the win. Earnhardt and Labonte came of turn four on the last lap side-by-side, and as they crossed the finish line the same way, a hush fell over the crowd and garage. No one could tell who'd won. The photo replay showed the number 3 ahead by a mere two inches (5.1 cm), a significant figure since NASCAR had just that week allowed Earnhardt's team to extend his front air dams two inches to improve handling. For an unexciting 2000 season, the photo finish was a welcome dose of drama.

LEFT: Dale Earnhardt hangs on tightly to his 1990 Winston Cup championship trophy, as if to make sure it doesn't jump out of his arms and scamper away. The crown almost did get away from him—Mark Martin finished the season a mere 26 points behind Earnhardt in the points standings. RIGHT: Winning a race can make a man do strange things... Bill Elliott poses for the traditional "now wear it like a hat" photo following his November 1985 Atlanta win. Actually, he probably would have liked to have hid under that trophy—despite the fact that it was his eleventh win of the year, he lost the championship to Darrell Waltrip by 101 points.

⚑ The 1992 Hooters 500

The fall Atlanta race had been the final event on the Winston Cup schedule each year since 1987. Through the years, championships had been decided well before the circuit reached the Peach State, but the 1992 battle came down not just to the last race, but to the last laps of that November 15 race.

Davey Allison had had an up-and-down year in 1992. He had won the Daytona 500 and led the points early on, but was set back by injuries from his last-lap collision in The Winston and the terrifying tumble he had taken at Pocono in July. With their fifth win of the year at Phoenix the week prior, the number 28 Texaco team was back on top

PAGES 84–85: Pole-sitter Bobby Labonte (number 18) and Mike Skinner (number 31) lead the field under threatening skies at the 1999 Cracker Barrel 500 (at Atlanta). ABOVE: A uniquely American success story, Alan Kulwicki had turned down rides with several top teams in order to be his own master. All season long, the Hooters team made the most of every opportunity and then used a careful pit strategy to pull out the 1992 championship at the final race in Atlanta. Here, Kulwicki hoists the hard-fought Winston Cup trophy high above his head. Kulwicki's success as an independent driver-owner was an inspiration to everyone in the NASCAR community.

of the points standings, albeit by a slim margin, going into the final race.

Meanwhile, Alan Kulwicki owned and drove for the number 7 Hooters Ford team. He had enjoyed increasing success over the last several years, but as an independent owner wasn't given much of a chance to win the championship (the nameplate on the front of his Ford T-bird was altered to read "Underbird"). Kulwicki was in the chase, though, at the end of 1992 at only 30 points behind Allison. Hometown favorite Bill Elliott had won four races in his first year with Junior Johnson and was third in the points, just 10 behind Kulwicki. Kyle Petty, Harry Gant, and Mark Martin all had remote, but real, shots at the championship as well, so the points race was in full gallop at Atlanta.

On top of all of that, the Hooters 500 was Richard Petty's very last race as a driver. The fifty-five-year old legend had announced his impending retirement before the start of the season, and had run a special Fan Appreciation Tour throughout the year. After Atlanta, Petty would be strategizing races from the pit box instead of the cockpit.

The starting lineup was a bit perplexing as most of the points leaders were starting mid-pack or back. Martin was the only one of them with a top-ten qualifying run. Earnhardt and Ernie Irvan had top-five spots, though, and swapped the lead throughout the first sixty laps of the race. Martin's car was strong early, but his normally stout Rousch powerplant went south, taking him out of contention. Gant and Petty moved up from dismal starting positions but not enough to matter (they finished thirteenth and sixteenth, respectively). That left only Allison, Kulwicki, and Elliott as championship contenders.

Allison struggled early on, running over debris on lap two that damaged his front air dam. The repairs put him far behind on the track; all Davey needed was a fifth-place finish to clinch but he was far from that. Then a timely caution let him catch back up to the pack and he started working his way, spot by spot, into contention. By lap 285 he was running in seventh and within sight of the fifth-place car. As he closed in on that car—Ernie Irvan's number 4 Kodak Chevy— it blew a tire and spun into the wall, then ricocheted back across the track, leaving Allison with nowhere to go. The damage to the number 28 from the collision was substantial. Allison's championship hopes lay broken on the track along with the pieces of his car. He put a brave face on it as he was interviewed on the way back to his trailer but couldn't mask the frustration and bitter disappointment he felt.

Then there were two. The race was much kinder to Kulwicki and Elliott. Both cars were intact and in position to challenge. When it became apparent that the title was between the two of them, there was no holding them back. By lap sixty, Elliott was in the lead with Kulwicki right behind. They swapped the lead back and forth, Kulwicki holding the point three times in the number 7 and Elliott taking seven turns up front. As the race wound down, Elliott was

The Superspeedways

The 1994 rookie class was a big and promising one. Jeff Burton took Rookie of the Year honors driving for the number 8 Stavola brothers team, beating out brother Ward, Jeremy Mayfield, John Andretti, Jor Nemechek, and Steve Grissom. Jeff Burton remained with the team in '95 and earned four top-tens before moving to Jack Rousch's number 99 operation in '96.

clearly in command and Kulwicki a good ways behind. It seemed the race was in the bag for the number 11 team.

Junior Johnson's Budweiser crew hadn't started celebrating, though, because the points just weren't adding up. If the two finished as they were running, in first and second, Elliott would gain only five points on Kulwicki, not enough to bridge the ten-point gap separating them for the season. With the extra five points that a driver can win by leading the most laps in a Winston Cup race, however, Elliott could tie Kulwicki. Then, as per the NASCAR rules, the win would go to the driver with the highest number of wins for the year—in this case, Elliott, who had five (Kulwicki had just one). But even if Elliott stayed up front for the rest of the race he would have only 102 laps, while Kulwicki already had 103. The Hooters crew had also been carefully calculating their stops, making sure that Alan stayed on track just long enough to get the critical bonus. The Winston Cup championship, it appeared, would come down to an earlier green flag pit stop. Elliott's crew had brought him in one lap too soon, giving up the lead to Kulwicki at a critical juncture.

With nothing to lose, Awesome Bill from Dawsonville put the hammer down for the remainder of the race and won,

his fifth victory of the season. Meanwhile, the Underbird did exactly what he needed to do to stay in second place. In the end, the Budweiser team won the battle, but lost the war. Victory lane photos show Elliott smiling broadly, giving the "we're number 1" sign, and hugging the beauty queen. But inside, he had to be crying.

Against all odds, Alan Kulwicki had worked his way to the pinnacle of the sport. Typically, the Wisconsin racer was low-key as he donned the Winston Cup Champion cap alongside Elliott in the winner's circle. It was clear how he felt, though, when he whipped the Underbird around at the start/finish line and slowly cruised the Atlanta speedway backwards in his trademark "Polish victory lap."

Alan Kulwicki had little time to enjoy his success. In April 1993, on his way to qualify at Bristol, the small plane carrying him and executives for his sponsor, Hooters Restaurants, crashed in a meadow just five miles (8km) short of the airstrip. All aboard were killed. Kulwicki's untimely death (the first for a current champion since Joe Weatherly's in '64) was deeply felt in the NASCAR community. Rusty Wallace, winner of the Bristol race the next week, commemorated his friend and competitor with his own reverse victory lap.

E ach season the Winston Cup teams run a full schedule of points races. At the end of the season, the driver with the most points wins the cup. There are several special events each year that do not count towards the points competition. Like the all-star games of other sports, these races are purely for money and bragging rights (mainly the latter). Since they don't affect the championship picture, teams can go all-out with only one purpose: get to the front. As a result, the events are often exciting, sometimes spectacular, and the fans love them.

American Challenge Cup

was the first of NASCAR's all-star races. This event was held during Speedweeks at Daytona in February from 1961 to '63. The ten-lap dash was by invitation to drivers who had won major races the prior year (a prelude of things to come for the smallest tracks). Eleven drivers competed in '61. Joe Weatherly won with a last-lap pass on Fireball Roberts. Roberts reversed the ending the following year in another close finish. Only half of the thirteen invitees accepted in '63. Many considered the risk of damaging their car—most teams back then only had one car—unacceptable. Fred Lorenzen took home the trophy. Attendance, both by fans and drivers, was insufficient to continue the race after '63.

The Bud Shootout

began in 1979 as the Busch Clash, sponsored by the Anheiser-Busch Brewery. Busch had previously sponsored weekly awards for pole winners and conceived of the event as a "quickest of the quickest" race for pole winners from the previous year. The Clash has been held since then at Daytona, in the week prior to the 500. It's a twenty-lap shootout (the name was changed to the Bud Shootout in '98) for a big purse. Dale Earnhardt has been the master of the event, with six wins over the years.

Daytona Twin 125s

are the two races in which drivers qualify for the Daytona 500, the lineup for which is set primarily by the finishing positions of the competitors in the two 125-mile (200km) races. The field is split in half and the top fifteen finishers from each race get into the Daytona 500. In the modern era these races are purely for that purpose, but until 1968 they also were part of the regular Grand National schedule and counted towards the championship points. When Daytona

Kyle Petty (number 44) and Derrike Cope (number 30) race under the lights at Charlotte in the Winston Open in 1998. The Open is a "heat" race preceding The Winston. Teams that don't qualify for The Winston can vie in the Open for one transfer spot—the winner gets to run in The Winston. It's well worth the attempt. The Winston is a non-points event run purely for bragging right and money. Mark Martin earned more than $250,000 as the '98 winner.

The IROC series today features U.S. cars, and all IROC events take place on oval courses. And as the format changed, so have the results: NASCAR drivers now dominate the races and standings, winning more often than not.

opened in '59 there was only one qualifier for the GN crowd—the other was run for the Convertible Division cars that were also in the 500 that year. The next year, without the convertibles, two races were run. As in so many events, Dale Earnhardt holds the record, with eleven Twin 125 victories.

International Race of Champions (IROC)

races answer the question, "Who is the best race car driver in the world?" A cooperative venture among different racing organizations, the IROC series puts the top drivers from each of the major racing organizations together for four races, in identically prepared cars. In theory the only thing that's different is the driver. The series started in 1973, when the hottest drivers in USAC, SCCA, FIA (Formula 1), and NASCAR were invited to compete. Over the years the World of Outlaws and Busch Grand National series have also been tapped for talent. Races have been run at the biggest NASCAR and Indy Car tracks in the country. As popularity grew, the races shifted to mostly oval tracks, which are able to host more fans.

So who has that best driver been? Unfortunately not all of the invitees have participated in the races so it's hard to say, but Al Unser Jr. and Dale Earnhardt have been fierce competitors over the series' history and share the record for number of IROC wins, with eleven each. Mark Martin has won the most championships (points are awarded based on finishing position in each race), with four over the last six years.

IROC races are run today in specially prepared Pontiac Firebird TransAms. Only the color of the paint job differs from car to car. With that kind of equality, the racing has often been tight. In fact, the 1992 Daytona race ended in one of those rare occurrences— a true tie. The video replay showed NASCAR's Ricky Rudd and Harry Gant literally dead even as they took the checkered.

The Winston

was launched in 1985, the same year that R.J. Reynolds unveiled its Winston Million program. The Winston is an RJR-sponsored all-star competition for race winners from the previous year. Originally a seventy-five-lap run, the race has evolved into a more exciting three-segment format. The pole order of the second and third segments is determined by the finish of each previous segment. The race has settled in at Lowe's (formerly Charlotte) Motor Speedway and is conducted with much hoopla.

There have been lots of fireworks over the years in the run for the money. Dale Earnhardt muscled past Bill Elliott in the action-packed 1987 finish, immortalized as "the pass in the grass." Darrell Waltrip got a taste of his own medicine when he was tapped and spun out by Rusty Wallace in the '89 event. Davey Allison won the '92 race, the first held at night under the lights at Charlotte, going backwards: he and Kyle Petty had been racing hard for the checkered, and touched going into the middle of the front dogleg. Allison spun around, hitting the wall hard, but beat Petty to the line, rear bumper first. Michael Waltrip's only Winston Cup win to date was the '96 Winston Select (same race, different name).

And off the track...

Another special event of sorts is the annual vote for the most popular Winston Cup driver. Any racing fan can vote by sending in an official form. The first winner was Curtis Turner, in 1956. Over the years Richard Petty's and Bobby Allison's fans have weighed in, giving those drivers nine and seven wins, respectively, but the uncontested champ is Bill Elliott, who has won almost every year since 1984.

Humpy Wheeler has positioned Charlotte (now known as Lowe's Motor Speedway) as a leader in quality and service, as this packed house for the 1996 Coca Cola 600 testifies. Wheeler came to the track from Firestone Tires in '75 to join new owner Bruton Smith. As director of racing at Firestone, then at Charlotte, Wheeler has also helped bring the sport much of its current talent, hooking up quite a few young drivers (Dale Earnhardt Sr., among others) with their first big-league rides.

Atlanta Today

Like its counterparts, Atlanta has been the site of tragedy as well as triumph over the years. The 1984 Atlanta Journal 500 was NASCAR rookie Terry Schoonover's second race. His number 42 Chevy went hard into the wall on lap 129 of the race, killing the thirty-two-year old Floridian. Another death at Atlanta resulted in big changes to race procedures. Through the '90 season, cars were allowed to enter and exit pit road at high speed. Mike Ritch, a tire-changer on the Bill Elliott number 9 team, was killed when Ricky Rudd lost control of his car coming onto pit road and pinned the crewman between his and Elliott's cars. As a result NASCAR instituted set pit road speed limits to lessen the danger to the exposed crewmembers. Any team that exceeds the set pit road speed during the race is black flagged and must revisit pit road for a stop-and-go penalty. Further, any car that loses control and spins out on pit road is hit with a stiff one-lap stop.

The Atlanta track underwent a significant overhaul after the 1997 season. The track was drastically reconfigured to a D-shaped oval much like the Charlotte or Texas speedways. The new setup was much faster; in fact, since Atlanta has no restrictor-plate limitations, it is now one of the fastest tracks on the circuit. Bobby Labonte has been the master of the new oval, with four wins at the track in just four years. Labonte's '96 victory in the season-ending NAPA 500 was a special moment that illustrated the family element of the sport. Bobby had won the race, but older brother Terry had just won his second Winston Cup championship (twelve years after the first, in '84). The number 18 and number 5 cars circled the track together for a shared victory lap.

LOWE'S MOTOR SPEEDWAY (FORMERLY CHARLOTTE MOTOR SPEEDWAY)

Location: Concord, North Carolina
Race length: 400–500 miles (640–800km) on a 1.017-mile (1.6km) paved oval
Number of races run: Eighty-two Grand National and Winston Cup, between October 31, 1965, and October 8, 2000
Speed record (average for an entire race): 160.306 mph (256.5km), set on October 11, 1999

Daytona may be the most famous, Talladega the fastest, and Bristol the most action-packed track, but Lowe's Motor Speedway (formerly Charlotte Motor Speedway) gets the prize for the best overall show. Vice President H.A. "Humpy" Wheeler hasn't missed a trick in ensuring that fans get the best value for their money at his track. From food quality, concession prices, and cleanliness of facilities to the incredible prerace shows that liven the long hours fans spend in their seats, the Charlotte track exudes hospitality.

For all its present polish, the speedway got off to a pretty rocky start. Curtis Turner, an entrepreneur as well as a racer, sensed the direction NASCAR was taking and decided to build a superspeedway of his own. He partnered with Bruton Smith and the two came up with enough cash to break ground in the summer of 1959. It wasn't long before construction costs escalated and exceeded the capital available. Juggling bills and commitments, Turner got the track open for its inaugural race in June a year later, though just barely.

Like the man behind the track, the race was meant to be the toughest on the circuit, so the length was set at a grueling—for cars, drivers, and track alike—600 miles (960km). The asphalt was so green that the racers mounted radiator screens before the race to protect them from the chunks of the surface that had been breaking up all through the practice and qualifying laps.

The strategy for teams in that first World 600, in 1960, was simple: avoid the holes in the track and the flying debris and survive until the end. Tom Pistone was doing just fine, with a five-lap lead, until a "meteorite" punctured his gas tank and took him out of the race. Running in second, Joe Lee Johnson had a pretty good lead over third place so he quickly went from being five laps down to four laps ahead. Less than a third of the sixty-car field made it through the day, with Joe Lee outlasting the competitors for his second NASCAR win. A number of drivers, including Junior Johnson and both Pettys, were disqualified during the race for "improper entry onto pit road."

The first World 600 was a success, but the creditors banging on Turner's and Smith's doors were almost as numerous as the fans in attendance. Turner approached the Teamsters Union looking for a loan to bail him out of debt, but the deal fell through. In addition, the track's board of directors took issue with the move and fired Turner as track president in June 1961. Undaunted, Turner figured that if he could get the debts paid off he could gain back control of his baby. He went back to the Teamsters, this time offering to organize a union of NASCAR drivers in return for the $800 thousand he needed to erase the red ink.

The Federation of Professional Athletes formed in August 1961, but met with immediate and intense resistance from Bill France. The group quickly dissolved, leaving Turner out in the cold—he not only lost the track forever, but was banned for life from NASCAR as well, although the rather severe ban was later rescinded. Little by little the Charlotte Motor Speedway became a profitable racing enterprise, and

It may not seem like much today, but in 1978 six hundred dollars was pretty good money, especially for an ancillary award (i.e., winning crew chief of the race). Darrell Waltrip (third from left) and his chief mechanic Buddy Parrott (second from left) accept the check on behalf of the DiGard number 88 team after winning the '78 World 600, the first of Waltrip's six career victories at Charlotte.

now (in its current incarnation as Lowe's Motor Speedway) is the keystone of Bruton Smith's Speedway Motorsports, Inc. empire.

Racing at Charlotte

Once the surface settled, Charlotte quickly became a racer's racetrack and hosted quite a few exciting duels. Joe Weatherly, for instance, took the lead in the 1961 National 400 with fewer than five laps left and held off Richard Petty's ferocious charge by a car length.

Jim Paschal gave up a three-lap lead on lap 339 of 400 in May 1967, when he "slid up into the marbles" (pieces of rubber on the track), and scraped along the guardrail for a couple hundred feet. He lost the lead in the pits but still returned as the leader. Paschal's lap speeds dropped by more than 10 mph (16kph) after the accident but he wrestled his ill-handling Plymouth around the last fifty circuits, holding off challengers David Pearson and Bobby Allison to take the win by a scant five seconds.

There are certainly many professions whose practitioners are frequently in harm's way, but few vocations are as consistently and conspicuously dangerous as auto racing. Today's driver is protected by the best equipment and contingency plans that technology and the racing community's considerable ingenuity can produce, but he is never entirely safe; each time that driver pulls out of pit road for a race, qualifying run, or practice session, he is at risk.

Over NASCAR's fifty-year history, twenty-five drivers have lost their lives in racing accidents, and of those years 1964 was a particularly black one, as the sport lost several of its brightest stars. First, NASCAR was robbed of its reigning champion when Joe Weatherly was killed at Riverside in January. Not long after that the NASCAR family suffered another devastating blow.

The 1964 World 600

Glenn "Fireball" (for his blazing baseball pitch) Roberts grew up in the Daytona area, so was exposed to racing from an early age. He ran in the very first NASCAR races and scored his first win in 1950 at age twenty-one (still one of the youngest of all winners). In an era when many of the big stars were brash and larger than life, Roberts' quiet intensity and broad smile made him a fan favorite. He hooked up with the factory team of Pete DePaolo and then Holman-Moody through the second half of the '50s and rode the number 22 Fords to victory lane nineteen times. In '59 he went to drive for mechanical magician Smokey Yunick, and in '62 they captured the Daytona 500 and two other wins. Ford's Jacques Passino lured Roberts back to the Ford factory team in '63 and Fireball drove the metallic purple number 22 Galaxie that year and the next.

The Ford team had only one win going into the World 600 on May 24, 1964, but had several top-fives at the track over the years and managed an eleventh-place starting spot, so had a chance at a good finish. Jimmy Pardue sat on the pole and sprinted out to the lead at the green flag.

It didn't take long for the first caution flag to fly. On lap seven, Ned Jarrett and Junior Johnson crashed on the backstretch. Roberts, trying to avoid the spinning cars, got turned around and backed hard into a concrete abutment. The impact burst his fuel tank and the number 22 was engulfed in flames as it flipped onto its roof. Ned Jarrett, whose car was also swathed in flames, scrambled out and ran to Roberts' car. Roberts, seeing Jarrett, cried for help. Jarrett pulled the badly burned racer from the car and Roberts was flown to the local hospital in critical condition.

The race eventually resumed, with Paul Goldsmith leading the most laps until the engine in his number 25 Plymouth blew out. Jim Paschal, having returned to driving duties in

ABOVE: Two three-time champions battle for the lead. Darrell Waltrip's Gatorade car leads David Pearson's Purolator car by a fender in the 1978 World 600 at Charlotte. Both Waltrip, who took the win that day, and Pearson, who finished fifth, had enjoyed repeated victories with their teams, but would soon leave for other rides due to controversy—in Waltrip's case, contract disputes, and in Pearson's, internal disagreements.
OPPOSITE: Charlotte (now Lowe's) Motor Speedway is considered the home track of several NASCAR teams, many of whose headquarters are located in nearby Mooresville, North Carolina. In this photo of the October 1997 race, Mark Martin (number 6) leads the eventual winner, Dale Jarrett (car 88). Prior to this event, R.J. Reynolds had announced the inception of the new "No Bull 5" program, to replace the twelve-year-old Winston Million award.

Petty Enterprise's number 41, led the last 125 laps and won by four circuits over his boss, Richard.

Roberts had been burned over more than 80 percent of his body. Over the next several months he appeared to be improving, but after an operation in June, infection set in and turned to pneumonia and sepsis. Fireball Roberts, one of NASCAR's true heroes and an instrumental part of its success in a turbulent era, died on July 2, 1964.

Tragically the Charlotte track saw another racing death later that same year. Jimmy Pardue was testing tires at the track in September. As he went into turn three a tire popped and he rode up into the guardrail. He broke through the barrier and flew out over the tall embankment outside the track. The car landed more than 100 yards (91.2m) away. Pardue died later that night of his injuries. Pardue was a two-time winner of the Grand National series.

The Early Winston Era at Charlotte

Tight racing at Charlotte continued into the modern era. Buddy Baker and Bobby Allison swapped the lead fifty times in a ten-lap shootout at the end of the 1972 spring race. Baker asserted that Allison tapped him out of the way to make the last pass (recalling the roughshod racing between him and Petty on the short tracks earlier that year). The strength of Benny Parson's number 72 in the '77 NAPA 500 was such that, despite running out of gas and giving up a one-lap lead over Cale Yarbrough, he was able to run

Dale and Theresa Earnhardt celebrate together in victory lane after Dale's Coca-Cola 600 win in 1993. Theresa is an integral part of Dale Earnhardt, Inc., as team owner of the Busch Grand National team and in other areas of the thriving business.

the number 11 down, resume the lead, and rebuild the one-lap cushion. Parsons beat six-time Charlotte winner Darrell Waltrip in a tense battle at the end of the '80 World 600. The two traded the lead eight times over the last twenty-six laps, with Parsons hanging on for the last two laps to win.

The winningest drivers at Charlotte are Bobby Allison and Darrell Waltrip, with six victories apiece. Dale Earnhardt has five wins there. Some special moments in the Intimidator's early racing career are tied to the 1.5-mile (2.4km) track. Earnhardt's very first Winston Cup start was at Charlotte in 1975 in Ed Negre's number 8 Dodge. He finished twenty-second, many laps behind future rival Richard Petty. He caught another ride at the track in the '78 World 600 and played a big part in its exciting finish—though not in the way he would have liked.

The 1978 World 600

The Charlotte staff was always looking for something extra to attract attention to the World 600. Wheeler was always looking to entice new talent to the track. Janet Guthrie's first Winston Cup ride was in the '76 Charlotte race in what was initially a special deal that turned into a four-year stint on the circuit.

In 1978, the Charlotte organizers planned to introduce Formula driver Willy T. Ribbs to the North Carolina crowd. Will Cronkite had prepped a car for Ribbs, but Ribbs missed two practice sessions and never showed up for the race (he had been stopped by local police for driving the wrong way down a one-way street). Track manager Wheeler suggested putting young Dale Earnhardt in the car.

Qualifying was "same old same old": David Pearson sat on the pole at Charlotte for the tenth consecutive race. Dave Marcis had a good run and started in third behind Pearson's number 21 and Cale Yarborough's number 11. Sterling Marlin, Dick Brooks, and Al Holbert were surprise top-ten starters.

Pearson, Benny Parsons, and Cale Yarborough battled for the lead throughout most of the event. Darrell Waltrip and Donnie Allison were also strong and contributed to the record forty-three lead changes. Those five men and Bobby Allison were the only drivers left on the lead lap when the last caution of the race flew. Dale Earnhardt spun Cronkite's number 96 with four laps left, which forced all of the leaders into tight formation. Those last two green-flag laps were among the most exciting ever at the track.

Waltrip moved out to the lead with Donnie Allison's number 1 behind him. Parsons, in third, tried a pass around the outside of Allison in turn one. Allison slid up a bit and bumped the number 72, sending him into the wall. As Parsons caromed off the wall he clipped Pearson's Mercury, sending him spinning as well. Donnie was able to keep going after the touch with Parsons, but fell a bit back from Waltrip. Darrell, who was breathing a sigh of relief to see the others beating fenders behind him, held on for a two-second lead over Donnie.

The very first "racing grooves" at Rockingham (North Carolina Motor Speedway). In this 1965 photo the track is being smoothed and leveled in preparation for surfacing. In keeping with the track's name (and probably solving an excavation problem), there's a large rock planted outside the main entrance, with the names of every winning driver who has ever won there inscribed.

Brother Bobby slipped through the mess and moved up to third. Yarborough ended up in fourth and Pearson recovered to take fifth place. Parsons limped over the line in sixth.

Charlotte Today

In the 1993 Coca-Cola 600, Earnhardt showed that you can put him down but you can't count him out. The number 3 team suffered two pit road penalties that kept them at the back of the pack for most of the race. On lap 327, as he was about to go a lap down to the leaders, Earnhardt tapped and spun Greg Sacks' number 68, bringing out a caution. NASCAR penalized him a lap for rough driving. Earnhardt fought back around the front runners and was back on the lead lap when Rusty Wallace spun on lap 350. The number 3 was the last of the eight cars on the lead lap but needed only eight laps to make it to the front around Ernie Irvan, giving Earnhardt another win.

Jeff Gordon's first NASCAR win, in the 1994 World 600, was a popular and emotional one. John Andretti made history that day by flying to the track after driving in the Indianapolis 500 and completing the WC event as well, racking up a total of 1,100 racing miles (1,760km) in one day. Rusty Wallace looked like the clear winner as the race wore down, but a risky two-tire pit stop put the number 24 Chevy ahead with only seventy-seven laps left. At that point, Gordon was running in second behind Ricky Rudd, who was trying to stretch his fuel to the end of the event. Gordon hung on to second place despite having two fewer fresh tires than his challengers, and took over the lead for good when Rudd ran dry with nine laps left.

NORTH CAROLINA MOTOR SPEEDWAY

LOCATION: *Rockingham, North Carolina*
RACE LENGTH: *400–500 miles (640–800km) on a 1.017-mile (1.6km) paved oval*
NUMBER OF RACES RUN: *Seventy-one Grand National and Winston Cup, between October 31, 1965, and October 22, 2000*
SPEED RECORD (AVERAGE FOR AN ENTIRE RACE): *131.103 mph (209.8kph), set on October 24, 1999*

Make no mistake: "The Rock" is a tough place to race 500 miles (800km). The high-banked track is situated in the sand hills of North Carolina and the surface compound has a grittiness to it, like Darlington Raceway, that just eats up tires. Teams use as soft a setup on springs and shocks as they can to reduce wear on the rubber. During races, pit stop strategy is straightforward: always take four fresh tires.

When Harold Brasington built the North Carolina Motor Speedway, in 1965, it was designed largely by eye and ended up as a 1-mile (1.6km) oval with a rounded front straight and relatively flat turns. Planned changes to the track accumulated over the next couple of years until the management decided to bite the bullet and start over from scratch. The facility was torn up and redesigned (with the aid of computers) in 1969, to the configuration we know today. The track was lengthened slightly to 1.017 miles and the banking increased. Turns one and two are sloped at 22 degrees and turns three and four at 25 degrees.

In 1994 a new program of growth was kicked off, with notable improvements to garage and media facilities and additional seating for fans. In 1997 the track became part of Penske Motorsports and the improvements accelerated. A new grandstand was erected along the backstretch and pit road was redesigned to allow all cars to pit on the front stretch.

Early Racing at The Rock

The 1965 American 500 was the first Rockingham race. Curtis Turner had returned to NASCAR only six races earlier and was

driving for the Wood Brothers in his familiar number 41. As one after another of the contestants fell out of the race with mechanical problems, Turner and Cale Yarborough found themselves alone on the lead lap. Yarborough yielded the lead in a late pit stop, getting back on track seventeen seconds behind the number 41. He chewed off a third of that but could not pull closer. Turner, driving in his usual no-holds-barred fashion, bounced his car off the guardrail a couple of times in the last run, trying to maintain his lead; it worked, and the victory was the last of his seventeen Grand National wins.

The second of Richard Petty's eleven Rockingham wins (the record) was the 1968 American 500. Petty hadn't won a superspeedway race for more than a year (despite having twenty-seven victories in the previous season). Petty started near the front but was concerned with the way some of the drivers were running, so dropped back a bit to give himself some space in case of a wreck. Petty knew he had one of the fastest cars, with Cale Yarborough as his biggest challenge. Once Yarborough, in the lead at the time, lost his engine, Petty moved to the front and built a sixteen-second lead over second-place runner David Pearson.

In 1972 Bobby Allison set a record at The Rock that has never even been approached, much less passed in the years since. Allison had led in each of the final nine races of the '71 season, and the first twenty-nine of the '72 season. When he

TOP: Curtis Turner looks like he could use a nice hot bath in this celebration shot, taken after his win in the first race at Rockingham, in 1965. ABOVE: Richard Petty (number 43) slides by and goes on to win the 1976 Carolina 500 after contenders Bobby Allison (upside-down) and Cale Yarborough (Holly Farms car) were taken out in a spectacular crash. Allison spent three days in the hospital but suffered no long-term injuries. Quipped the plucky driver after the crash, "The car didn't handle worth a darn—while it was upside down!"

The Superspeedways

put Richard Howard's number 12 Chevy in Rockingham's victory lane in the American 500, he set the all-time record of leading in thirty-nine consecutive races. Despite starting and finishing in fourth place the next week, he never managed to lead, ending the formidable streak. (Cale Yarborough and Darrell Waltrip share runner-up status with twenty-five.)

David Pearson's racing career started in 1960. He had tremendous success with the Holman-Moody team and with the Wood Brothers and became only the second NASCAR driver ever to win a hundred events. His 100th was in the March 5, 1978, Rockingham race, though the victory almost didn't take place: Benny Parsons rubbed fenders with the Pearson's number 21 Mercury and sent it spinning with only forty laps left in the race. A caution came out, so Pearson didn't lose a lap when he pitted to replace the flat-spotted tires (the spin had left a bald spot on the rubber). When the race resumed, Pearson was the third of the three cars left on the lead lap. Pearson later commented that he was "hot" because of the incident and determined to catch Parsons. After the green, he quickly passed Allison to take second place, then dove under Parsons to retake, and maintain, the lead the rest of the way.

Rockingham has seen some pretty close finishes over the years. One of those was Neil Bonnett's win in the 1985 Carolina 500. It was his first year on Junior Johnson's two-car team; his mate was Darrell Waltrip. Bonnett had not been to victory lane for more than thirty races so he pulled out all the stops in a late-race duel with Harry Gant and Terry Labonte. Coming out of the fourth turn on the last lap Gant had the lead, with Bonnett in second. Bonnett used his bumper to move Gant up a lane and draw up alongside. Bonnett pulled Gant down the straightaway and edged ahead, winning by eight inches (20.3cm).

Hoosier tires helped Bonnett win again at The Rock in 1988. When Hoosier stepped up to challenge Goodyear in Winston Cup competition, the number 75 team of Bob Rahilly and Butch Mock decided to go with the "purple H" brand. Bonnett actually earned two wins in a row on the circuit, including the Goodwrench 500 at North Carolina. Bonnett made steady progress through the field in the latter race, going from the thirtieth starting spot to put the number 75 in the lead, overtaking Lake Speed with ten laps to go.

The 1989 AC Delco 500

Mark Martin's path to Winston Cup victory lane was long and winding. The Batesville, Arkansas, driver started his racing career at a young age and enjoyed considerable success in the Midwestern ASA league. He got his feet wet in NASCAR in 1981, then jumped all the way in for the '82 season with his own team. The independent operation didn't do well, however, managing only one top-five, and Martin wound up selling his equipment and going back to the ASA.

Jeff Gordon began the 2000 season with a new pit crew. The Rainbow Warriors of '99, whose primary jobs were to handle race day pit stops, defected en masse to Robert Yates' organization at the end of that season.

Jack Rousch decided to form a NASCAR team in 1988 and selected Martin to drive his number 6 Fords, having been impressed by the intensity and fire he had seen in the young driver. The first season was tough, but as the '89 season neared its finale they'd earned six poles and twelve top-fives, though no wins. By the October 22 Rockingham race, they were nearly out of chances to notch one in their promising sophomore season.

When the race started, Alan Kulwicki had the pole and Martin was in seventh. The lead was soon in contention, and was traded among ten different drivers through thirty-five changes over the course of the race. Dale Earnhardt led the most laps, eighty-seven. He fell victim to one of the race's record-setting fourteen cautions, however, ending up eight laps off the pace in thirtieth place. Harry Gant was making a bid for the lead when he was taken out by an inadvertent tap from Kulwicki.

Rusty Wallace seemed in position to win the race but was caught up in the incident with Earnhardt and fell behind. When the race resumed after the last caution flag,

The Rock in 2000. Bobby Labonte's win in the spring race put him in striking range of the NASCAR points lead, only 5 points behind Dale Jarrett. Jarrett got his first Rockingham win later that year in the October event, but wasn't able to make up enough ground on then–points leader Labonte to challenge for the top spot in the standings.

Mark Martin's number 6 Stroh's Light Ford was out in front. Wallace wasn't far behind and made a strong charge at Martin, but couldn't catch him. After 113 starts, Martin got his first WC win to a standing ovation from the crowds and his peers. Martin still races for the Jack Rousch number 6 team, at this writing more than thirty victories later.

The Rock Today

As a driver, Richard Petty has winning records at many tracks. He hasn't had quite the same success with others behind the wheel of his vehicles, though. In '96, Bobby Hamilton finally brought "the King" his first win since leaving the cockpit, but as the '97 season wound down, the team continued to struggle, unable to duplicate that success. Their next win, at the Rock, was due in no small measure to Petty's motivational tactics.

When Hamilton made plans to move to the Kodak number 4 team in '98, Petty had loudly proclaimed that with those plans laid, there was little chance Hamilton would win a race for him the remainder of the season. He put his money where his mouth was, offering Hamilton $100,000 to prove him wrong. Despite a poor qualifying start in the October AC Delco 400, Hamilton had a strong car and moved up steadily throughout the race. After moving into the lead with a few laps left, he broke Petty's slump for the second time, radioing "Ka-ching!" to his crew and car owner as he took the checkered flag—and the $100K.

TALLADEGA SUPERSPEEDWAY (FORMERLY ALABAMA INTERNATIONAL MOTOR SPEEDWAY)

LOCATION: *Talladega, Alabama*
RACE LENGTH: *500 miles (800km) on a 2.66-mile (4.3km) paved tri-oval*
NUMBER OF RACES RUN: *Sixty-three Grand National and Winston Cup, between September, 1969, and October 15, 2000*
SPEED RECORD (AVERAGE FOR AN ENTIRE RACE): *188.354 mph (301.4kph), set on May 10, 1997*

If there's one word that summons up a vision of speed and excitement in motorsports it's "Talladega." The Alabama track is known for white-knuckle, asphalt-scorching motorsports drama. The "superest superspeedway," with its 33-degree banking and 2.66-mile (4.3km) sweep, is the fastest raceway in the world.

The track almost came to be as the South Carolina Superspeedway. Bill France had been planning to replicate the immensely successful Daytona track at a location near Spartansburg, South Carolina, when a casual conversation with an acquaintance changed his mind. The race fan sug-

gested that France build the track in Alabama instead, and came up with a suitable site for Big Bill to look over. Lots of land, close access to a highway, nearby population centers, and support from the local community all made Talladega, Alabama, the perfect NASCAR locale.

Planning for the Alabama International Motor Speedway began in 1966. It was to be a 2.5-mile (4km) quad-oval, with rounded front and back straightaways. Groundbreaking took place in May '68, and the track took shape over the next fifteen months. A few things changed between planning and execution, and the track ended up 2.66 miles long and a tri-oval. The facility also featured an airstrip (it was partly built over an old airport and the Federal Aviation Administration required that a runway be maintained there).

The speedway was completed well in time for the scheduled inaugural race in September 1969. The track was awe-inspiring, and to the drivers who'd run tire tests there in August and September at speeds nearing 200 mph (320kph), it inspired fear as well. As marvelous as the facility was, its history began under a cloud of misgivings.

The 1969 Talladega 500

What the Talladega construction plan hadn't taken into account was the time needed for the tire companies to test and develop suitable compounds for the unique track. Neither Goodyear nor Firestone had a tire that could hold up at the tremendous speeds possible at the track for any length of time. Test runs resulted in shredded rubber within fifteen laps and drivers shaking their heads in consternation. The companies tried formula after formula in the short time remaining before the September 11 race, but nothing was working. Firestone decided to pull out—they would not supply tires for the event. Goodyear was about to do the same but was persuaded by France to give it one more shot on the

TOP: Talladega Superspeedway in 1991. The airport runways still in use inside and outside the track are clearly visible in this shot. The runways have been used occasionally during races, most notably to land and launch Air Force One when the U.S. President makes an appearance at a race. ABOVE: Richard Brickhouse was a member of the Professional Drivers Association (PDA) at the time, but decided to race in the 1969 Alabama 500 despite the organization's boycott of the event. The insubordination paid off: he drove the winged number 99 (upon the hood of which he and the go-go victory queen share a tender moment) to victory lane for the first and only time in his five-year NASCAR career.

David Pearson (wearing the lei) and the Wood Brothers crowd victory lane after the 1972 Winston 500. Pearson stole the victory from Bobby Isaac when the number 71 was pushed into the wall by a lapped car on the white flag lap. Isaac took second place despite getting a black flag earlier in the race for a missing gas cap (the determined racer ignored the flag, opting to pay the stiff fine later).

Saturday before the race. To quell the escalating fears among the drivers, France went so far as to take a car out on the track himself to demonstrate its safety. His exhibition was not enough, though, and most of the leading contenders and factory-based teams packed up and left.

Much has been made of the role of the Professional Drivers Association (PDA) in the Talladega boycott. The group was formed not long before the track opened as a union of sorts for the drivers, headed by Richard Petty. Since the PDA had just organized in mid-August it appeared that the action at Talladega was a direct outcome of the group's formation. Evidence suggests that most of the drivers who had run and tested at the track had serious misgivings about safety. The PDA simply gave them a forum through which to advise NASCAR as a group, rather than one at a time, that they weren't going to unnecessarily risk their lives just to meet the sanctioning body's schedule. PDA or not, most of the drivers who went home that weekend likely would have done so anyway.

More than thirty teams elected not to run, the Holman-Moody, Cotton Owens, Junior Johnson, Mario Rossi, Petty, and Banjo Matthews outfits among them. Bobby Isaac was the biggest name among the thirteen Grand National crews that remained. Regardless, France was determined to run a race on Sunday. The GT Touring Car series was the opening act for the weekend, running a 400-mile (640km) race on Saturday—without tire problems or crashes. NASCAR asked the GT drivers to hang around and added their cars to the Talladega 500 starting lineup (in finishing order from their race, behind the GN cars that had qualified). This was obviously not the field that 62,000 fans had bought tickets to see. To compensate for the difference, France ran the race on the house. Fans could reuse their tickets at another Talladega or Daytona race.

On Sunday, thirty-six cars lined up on the long Talladega pit road, with Bobby Isaac's number 71 on the pole and Jim Vandiver (subbing for PDA driver Bobby Johns) in Ray Fox's number 3 to his right. Coo Coo Marlin, Dick Brooks, Ramo Stott, and Richard Brickhouse were among the other GN drivers who stayed to race. Tiny Lund sat in the number 53 that Bill France had used to run laps just days before. Dr. Wilbur Pickett's Camaro was the fourteenth starter and the first of the GT crowd.

The Superspeedways

The race itself was almost a footnote to the affair. Isaac led the first circuit but got caught a lap down from two unscheduled pit stops and finished in fourth place, one lap off the pace. The surprise leader was Dr. Donald Tarr, in a Ray Fox Dodge, who rocketed from sixteenth to the lead for laps two and three. Lund, in France's number 53, led almost thirty laps before dropping out with transmission trouble. Jim Vandiver led the most laps (102) and his Dodge Charger was at the point with ten laps to go, but the car was outclassed by the other Dodge model in the field: the Daytona, with its high wings. Richard Brickhouse, in the number 99 Daytona, ran laps at more than 198 mph (316.8kph) to catch, then pass, Vandiver, scoring the inaugural Alabama victory.

Charlie Glotzbach (the regular driver of the number 99), and indeed all of the PDA drivers, returned to their seats for the rest of the year. No further actions were taken by the organization. France had made it clear that the races would run with or without the drivers. The group eventually disbanded in 1973.

Brickhouse, out of his fleet number 99 ride, picked up a seat in Bill Ellis' cars for several races that year. Actually he did have another opportunity to race the number 99, but was unable to repeat his Talladega success.

A Tricky Place to Race

In addition to hosting the fastest races, Talladega speedway has the record for races with the most lead changes. Starting in 1971, R.J. Reynolds sponsored the spring race, which was renamed the Winston 500. The drivers did the new NASCAR sponsor proud, producing a thriller featuring a record total of forty-six lead changes. Donnie Allison just beat his brother, Bobby, to the finish line for the victory. Bobby upped the ante in the fall race, which had a total of fifty-four lead changes (the record for any auto race). And the trend continued: sixty-three in '73, then sixty-seven in '78, and culminating in a scorer's nightmare, the '84 Winston 500, which saw seventy-five changes.

Talladega has a reputation as a track where anything can happen. It's been an especially good stop for underdogs and first-time winners. James Hylton surprised the crowds in 1972 with one of his two career wins there. Dick Brooks got his only WC win in '73, Lennie Pond his sole victory in '78,

Talladega's high banks and long sweeping turns allow drivers to run the entire track without braking or even lifting their feet from the gas pedal. Bill Elliott repeatedly set the record for stock car speeds at Talladega during the mid-1980s, topping out at a pole-qualifying speed of 212.809 mph (340.5kph) in '87. He only led a handful of laps in that race, dropping out when the engine in the "world's fastest race car" blew up with forty-four laps remaining.

Ron Bouchard in '81, Bobby Hilling in '86, and Phil Parsons in '88. Davey Allison won his first race there in '87—in his rookie season.

With the highest speeds on the NASCAR (or almost any) circuit, Talladega is also, unfortunately, the scene of often stupendous and sometimes tragic crashes. The 1970s was an especially costly decade as several Alabama races were marred by serious injuries and, in some cases, deaths. The '72 Winston 500, for instance, might have more appropriately been sponsored by a towing service: only nine laps into the event, oil from Ramo Stott's blown engine turned the sixty-car field into a "million-dollar junkyard." Twenty-one cars were involved in the crash as the field ran through the slick spots, with nineteen of those vehicles going to the garage. Several drivers were injured, Wendell Scott seriously enough to put an end to his racing days. David Pearson's was the only top car to make it through the melee and he beat the remaining opponents by a lap.

Second-year driver (and 1972 Rookie of the Year) Larry Smith was killed in the '73 Talladega 500 when his car hit the retaining wall at top speed. Later that day, '70 champion Bobby Isaac decided to call it quits on racing—not after the race but during an unscheduled pit stop on lap 182. "Something told me to quit," said Isaac, so he parked the number 15 and walked away, ending his career.

Dwayne "Tiny" Lund lost his life in the 1975 race at Talladega when his car was T-boned on the driver's side by another car. Buddy Baker, the race winner and long-time friend of Lund's, first heard the news as he celebrated in victory lane. The big guy's knees buckled in shock. Lund, a six-foot, five-inch (195.6cm) brawler, had been a fixture in NASCAR racing since '55 and had won a handful of races as well as a medal for heroism when he pulled Marvin Panch from a burning car early in '63. The Wood Brothers, the owners of Panch's car, put Lund behind the wheel of their car (by Panch's request) for that year's Daytona 500. Lund won the race, the biggest of his five GN victories.

The 1996 Winston 500 came close to tying the '73 race for number of cars involved in a wreck. The battle for the lead was furious and tight, so when Jeff Gordon and Mark Martin touched going into turn one on lap 129, a pile of cars were caught up in the whirlwind. Ricky Craven's number 41 got the worst of it, flying into the air near the retaining wall and across the track, over the intervening cars, and landing on the apron. The car was destroyed beyond recognition but the roll cage held up and Craven escaped without critical injuries.

The 1985 Winston 500

As racing technology progressed, speeds at the track began to creep up to the 200 mph (320kph) mark. Benny Parsons, in Harry Ranier's number 28, was the first to break the barrier, with a qualifying lap of 200.176 mph (320.3kph) in the 1982 Winston 500. Ranier's car remained the quickest for a couple of years, with Cale Yarborough replacing Parsons

Every driver fears becoming a victim to a "big one" at Talladega. In the 1996 Winston 500, this mess was set off by contact between two cars that soon embroiled half the field. Luckily, despite the damage to the machines, no one was seriously injured. Sterling Marlin avoided the carnage and took the point after the race resumed, putting the number 4 in victory lane for the second time that year.

The Superspeedways

at the helm and taking poles in all four Talladega events in '83 and '84 at speeds in excess of 200 mph (320kph). Amazing as these speeds were, they would be eclipsed the very next year, by a redhead in an asphalt-scorching red Ford.

R.J. Reynolds had sponsored the NASCAR Winston Cup since 1971, and the sport had since grown by leaps and bounds. Even into the mid-'80s, though, NASCAR was still big news only in the South. There was little national coverage or recognition. NASCAR, and RJR, needed something big to catch everyone's imagination.

In 1985, the tobacco company came up with just the thing: the Winston Million program. Any driver who won three of the four big races—the Daytona 500, Winston 500, World 600, and Southern 500—would get $1 million and surely grab headlines from Boston to Los Angeles. Only two drivers, LeeRoy Yarbrough and David Pearson, had ever won three of those races in a season. The pot of gold seemed secure for a while. So nearly everyone was surprised when a team from Georgia found a magic bullet that let them shatter all the records.

Harry Melling's number 9 team started the 1985 season with a bang. Their Daytona 500 qualifying lap was more than 205 mph (328kph), and during the actual race they outclassed the field, giving driver Bill Elliott his first Daytona win. Going into the April Talladega race Elliott had won all three of the big superspeedway races (including Atlanta and Darlington).

Elliott's early practice runs for the Winston 500 were frighteningly fast—more than 206 mph (329.6kph) on some laps. Up to then, only a few drivers had exceeded the 200-mph (320kph) mark. By Daytona, earlier in the year, a handful of other teams had landed in the 200-to-201-mph range, but were still far behind Elliott's times. At Talladega, sixteen teams broke 200 mph and it looked like the secret to running with the red and white T-Bird was out. But only until Elliott's turn came. The young driver had every right to be shaken and breathless when he climbed from the car after his qualifying run. At 209.398 mph (335kph), he had held his breath the whole way around the track.

On Sunday, thirty-eight teams figured to be racing for second place behind the Coors Ford. Surprisingly, the number 9 did not jump out to an early lead. Indeed, outside pole-sitter Cale Yarborough led the first four laps and Kyle Petty the fifth. Elliott then made it to the front, but only for twenty-odd circuits. Then on lap forty-eight Elliott's car began smoking, and eyebrows were raised along pit road as the number 9 pitted and the hood went up. It was just a loose oil line, which was quickly fixed, but Elliott returned to the track a hair from being two laps down. The contenders felt they had a chance at the win after all. It didn't matter how good Elliott's car was—there was no way he could make up that kind of ground, not at Talladega where two laps translated to more than 5 miles (8km).

They should have known better. The race leaders—Petty, Yarborough, and Earnhardt—were fast, but Elliott was crank-

Number 28 team owner, Harry Ranier, was used to winning drivers—Buddy Baker, Bobby Allison, and Lennie Pond had all been to the winner's circle with him—so it was par for the course when Cale Yarborough joined the team in 1983 and continued the trend by taking nine wins in their four seasons together. Here, Cale sprays champagne in victory lane after winning the '84 Winston 500 in a last-lap pass. That race still holds the official record for highest number of lead changes—seventy-five in 188 laps.

ing out laps consistently at or above 205 mph (328kph). Lap by lap he narrowed the gap by more than 1 second each time around. A caution would have helped him, but no yellow flags flew. Through horsepower and nerves, Elliott closed on the lead pack. On lap 125 he shot past Yarborough's number 28, having made up nearly a whole lap.

Elliott was back on the lead lap, but still 2.6 miles (4.2km) behind. Again, a caution would have put him nose-to-tail with the leaders, but the racing gods had something different in mind and the race stayed green. What happened next was an unparalleled, indeed unimaginable, feat. Whereas the first 2.5 miles (4km) had taken him seventy-five laps to make up, the next 2.5 took only twenty. At a track where lap-by-lap gains are usually measured in car lengths, Elliott had chewed up ⅛ mile (0.2km) each time around. On lap 145 Elliott waved goodbye to Yarborough for the second time and resumed the lead of the race. For the fans who had stuck it out, this was an epiphany.

Ironically, the caution flag came out only fourteen laps later. Yarborough again assumed the lead after the pit stops

Only the blur of the background belies their speed. Today's Winston Cup drivers race inches apart, three-wide, at speeds approaching 190 mph (304kph) for lap after lap at Talladega. The number 24 (driven by Jeff Gordon) and number 31 (driven by Mike Skinner) were running strong in the April 2000 race, and both made their way to the front. Gordon won the event, breaking a thirteen-race losing streak, and Skinner finished second.

and held it for eight laps. With twenty laps left, the number 9 motored around the Hardee's Ford and pulled away to win the race by nearly two seconds.

It was the most amazing comeback in NASCAR history. Drivers had made up as many as five or six laps before, but never at a track the size of Talladega. And more importantly, never against leaders running at record speeds. The race was run at an average speed of 186.288 mph (298.1kph), a NASCAR record. But if you had looked at the fastest car in the field rather than the leaders, his average speed would have been more than 203 mph (324.8kph).

Elliott continued his superspeedway dominance through the rest of the year and racked up eleven wins altogether, including the Southern 500, the third jewel in the Winston Million crown, earning him the bonus in the first year it was offered; amazingly, the big prize wasn't won again for another twelve years.

Elliot wasn't quite through with speed records. Although by 1987 the rest of the field had caught up—Bobby Allison posted a qualifying lap of 211.797 mph (338.9kph) in the spring '87 event—Elliott took the pole at 212.809 mph (340.5kph), the fastest ever recorded for a stock car.

The Birth of the Restrictor Plate

The last year that speeds at Talladega exceeded 200 mph was 1987. Bobby Allison had a horrendous crash in the Winston 500 that year, which had a profound effect on the series. He blew a tire on the front straight and smashed into the fence separating the track from the grandstands. The force of the crash breached the fence, and debris from the disintegrat-

ing car flew into the crowd. Luckily, the car careened back towards the track instead of landing in the crowd and tumbled to a stop. Allison suffered minor injuries, but several spectators were more seriously hurt.

The NASCAR community was in shock. The possibility of a 3,700-pound (1,676.1kg) car landing in the stands was terrible to contemplate. Something had to be done to bring speeds, and the cars, back under control.

At more than 200 mph (320kph), a driver's control over the vehicle is marginal. NASCAR instituted a speed-reducing measure to be implemented at the two fastest tracks on the circuit, Daytona and Talladega. A special carburetor restrictor plate would be issued by NASCAR and its use would be required at those two tracks. With the plate in place, speeds immediately dropped by 10 mph (16kph). Although 1988 wasn't the first time NASCAR used them—in the 1960s and '70s, they were mandated, off and on, for certain engines to equalize performance across car makes—requiring restrictor plates throughout the entire field had a profound impact.

Restrictor-plate racing, a style of competition all its own, was born. Such races feature long lines of cars, sometimes three abreast, that need the drafting help of several other cars to make a pass. Race tactics have changed: drivers now form fleeting "alliances" with other drivers to draft together to the front, and if a car gets caught out of the draft it looks like it's standing still as the pack rockets by.

Dale Earnhardt is a master at the drafting game and has won seven races at Talladega since the restrictor plates went into effect. He also has the overall track record with nine wins. Earnhardt swept the 1999 events there, quieting any garage gossip about his salad days being behind him. The superspeedway was never a favorite of Richard Petty, who only managed two wins at the track over his long career. Bobby Allison, Buddy Baker, and Darrell Waltrip each have four wins at Talladega. Superspeedway ace David Pearson has three wins, as does second-generation driver Davey Allison. Sadly, Allison lost his life at the track where he ran so well, in a helicopter accident in '93.

DOVER DOWNS INTERNATIONAL SPEEDWAY

LOCATION: *Dover, Delaware*

RACE LENGTH: *300–500 miles (480–800km) on a 1-mile (1.6km) paved oval*

NUMBER OF RACES RUN: *Sixty-two Grand National and Winston Cup, between July 6, 1969, and September 24, 2000*

SPEED RECORD (AVERAGE FOR AN ENTIRE RACE): *132.719 mph (212.4kph), set on September 21, 1997*

If you haven't spent all your cash on auto racing after a weekend at Dover, don't fret—the track also has pari-mutuel horse racing and casino slots to help you get rid of that spare change. Dover Downs, the only track NASCAR has ever run in the state of Delaware, was built in 1968 for horse and auto racing. A NASCAR date was scheduled in '69 and the track prospered, so a second yearly race was added in '71.

Dover Downs International Speedway is a high-banked, 1-mile (1.6km) oval. The corner banking is 26 degrees—not much less than at Daytona and Talladega—and the straights are banked at 9 degrees. With that much slope all the way around, Dover is a "self-cleaning" track (stalled or wrecked cars usually roll down towards the inside of the track). It is also one of only two concrete tracks left on the circuit, resurfaced from black top in 1995. Concrete is a particularly unyielding surface (more so than asphalt) that is tough on cars and drivers. All of these factors combine to make Dover, nicknamed the "Monster Mile," one of the most challenging tracks on the circuit.

The King's Reign at Dover

Richard Petty and Bobby Allison share the record for NASCAR victories at Dover, with seven apiece. Petty won the first two races, the inaugural one—the 1969 Mason Dixon 300—by six laps. Most of the field in that event were independents, and Petty's only serious rivals, David Pearson and LeeRoy Yarbrough, were both sidelined by problems. Similarly, Cale Yarborough was the only driver who could run in the '74 Delaware 500 with the number 43; when Cale's engine let go, Petty coasted to a three-lap lead and the win.

Victory lane at Dover Downs was like a second home to Richard Petty. In the 1975 Delware 500, Petty (leading the pack here in the number 43) overcame a six-lap deficit to win his sixth race at the track. Second-place finisher Dick Brooks felt cheated out of the win by a controversial yellow flag late in the race that benefited Petty's team.

TOP: Dover Downs Speedway under construction in 1969. The horse track, inside the 1-mile (1.6km) automobile track, is clearly visible in this photo. The high banks and abrasive surface make Dover a drivers' track, where handling and finesse are critical to success. ABOVE: The Dover speedway today is ringed by stands. The steep banking of the turns poses a bit of a problem for spectators, solved by the towering bleachers that provide a clear view over the intervening obstacles. A couple of tips for race fans heading to Dover: spring for the best seats, which are high up; and bring your bathing suit and sunscreen because the Dover races are run in the summer, and the Delaware beach is close by.

In the September '75 Delaware 500, Petty made up six laps to win, but competitors complained that the race was fixed. Partway through the event Petty lost a one-lap lead when he ran over some debris; the repairs cost him six laps in the pits. Amazingly, he made up difference to get back on the lead lap, but was still a good part of a mile (1.6km) behind the leaders as the race wound down. It didn't look like Petty would have time to run them down unless there was a caution.

With just fifteen laps remaining, Buddy Arrington, driving the number 67 car many laps off the pace, stopped in one of the turns. Everyone expected the yellow flag, but Arrington was well out of the way so the officials let them run. The number 67 then restarted and drove to the pits, only to quickly return to the track and stop again, this time close to the racing groove. The officials had no option but to fly the yellow. This was the break Petty needed. He closed up on the leaders and, after having run down six laps already, had no trouble shooting by to take the checkered. As soon as the caution flew, Arrington drove back to the pits and parked, suggesting that he had been deliberately trying to bring out a caution flag. Rumors circulated that he had concluded a business deal with Petty Enterprises earlier that week, so the action looked pretty suspicious to the teams that had to settle for second place on back. Was it rigged? Only Arrington knows—and he wouldn't comment.

Difficult Driving at Dover

The 1971 Dover race was lengthened from 300 laps to 500 and turned out to be a test of endurance. Temperatures soared on race day, turning cars into rolling convection ovens. Making matters worse, the entire race was run without a single caution. Driver after driver hit the pits looking for someone to relieve them. Bobby Allison was used to the heat, though, whether because he came from farther south than the rest of the crew (as he jokingly suggested afterwards) or because he'd conditioned himself for it by driving his family car in the summer with all of the windows shut and the heater turned up. He finished the race a lap up on second-place Fred Lorenzen.

Both 1973 races went to David Pearson, though in very different fashions. The June race was all Pearson—the number 21 led more than 300 laps and won handily. He had the field lapped in the September race, too, but his ride took a shot in the side when Dick May's wrecked car slid down the banking into him. The contact took off the sheet metal along the right side of Pearson's car and put him in the pits for two laps. He was a lap down to the leaders when he returned to the track. Drivers often complain of exhaustion after wrestling their cars around the difficult track for 500 laps, and the Wood Brothers Ford was even harder to handle with one side stripped, but Pearson worked his way back to the lead lap within a hundred circuits. A timely caution put him back in the hunt. He took advantage of it, passed leader Bobby Allison with a handful of laps left, and got the win.

Dover is the kind of track where a car that is really on the mark can thoroughly dominate the day. By the same token, if the handling's askew, not only will the lap speeds suffer but the driver will soon be worn out from wrestling with the Monster. Year after year, top cars have negotiated multilap

Two members of the first family of stock car racing—Richard and Kyle Petty—race side-by-side in the Bud 500 at Dover in 1990. In the end, Derrike Cope took the win, backing up his earlier Daytona 500 vicotry with a convincing performance at the Delaware speedway.

LEFT: Stock car racing has lead to many technological breakthroughs, not all of them specifically automobile-related. The paving equipment shown here was specially designed for use on the broad, sloped surfaces of racetracks. This photo was taken at Dover Downs, where the machine was used to repave the asphalt surface with concrete, a.k.a. "white lightning," between the September 1994 and May '95 events.
RIGHT: Mark Martin's pit crew hustles to get the number 6 Folgers car back on track during the Bud 500 at Dover Downs International Speedway, June 2, 1991.

comebacks. Cale Yarborough fought back from three laps down to win in 1976 and Pearson from two laps in '78. Allison's fifth win at the track was by three laps in '82. Darrell Waltrip robbed Harry Gant of his first potential win in '80, coming back from a lap down and taking advantage of a late-race caution to get around the Race Hill Farms number 47. Gant finally got his turn to leash the beast as well, adding the fall race to a string of consecutive wins in '91 by lapping the field. Ricky Rudd added "superspeedway win" to his racing resume in '86 when he came back from a one-lap deficit to win.

Despite its ferocity, Dover has seen its share of first-time winners. J.D. McDuffie's only pole position was in the September 1978 Delaware 500. McDuffie used McCreary tires—the company had just hit the NASCAR scene—to win the pole, but once the race got underway was forced to make unscheduled (and costly) pit stops due to blistering rubber. Another surprise first was Jody Ridley's victory in the '81 Mason Dixon 500. Ridley drove the number 90 of old-timer Junie Donlavey. Donlavey had been a regular on the NASCAR circuit since its second season but in nearly 300 races he had never won. A rain cloud hung over their parade, though. NASCAR admitted they had been having scoring difficulties and there was the possibility that Ridley was actually a lap down to Harry Ranier's number 28 team. But the win was upheld and Donlavey took home his only Winston Cup trophy (to date).

Dover Highlights

Derrike Cope had won the 1990 Daytona 500, but many observers felt he had won the race by chance rather than

prowess. Cope had been running in second on the last lap when Dale Earnhardt's Daytona curse reared its head and the number 3 blew a tire. Cope went on to win. At Dover in June, though, the Washington native demonstrated that he was the real thing (in a race that oddly didn't have a sponsor or even a name). Cope put Bob Whitcomb's colorful number 10 Purolator Chevy up front for ninety-three laps over the course of the race, only to run out of gas while leading on lap 160. He recovered without losing a lap and returned to the lead for good with fifty-five laps to go.

The Miller Genuine Draft number 2 Ford made it to victory lane at Dover three times over the 1993 and '94 seasons. The finish of the '94 Splitfire 500 came down to the very last lap. With five laps left, leader Mark Martin lost a tire and Rusty Wallace slipped past him as the yellow flew. Earnhardt was right behind Wallace and the crowd was expecting the familiar door-to-door duel between the fierce competitors. Before the cleanup was complete, though, Rick Mast's number 1 car stalled on the track, requiring a tow. Then Sterling Marlin's number 4 ran out of gas. The race finished under caution and the win was up in the air until the moment Wallace crossed the finish line. Both he and Earnhardt were running on fumes. To boot, Wallace was rolling around on a flat tire, cut down when he ran over debris from Martin's wreck. Ol' DW was sitting in third—no fuel worries there—with a big grin on his face, just waiting for the two cars in front of him to go dry. Perhaps through sheer willpower, the two lead drivers coaxed their cars to the checkered flag, Wallace in front.

Mark Martin has had his share of stressful encounters with the Monster, but over the 1997–99 seasons ran off a string of three successive wins in the fall 400-miler. The race format was changed from 500 to 400 laps in '97—to a chorus of cheers from the drivers—and Martin set the track speed record with his win at that race.

MICHIGAN INTERNATIONAL SPEEDWAY

LOCATION: *Brooklyn, Michigan*
RACE LENGTH: *400–500 miles (640–800km) on a 2-mile (3.2km) paved oval*
NUMBER OF RACES RUN: *Sixty-three Grand National and Winston Cup, between June 15, 1969, and August 20, 2000*
SPEED RECORD (AVERAGE FOR AN ENTIRE RACE): *173.997 mph (278.4kph), set on June 13, 1999*

In 1967, Larry LoPatin built the Michigan International Speedway in the Irish Hills of southeastern Michigan, not far from Detroit. The track is a large D-shaped oval, designed by the same man who crafted Daytona and Talladega. The track features 18-degree banking and a wide racing surface.

Despite high speeds, the track is relatively forgiving and long green-flag runs are the norm. Fuel management is thus an important part of race strategy. The 2-mile (3.2km) track first hosted Indy cars races and still does today.

LoPatin's American Raceway, Inc. went bankrupt in 1972, at which point Roger Penske purchased the speedway. The plans for improvements were immediately put into motion. The track has been resurfaced several times over the years, a consequence of the harsh Michigan winters. In '77 the weather had caused severe buckling at several points and drivers were worried that their engines would over-rev as their cars actually lifted up off the surface when they hit the uneven spots. In 1995, a special polymer-enhanced asphalt was used to help the track better retain its shape through the freezes and thaws.

Footprints of the Silver Fox

The first NASCAR race at Michigan, the Miller 500 in June 1969, got rave reviews. There were thirty-five lead changes, mostly between Cale Yarborough and LeeRoy Yarbrough, who were side-by-side as they took the white flag. Cale's number 21 and LeeRoy's number 98 brushed as they went into turn three for the final time and Yarbrough's car slammed into the wall. Cale fishtailed through the turn but reeled it in and took the checkered flag.

By 1984, top-ten finishes were few and far between for the number 43 STP team. Just the same, Richard Petty picked up his last two career wins that year (at Dover and Daytona), which, in addition to a ninth-place finish (in the August Champion Spark Plugs 400 at Michigan), helped the team to tenth place in the points standings. Petty was with Mike Curb Motorsports at the time. Petty returned to RPE after '85, and the Curb team, unable to find victory lane with other drivers, dropped out of NASCAR following the '88 season.

David Pearson, the Silver Fox, had great success at Michigan and holds a couple of track records, with nine wins and ten poles. His first win was in the 1969 Yankee 600, a 600-miler (960km) that was rained out just past the halfway mark. On top of that, half of the laps that were completed were run under yellow due to intermittent showers. Pearson's eighth win, in the '76 Champion Spark Plug 400, was something of a surprise. His ill-handling Mercury was at the tail of the lead lap all afternoon. When the day's final caution flew, with thirty-seven laps left, he was just a hair in front of leader Yarborough, but nearly a full lap behind. The adjustments Pearson's crew made during that pit stop did the trick, however, allowing Pearson to get around Yarborough for the win. It wasn't until Pearson left the Wood Brothers ride in '79 that the rest of field finally had a chance at Michigan's victory lane.

The Waltrip Way

The races Darrell Waltrip almost won at Michigan were in some ways more awesome than the two he did win. Waltrip finished fifth in the 1974 June race, despite failing to qualify.

TOP: Dale Jarrett bounced around for a few years among several teams after his 1987 debut without much success. His first victory came in '91 after a side-by-side duel with Davey Allison over the last two laps of the Spark Plug 400 at Michigan in August. ABOVE: It looks clunky compared to current technology, but the CBS in-car camera brought the behind-the-wheel excitement of stock car racing alive for the television audience. It also brought Cale Yarborough and the number 28 team good luck in 1983, a season in which he won three of the four races he ran with the camera aboard. "CBS, you can ride with me anytime," he told viewers after his Gabriel 400 win at Michigan.

Michigan has always been a state-of-the-art track, with wide, broad turns that support high speeds (for both NASCAR and CART races). Ernie Irvan credited the top-notch emergency rescue crew at Michigan with saving his life after the crash there in 1993 that interrupted his career. Steve Park (Pennzoil car) and Jeff Gordon (DuPont car) are at the front of the field here at the '99 Pepsi 400.

During the qualifying round, two blown engines kept him out of the starting lineup—until he bought his way in. The race had thirty-five starters and eleven alternates. Waltrip paid off each of the alternates and the last-place qualifier in order to get a spot in the field. He ended up spending more money than he won, but the points he added to his season total helped him to a top-ten finish for the year.

Waltrip's first win at Michigan was in 1977. He led most of the race and held off David Pearson at the end. Benny Parsons finished third, though at about the halfway point he thought he'd blown his engine when the cockpit filled with a cloud of white smoke. In fact, his fire extinguisher had come loose and triggered as it rolled about, covering him with the white powder.

Waltrip couldn't hold Pearson back in a last-lap duel in 1978. Petty had torn down several fence posts when his new number 43 Chevy (he'd switched from the unsalvageable Dodge Magnum just that week) crashed into the steel guardrail. The race went back to green with only a lap left and Pearson was able to slip by Waltrip for the win (his last at Michigan). Waltrip again failed to qualify due to engine problems in the August '80 race. This time he took over the seat in Joel Halpern's number 2 car instead of the garaged DiGard number 88. Waltrip led much of the race in the independent owner's car and was pulling away from the field when a late-race caution relegated him back to fourth, where he finished. Ongoing trouble with the DiGard team led Waltrip to buy his way out of a long-term contract at the end of that year.

Michigan Marches Forward

While the field often stretches out over the course of a Michigan race, the track has seen more than its share of competitive events. For instance, there were sixty-three lead changes (a track record and not far below the series record) in the August 1981 race. Richard Petty came out on top, one of his four Michigan wins.

The first of Bill Elliott's many superspeedway wins took place at Michigan, in 1984. The following year—his amazing eleven-win, Winston Million season—he won both races there without even breathing hard. Elliott also won both races in '86 (including the one in June, which was his fourth in a row and also happened to be Richard Petty's 1000th career start). Wins at Michigan in '87 (in what would be Tim Richmond's last race) and '88 brought Elliott's total up to seven.

Davey Allison earned his third Winston Cup win at the track in 1988, won again there in '91, and came within 1 foot (30.5cm) of taking the second event in '91 as well (Dale Jarrett, in the number 21, edged him out for his first WC win by 10 inches [25.4cm], the smallest margin in track history). Allison and Jarrett carried on a heated battle over the last two laps, literally running door-to-door.

Harry Gant won his last race in the Champion Spark Plug 400 in 1992 at Michigan. He got the win on gas mileage, his second such that year. In doing so he broke his own record as the oldest driver to win a major auto race, setting the bar at fifty-two years young.

Pocono Raceway is located in the midst of "honeymooners' paradise," the Pocono region of north central Pennsylvania. The track features the longest straightaway in the country, which leads into one of the toughest turns (turn 1) in NASCAR.

Rusty Wallace and Mark Martin each have four wins at Michigan. Wallace's 1994 win, his first there in the Roger Penske–owned number 2, was particularly sweet, coming as it did at Roger Penske's track. Bobby Labonte, in his first year with Joe Gibb's number 18 team, won both '95 races. His Pepsi 400 win in '99 was one of five that year. Jeff Gordon's '98 victory was his fourth win in a row, putting him in a seven-way tie for the modern-era consecutive-wins record.

POCONO RACEWAY

LOCATION: *Long Pond, Pennsylvania*
RACE LENGTH: *500 miles (800km) on a 2.5-mile (4km) paved triangular course*
NUMBER OF RACES RUN: *Forty-six Winston Cup, held between August 4, 1974, and July 23, 2000*
SPEED RECORD (AVERAGE FOR AN ENTIRE RACE): *144.892 mph (231.8kph), set on July 21, 1996*

Pocono Raceway is categorized as an oval track since racers only turn left there, but seen from the blimp, it's really a triangle. Unlike any other track on the circuit, Pocono has three turns and three straightaways. The front straight is 3,740 feet (1,137m) long, and wide enough to allow cars to fan out five or six across as they try to outpower the competition before funneling back down to single file through the first turn. The "north" straight (between turns two and three) is shorter than the main or "long pond" straight (between turns one and two), so that gearing set up for it would cause the car

to overrev on the longer stretches. To compensate, drivers downshift to get the needed power for the shorter chute, then upshift for the long straights. With those long straights, a heady engine is a key to success at Pocono.

To further complicate things, each of the three turns has a different radius and different banking—a nightmare for crew chiefs trying to work out the best setup for the track as a whole. It's a big track—2.5 miles—but the turns are pretty flat, so teams treat it like a huge short track. Since the cars carry tremendous speed into the flat turns, the shock and spring configurations are heavy, like a short-track package, to keep the cars from leaning over and bottoming out.

Pocono is also one of the fastest non–restrictor plate tracks on the schedule, with qualifying speeds now in excess of 170 mph (272kph). As a result, there have been some frightening incidents when cars have spun out and then become airborne.

Doctors Joe and Rose Mattioli first built a ¾-mile (1.2km) track on the site, in verdant northeastern Pennsylvania, in 1969; the big track was finished in '71, originally hosting USAC Indy car races. In '74, Pocono joined the Winston Cup schedule. A second race at the site was added in '82, when Texas World Speedway dropped off the circuit due to financial difficulties.

In the Beginning...

Richard Petty won the inaugural NASCAR race at Pocono, the 1974 Purolator 500. In '75, Petty lost the lead to David Pearson near the end of the event. Then, with only fourteen laps left, Pearson's car started smoking steadily. Normally a sign that a car is leaking oil or water onto the track, a smoking car would be black-flagged to the pits to be looked over by NASCAR and the crew. No flag flew for Pearson until just two laps remained; since a driver has three laps to respond to a black flag before his score card is pulled, Pearson ignored the call and finished the race to take the win. The STP team cried foul play, feeling that Pearson—who was driving the number 21 Purolator car—was unfairly assisted in winning the Purolator 500 race. Petty had his revenge, though, winning the event again in '76.

At Pocono, more than at any other track, fuel economy has played a key part in determining the outcome of races. Bobby Allison has several wins at Pocono, including the 1982 Van Scoy Diamond Mine 500, a victory that cost Dave Marcis his sponsor. That day, Allison also beat Tim Richmond, in a J.D. Stacy–owned car, partly thanks to a push to the pits Allison got from Marcis earlier in the race when he had run out of gas. Marcis' car was also sponsored by J.D. Stacy, who didn't appreciate the helping hand to a competitor. Within the week, Marcis was advised that Stacy was pulling his sponsorship from the team.

Allison's career ended at Pocono in 1988. In the first lap of the Miller High Life 500, the number 12 Miller Buick driver advised his crew that he had a tire going down. Before he could make it back to pit road, he spun on the north straight.

The car bounced off the retaining wall into the path of the number 63 of Jocko Maggiacomo, who hit him at full speed. Allison was critically injured, forcing an end to his career. Maggiacomo, though not seriously hurt, also called it quits after the horrible incident.

Cale Yarborough twice won Pocono races when the closest competitor ran out of fuel, and four-time winner Darrell Waltrip took the 1992 race when he and Harry Gant (who finished second) outdistanced the rest of the field on mileage.

Bill Elliott and Tim Richmond tied Waltrip at the top of the Pocono wins list with four apiece. Elliott swept the 1985 events at the track during his incredible million-dollar year, and won again in '88 and '89. Richmond got his first superspeedway win there in '83, swept the '86 races, and won again in the '87 June race .

Rain is also frequently a factor in the outcome of the races at Pocono. The June 1986 race was concluded under yellow due to rain. A tremendous downpour had started just four laps short of the halfway point. NASCAR, not expecting to get a clear window to restart, ran those extra four laps under caution, in a torrential downpour. The cars inched around the track at less than 25 mph (40kph), with the drivers leaning out of their windows in order to see where they were going.

The number 25 Folgers team went through a roller-coaster season in 1987. It started with a search for a new driver, as wunderkind Tim Richmond was too ill to compete. Richmond did return, the high point of comeback being this win in the Miller High Life 500 at Pocono. Within two months though, the team would once again be without a driver, as Richmond suffered a relapse.

Technically, the very first Strictly Stock race was not held at the well-known Charlotte Speedway. On February 17, 1949, Bill France ran an "experimental" Strictly Stock race as the lead-in event of a three-race bill at Broward Speedway, in Broward, Florida. The Broward track was a huge, for the time, 2-mile (3.2km) paved track. France's crew ran a five-lap race—only 10 miles (16km)—to see how the stock car concept would go over. Many of the top drivers of the day were at Broward, but most were in the other races being held. Bob Flock and Jim Rathman competed in the roadster race, the main event. That very first Strictly Stock race was won by Benny Georgeson of Florida. Since it was not a points event, Benny, who only participated in one other NASCAR event, didn't get credit in the record books.

The 1987 Miller High Life 500

Tim Richmond ran two very different seasons in 1986. Richmond had signed on as driver for Rick Hendrick's second team, leaving the Blue Max team and turning down a multiyear opportunity with the DiGard team. It turned out to be the best move of Richmond's career.

Richmond was a devil-may-care character who first strapped into a stock car in 1980 after having given sprints, Modifieds, and Indy cars a try. Shortly after finishing ninth in the '80 Indy 500, he was asked to drive at Pocono by track owner Joe Mattioli. That trial was enough to get Richmond hooked on NASCAR. He earned his first win in '82 and got three more before joining Hendrick's organization.

Off the track, Richmond had earned a reputation as a daredevil who wasn't afraid of pulling any stunt. With his wild hair, beard, and mustache he certainly looked the part. On the track, he was talented and aggressive, a real hard-charger. This sometimes caused problems as the equipment often didn't hold up under his full-tilt style. The move to Hendrick's team was a big one for him, in more ways than one. He started the '86 season with a more sober image: well-manicured and dressed, and apparently with a newfound dedication to his career.

Hendrick gave Richmond the chance to work with top equipment and a legendary crew chief, pairing the flam-

boyant driver young driver with crusty veteran Harry Hyde. Hyde, who had guided Geoff Bodine and the number 5 Hendrick team to success, was moved to the new team in the hopes that he would be a stabilizing influence on Richmond. To his dismay, Hyde had acquired a reputation of being the crew chief who could temper aggressive but unschooled young pups. He'd repeatedly lived up to the challenge (and had a championship with Bobby Isaac in 1970 to show for it), but also chafed at the role. What he really wanted was to work with a proven commodity like Petty or Pearson.

Be that as it may, Hyde's charge was to bring Richmond's aggressiveness into focus, a task that proved to be something of a challenge. Through the first ten races of the 1986 season, the team could not get on track. They had three top-tens but were not serious contenders. With his many years of experience, Hyde certainly had ideas about what could be done to improve their track record, and he was used to being listened to. Alas, Tim Richmond was not a guy to meekly take orders, and the two butted heads over how to set up and run the Folger's number 25 car.

The two apparently came to terms after a tire test session at North Wilkesboro. Richmond had been tearing up tires and wasn't listening to Hyde's admonitions about saving his rubber to get better speeds. Hyde challenged Richmond to a comparison test—fifty laps run Richmond's way, all out, then fifty laps without sliding and abusing the tires. The results were dramatic. On Richmond's run, the tires became blistered and slick, while on Hyde's more conservative run the tires still had solid rubber and the track time was much better.

The team finally started pulling together in May and produced back-to-back runner-up finishes at Charlotte and Riverside. Then they really mashed the accelerator: in the second half of the season they won seven out of sixteen races, plus two more top-fives and three more top-tens. With that kind of performance, Hyde and Richmond were clearly the team to watch in 1987.

There aren't many things that can keep a Winston Cup racer out of his ride come raceday. A life-threatening case of double pneumonia is enough to do it, though, even for a risk-taker like Richmond. It wasn't until early January that the number 25 team learned that what they thought was a case of the flu was something more serious. Though Richmond came down with the illness shortly after the Winston Cup banquet in December, he kept it and his hospitalization a secret for almost a month. With the season fast approaching and Richmond just out of a three-week hospital stay, Hendrick knew he'd need a replacement for a good bit of the season. He lured veteran Benny Parsons from his part-time arrangement with Leo and Richard Jackson's Skoal car. The team kept Folger's on the car but changed the number to 35.

Jeff Gordon leads the field in the number 24 DuPont car on the parade lap prior to the start of the UAW-GM Teamwork 500 at Pocono in 1996. One after another, the strongest cars dropped out of the race after crashes or because of engine problems, leaving Gordon to cruise to an easy win.

Richmond finally made his 1987 debut on May 17 at The Winston in Charlotte, but had to drop back out again after that race—his health hadn't returned in full. Rumor had it that he was too debilitated to race in any other event that year. That rumor was at least partly put to rest when it was announced that he would appear in the June 14 Miller High Life 500 at Pocono. It was to be an amazing weekend for Richmond. Pocono was the track where he had made his first Winston Cup start and so was a special place for his comeback. "I thought about that when I started thinking about which race I wanted to come back in," Richmond confided in a June 13 conference.

Richmond started the event off well by qualifying third for the race, behind pole-sitter Terry Labonte and teammate Benny Parsons, and was one of five drivers to break the old track speed record that weekend. Despite that achievement he was asked repeatedly about his health and whether he had the stamina to hold up for a 500-miler. "I'll tell you when it's over," said Richmond. "I feel good and ready to go five hundred."

Come raceday, Richmond showed no signs of fatigue. Terry Labonte led from the green flag in Junior Johnson's Chevy, but Richmond wasted no time in coming to the front, first sliding by the Folger's number 35 car and then past Labonte's number 11 on lap five. The first half of the race was a battle among Richmond, Bill Elliott, and Dale Earnhardt, who had moved up from fourth and seventh places, respectively. Richmond's red Chevy was at the lead through lap twenty-two, then again for laps forty-one to fifty-seven, and was clearly fast enough to contend with the top dogs. Earnhardt had been the dominant driver so far that season and many fans were excited that Richmond might be the one to finally pose a challenge to the number 3 team.

Mechanical gremlins took out several good teams early on, and the tight first turn was causing headaches for many drivers. A number of teams complained that the asphalt in that turn was breaking up and posed a hazard. Several yellow flags kept the field from stretching out too much, and as a result plenty of cars were still on the lead lap near the halfway mark. The caution on lap sixty, originally for Jimmy Horton's spin, was extended when J.D. McDuffie's car exited pit road without lug nuts on one tire and, to the crew's embarrassment, lost the tire on the track.

After Michael Waltrip spun his number 30 car on lap ninety, the field lined up for the restart with Richmond in second behind Bill Elliott's number 9. As the field came up to speed, though, Richmond began falling back through the pack. He had been shifting gears so energetically throughout the day that he had bent the transmission shift linkage, and folks

For Bill Elliott, the July 1989 AC Spark Plug 500 ended on a much better note than it had started, as this victory-lane shot shows. Elliott lined up fourteenth for the green flag and had to pit on the first lap to replace a punctured tire, but managed to stay on the lead lap (pit stops at the long track often allow that). In the end, Elliott ran down Rusty Wallace with six laps left to take the lead and win.

The Superspeedways

had earlier questioned whether Richmond had the stamina for the race. On lap ninety-five, the Folger's car pulled into the pits, where the crew worked feverishly to get at least fourth gear back on the car. This accomplished, Richmond went back out onto the track, but had lost a lap in the process.

Over the next twenty laps Richmond demonstrated why he was such a hot commodity, managing to move back around leader Bill Elliott on lap 114 to regain the lead lap. What he needed now was a caution to let him stay there. On lap 120, teammate Benny Parsons obligingly provided the needed yellow flag as he hit the wall in turn one. Richmond restarted in fifteenth place, on the lead lap.

Though certainly not what they had hoped for, Parsons' early exit from the race was actually a break for the second Hendrick team. The Folger's crew had faced a special challenge during pit stops that weekend. The organization wasn't really set up to run two cars for the team, but with Richmond's return that's just what they had. They had hired on some extra help for the weekend, but some of the pit crew was actually shared between the two teams during the race. They chose adjacent pit stalls for the number 25 and 35 cars to make the situation easier to manage. They even staggered their green flag stops to allow the crew members to service both cars without conflict. With Parsons out, the team could focus on just one car for the remainder of the event. The awesome strength of the number 25 car and its driver were clear when the race returned to green. Within five laps Richmond had moved from lead-lap caboose up to fifth place. A caution helped him move up to third, and on the restart lap into second. Then he passed Dale Earnhardt for the lead in turn two.

Three more cautions slowed the race. Earnhardt was clearly Richmond's strongest challenger and dogged him through lap 195, when Richmond watched with surprise as his nemesis faded back in his rear-view mirror, giving up second place to Bill Elliott—the number 3 car had a tire going down in the closing laps. Kyle Petty, who'd had a strong run going all day, passed Earnhardt for third, and Cale Yarborough had one of his better finishes that year, taking fourth at the end. Earnhardt nursed his car to fifth place.

Richmond went on to the storybook finish, winning in his first race back from a long illness, at the track where he had gotten his stock car racing start. It was an emotional victory for team and fans alike. Even the normally staid Hyde was choked up by the win, "There's never been a win any more sentimental. I'm not a crying sort of man but I cried on the inside." Richmond had to take an extra victory lap in an effort to regain his composure before hitting victory lane. "I had tears in my eyes when I crossed the finish line and I couldn't stop, so I took another lap. I was the last car into the pits—all of the drivers were congratulating me."

When asked about his health, following the race, Richmond said, "I feel as good now as I was last year, but tomorrow could be another story." Richmond was well enough to return the following week for the Budweiser 400 at Riverside, California, and qualified fifth for the road course race. With ten laps to go he powered around leader Phil Parsons, and pulled away to beat Ricky Rudd by 1.5 seconds. Two races in 1987, two wins. The team seemed to be picking up right where they left off at the end of '86—unbeatable.

Richmond's dramatic return and win at Pocono are part of NASCAR lore. Sadly, the story took a dark twist after the Riverside race. The team was unable to return to winning form, and by mid-August Richmond was once again showing signs of illness. He finished twenty-ninth at Michigan in what was to be his last NASCAR race. A number of drivers expressed concern after the Michigan race over Richmond's ability to drive safely. Shortly thereafter, citing ongoing health problems, Tim Richmond resigned as driver of the number 25 Folger's car. Rumors burned like wildfire through the racing community. Were drugs at fault or, the prevalent story, did Richmond have AIDS (acquired immune deficiency syndrome)? Richmond never returned to Winston Cup. In February 1988 he was working on a deal to drive a Busch car at Daytona, but was denied permission when he failed a drug test (though apparently due to the prescription drug AZT rather than an illegal substance). Though he publicly denied the allegations of AIDS, his health continued to deteriorate, and he passed away from complications of the disease on August 7, 1989.

With raw driving talent and a burning drive to succeed, Richmond had the makings of a champion racer. His victory in the 1987 Miller High Life 500 at Pocono Raceway was perhaps the high point of his meteoric career and certainly a high point of that Winston Cup season.

Pocono in Passing

Alan Kulwicki won the June Pocono race in 1992 using a Jerico transmission, a new device that helped drivers shift smoothly, with less stress on the hardware. Davey Allison's Texaco Ford tumbled along the north chute, eventually coming to rest in the infield after contact with another car. (Allison was hospitalized with several broken bones in his arm and wrist but returned to start the next week's race.)

Kyle Petty had clean track ahead of him for much of the 1993 Champion Spark Plug 500—except for the inebriated fan who climbed over the infield fence and ran across the track in front of the oncoming cars. Luckily the fan had time to dive over the retaining wall before the thundering pack had to try and dodge around him. Dale Earnhardt won the July '93 Pocono race, the first event after Davey Allison's death in a helicopter accident. Earnhardt commemorated his fallen comrade with a Kulwicki-signature Polish victory lap carrying a large flag bearing the number 28.

Jeff Gordon had three wins at Pocono and was on his way to a record-tying fourth in June 1995 when "pilot error" sent

ABOVE: Can you figure out the sponsor of this race? (Hint: check out the trophy.) Tim Richmond looks relieved in this shot, taken after his 1987 Pocono win. Richmond's absences from the driver's seat in '87 gave veteran Benny Parsons his first chance to run full-time (first as Richmond's replacement, then as his teammate) and his best end-of-season standing, sixteenth place, since 1981. OPPOSITE: This aerial view of Phoenix International Raceway shows the differences between the front straight, on the right, and the "dog-legged" backstretch. Spectators are visible all around the hillside outside of turns three and four (at the bottom of the photo), one of the best seats in the house. This photo as taken at the 1999 race, where rookie Tony Stewart earned his record-breaking third win of the year and Dale Jarrett cinched his first Winston Cup championship.

him to the back of the pack. With ten laps to go, the field was restarting after a caution with Gordon in the lead and teammate Terry Labonte right behind him. As the field came up to speed, Gordon slowed drastically and cars frantically fanned out across the track to get by. Gordon had missed a shift, giving Labonte the lead and the win. Later that year, Dale Jarrett earned his first victory with Robert Yates' number 28 team (taking over for injured Ernie Irvan), using judicious fuel management to control the last segment of the race.

Rusty Wallace got his third win at the track in July 1996. His first, in '91, had been accomplished with the help of friend and rival Dale Earnhardt. The race was red-flagged for rain, and as the two talked Wallace mentioned that he didn't have enough gas to go on if it went back to green. As the rain appeared to clear, the cars took to the track under a yellow flag. Earnhardt, laps down, tucked under Wallace's bumper and pushed him around for several laps, allowing him to conserve fuel. The rain returned, the race was called, and Wallace was able to stay in the lead for the win.

In 1998 the number 37 Kranefuss team partnered with Penske Racing, changing to number 12. Jeremy Mayfield and Rusty Wallace, now teammates, were both strong in the first half of the season. Mayfield was at the top in points for several weeks, but had yet to win a race. That would change in the June Pocono event. Mayfield started in third and led several times, but had stiff competition at the end. On a late-race restart, Jeff Gordon in the number 24 and Dale Jarrett in the number 88 loomed behind him, ready to blow past the

Mobil 1 Ford. But Mayfield pulled away from the duo, taking the checkered by three car lengths over Gordon, earning him a big kiss from his boss, Michael Kranefuss, in victory lane.

Bobby Labonte swept both Pocono events in 1999 on his way to a career-high second-place finish in the championship race. Mayfield won the first of the Pocono Races in 2000 as well—courtesy of a last-lap love tap to leader Dale Earnhardt that moved the number 3 car out of the groove in turn three. The Intimidator (often the one doing the tapping) took the turn of events gracefully. When Mayfield's number 12 team was half a lap from sweeping the season there, though, a flat tire robbed them of the victory. Karma?

PHOENIX INTERNATIONAL RACEWAY

LOCATION: *Avendale, Arizona*
RACE LENGTH: *312 miles (499.2km) on a 1-mile (1.6km) paved oval*
NUMBER OF RACES RUN: *Thirteen Winston Cup, between November 6, 1988, and November 5, 2000*
SPEED RECORD (AVERAGE FOR AN ENTIRE RACE): *118.132 mph (189kph), set on November 6, 1999*

Heavy traffic, indigestion from track food, loud neighbors in the stands—these are hazards a race fan expects and knows

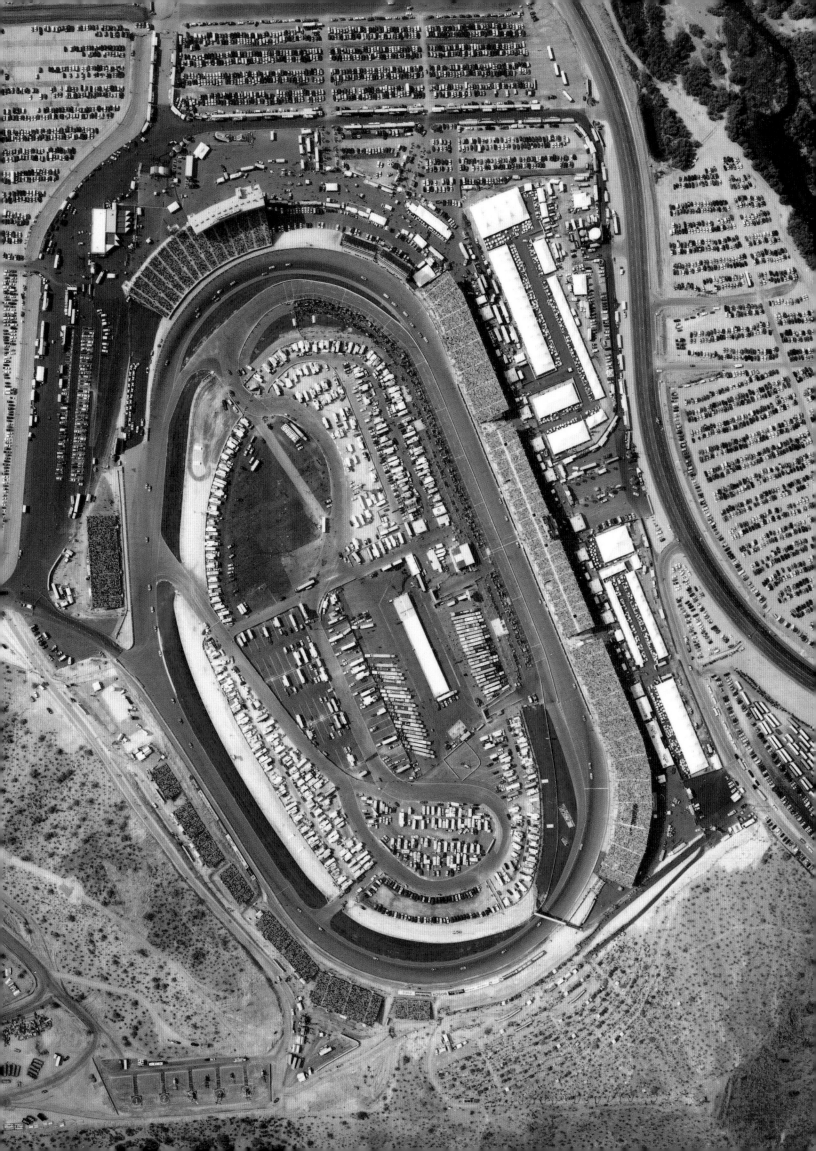

how to deal with. But rattlesnakes? At Phoenix, depending on your seat, rattlers can be a real concern.

The Phoenix International Raceway sits in the scrub desert of Avondale, Arizona, near Phoenix. One of the most popular seating areas at the track is up on the hill overlooking turns three and four. Fans pitch tents, erect canopies, and camp out on the cactus-dotted hillside, turning it into a pseudo-grandstand. And they occasionally share their spot with a startled reptile.

The Phoenix track was built in 1964 for USAC Indy competition; fittingly, the venerable A.J. Foyt won the first event held there. The IRL and USAC series still races at the track each year. NASCAR first visited the track with its Winston West series. In 1988, when the Riverside, California, road course closed, Phoenix was added to the Winston Cup schedule to maintain a presence for the series out west. More recently, Phoenix Raceway was purchased by International Speedway Corporation and is operated by longtime track president Emmett "Buddy" Jobe.

The track configuration is a bit unusual. It's a flat, D-shaped track, with only 11 degrees of banking in turns one and two, and 9 degrees in three and four. Unlike most D's, the front stretch is straight and the curve is on the backside, an off-center kink that gives the track an asymmetrical shape. Teams set up their cars for flat-track racing. Smooth handling through the turns is the key. The driver who can roll into the turn and get back on the gas quickly will be the one to beat.

Surprisingly, having a fast qualifying lap doesn't seem to mean much during the 312-mile (499.2km) race—no one has won from the pole. In the twelve events so far there have been eleven different winners. Only Davey Allison managed repeat wins (in 1991 and '92).

Phoenix Facts

Wisconsin native Alan Kulwicki, who had started his WC career in 1986 with his own team, won the inaugural Checker 500 in November '88. With sponsorship dollars from Zerex, he'd started collecting top-five finishes in the '88 season and seemed poised for a win. Geoff Bodine had the pole for the Phoenix race, but led only the first two laps. Kulwicki started twenty-first, but made it to the front by lap forty-six and swapped the lead throughout the race with Rusty Wallace and Ricky Rudd. Rudd was in charge in the last half of the race, but was sidelined when his engine let go. Kulwicki, in the right place at the right time, went on to win.

Kulwicki, normally staid and serious, poked fun at himself by driving a victory lap the wrong way around the track, inaugurating his famous "Polish victory lap." The fans loved it. After Alan's death (1993), the Polish victory lap has been repeated by several drivers as a tribute or to signify some special occasion (most recently Rusty Wallace's fiftieth win).

The list of other winners at Phoenix is a *Who's Who* of the top drivers of the last decade of the twentieth century: Bill Elliott, Dale Earnhardt, Mark Martin, Terry Labonte, Ricky Rudd, and Rusty Wallace. Bobby Hamilton added his name to that list and earned his first WC win in the 1996 Dura-Lube 500. Hamilton claims he doesn't like flat tracks, but seems to run very well on them. The victory was popular with fans and competitors alike—not just because it was Hamilton's first, but because it was Richard Petty's first as a car owner.

Tony Stewart didn't get his first win at Phoenix, but did get a record-tying second win there in 1999, his rookie season. He led most of the last half of the race, and 150 laps overall. As he motored away from the field at one point, his crew chief cautioned him not to get too excited. He replied, "If I was any calmer I'd be in a coma."

Alan Kulwicki in the middle of his first "Polish victory lap," after his first win, at the 1988 Checker 500 in Phoenix. The win and eight other top-ten finishes that year caught the attention of many of the top dogs of the sport. Kulwicki, armed only with an engineering degree, experience in the ASA series, and dogged perseverance, made his own way in NASCAR after he moved south in '85.

Michigan State Fairgrounds

was one of the oldest tracks visited by NASCAR. First opened in 1899, the venue hosted only two Grand National races, in 1951 and 1952, but they were important events. The Motor City 250 was NASCAR's chance to put on a show for the Detroit auto manufacturers in their hometown. There were fifteen different makes of cars in the field of the first race, representing all of the major factories. The excitement of the race—there were fourteen lead changes, many crashes, and a fender-banging battle for the lead between Curtis Turner and Tommy Thompson near the end—caught the attention of the auto industry and the more than 16,000 fans, and helped draw the manufacturers into sponsorship of NASCAR teams.

Lakewood Speedway,

in Atlanta, Georgia, first saw auto races on its 1-mile (1.6km) dirt oval in 1917. The track hosted AAA Indy car races through the '50s and NASCAR races from '51 to '59 (closing in '60 when the Atlanta International opened). Promoter Sam Nunis ran a last-minute NASCAR race at the track after the official end of the '49 season. It was not a points race, though it was extremely popular and drew more than 33,000 fans. As a result, Nunis scheduled another race for three weeks later.

In the middle of the 1950 season, Nunis announced that he would hold the first 500-mile (800km) stock car race at the track that year. NASCAR was cautious about holding that long of a race on the dirt oval (the previous two races had been plagued by accidents), but knew the time for a major event had come. Rather than go with Nunis, though, NASCAR signed with Harold Brasington and the CSRA to cosanction the Labor Day race at the new Darlington Raceway. How different NASCAR might have been if that first 500 had been at Lakewood instead of Darlington.

As the result of his actions in the 1958 Lakewood race, rookie Fred Harb was given a special award, though he finished only sixteenth. When the number 56 car rolled during the race and its driver was thrown from the vehicle, Harb pulled his car up and stopped it to protect the injured man from traffic. Richard Petty almost got his first win in the last race at Lakewood, in June '59, but the victory was protested, and reversed. The plaintiff? His father, Lee Petty.

Raleigh (or Dixie) Speedway

was a 1-mile (1.6km) track that featured long straightaways and extremely tight turns with high banking. It could be a dangerous track: September 19, 1953, became known as "Black

Appropriately named Lakewood Speedway, this Atlanta, Georgia, racetrack features a beautiful setting and a treacherous raceway. A glance at the NASCAR record books for 1949 shows ten race winners that year—even though there were only eight sanctioned events. Why? Sam Nunis ran two non-points events at Lakewood featuring NASCAR drivers after the regular season and the victors, June Cleveland and Tim Flock, were erroneously credited with wins on the Strictly Stock ledger. Lakewood closed its doors in '79.

Saturday" when several drivers were killed in a horrific accident during a Modified race there. No one noticed that a car had stalled on the backstretch on the last pace lap, and the field was given the green flag. As they roared around the second turn, they ran right at full speed into the stationary vehicle, sitting in the racing groove. The race was quickly red-flagged, but a dozen cars were involved in the wreck, and two drivers were dead. The inaugural Grand National race the next day went caution-free.

There are a number of interesting facts associated with Raleigh. It was North Carolina's first superspeedway, and the first track to install lights and run a night race (in 1955). It was also the only track where a team pitted to remove a wild animal from a car. Tim Flock had a small monkey riding with him, Jocko Flock, as a promotional stunt during the '53 season, and it got loose in the car during the Raleigh 300. Flock gave up second place to pit and extricate the frantic animal from the cockpit.

The races at Raleigh were originally scheduled opposite the Indy 500, on Memorial Day. They later moved to the Fourth of July. When the new Daytona track opened in 1959 and took the July 4 date,

RIGHT: The advertisement posters for the first NASCAR race at Raleigh clearly demonstrate that Bill France's name was so well recognized that its appearance on the ads was a drawing card for stock car drivers. BELOW: Raleigh Speedway in 1953. The facility featured both a superspeedway with very long straights, and a short track with short, tight turns. Despite the track's size, the record speed there was only 79.8 mph (127.7kph).

Raleigh was dropped from the Grand National schedule and closed its gates.

Memphis-Arkansas (or LeHi) Speedway was a real corker. The 1.5-miler opened in 1954 as the largest track dedicated to stock car racing in the country (larger even than Darlington) and was certainly the biggest dirt track around. With the track's high banks and relatively high speeds, the 250-mile (400km) events

America's Newest Big Time Speed Classic

THE
"Raleigh 300"
Championship Late Model Stock Car Race

MEMORIAL DAY
Saturday, May 30, 1953
STARTING TIME: 2:00 P. M.
Sanctioned By

NASCAR

$15,000.00 PURSE

Over The New Half-Million-Dollar
One-Mile Banked Asphalt

**RALEIGH
SPEEDWAY**
RALEIGH, N. C.

Under The Personal Direction Of
BILL FRANCE
President, National Association For Stock Car Auto Racing, Inc.

GRAND NATIONAL CIRCUIT
300-MILE LATE MODEL STOCK CAR RACE
TIME TRIALS: TUESDAY, WEDNESDAY, THURSDAY, MAY 26-27-28, 1:00 TO 5:00 P. M.

were extremely demanding on the drivers, and the facility acquired a reputation as NASCAR's most dangerous speedway. Several drivers required medical attention after the '54 race for heat exhaustion, exposure to fumes, or injuries from crashes. In '56, two drivers, Clint McHugh and "Cotton" Priddy, were killed when their cars flipped (one over the steep embankment outside the turns). The last event at Memphis-Arkansas, in '57, was flagged twice—not for rain or accidents, but for thick, blinding dust. The crowd, if not the dust, thinned out noticeably after the first flag.

Trenton Speedway

first opened in 1900 as a ½-mile (0.8km) dirt track. A 1-mile (1.6km) track was configured in the '40s and paved in '57. In 1969, the track was expanded to 1½ miles (2.4km) and reshaped to a "kidney bean" oval. Was it a superspeedway or a road course? After all, it did have a right-hand turn... Trenton was one of the last tracks to drop off the abbreviated Winston Cup schedule, and it did so abruptly. Time trials were held for the '73 race, but the event itself was rained out—and never rescheduled.

Texas International Speedway

was the site of Bobby Isaac's first superspeedway win, in the inaugural Texas 500 in 1969. Cale Yarborough was seriously injured in a crash in that race. Doctors predicted a nine-month convalescence, but the tough Carolinian was back in the driver's seat in February.

A number of USAC drivers had entered the field for the 1971 running, but backed out after that sanctioning body issued stern warnings about the penalties that would be issued to participants in the NASCAR event—including planned pace-car driver Johnny Rutherford. Financial troubles lead to a six-year hiatus in NASCAR action following the '73 race. Racing resumed in '79, but the track dropped off the schedule again following '81 due to sparse attendance. The track closed for good in '89.

Ontario Motor Speedway,

in Ontario, California, was considered one of the premier race facilities in the country in its heyday. Opened in 1970, the large, Indianapolis-like track originally hosted USAC Indy cars. NASCAR came to town in '71 to run its 1,000th race there and offered its biggest purse to date: $207,675. Taking a page from the Indy book, the race was started with cars three-abreast, the first time since the '60 Southern 500 that that had been done in a NASCAR race. Indy car champion A.J. Foyt won the inaugural race from the pole, and came back to take the checkered the following year as well.

Buddy Baker won the Southern 500 in 1975 as a last-minute entrant. Norris Industries had just signed

on as sponsor of the Bud Moore team and wanted to see their car run, so Moore hustled the team out west. They got their money's worth, as the number 15 went on to the win.

A bit of NASCAR history was made in the 1977 race, when Janet Guthrie led the event for several laps in her Kelly Girl number 68 Chevy. This was the only time a woman has ever led a Grand National/Winston Cup event.

Richard Petty sewed up his seventh and last championship in 1979 at the facility. Darrell Waltrip was only 2 points ahead of Petty going into the season finale. On lap thirty-eight of the race Waltrip spun his car to avoid a wreck. He pitted to replace his flat-spotted tires and was caught a lap down when a caution flag fell several laps later. He was never able to make up the loss and finished a lap down in eighth place. Petty managed fifth place and won the championship by a meager 11 points.

Despite the quality of the facility and of the racing there, Ontario continued to suffer financial difficulties and was sold to Chevron Oil after the 1980 race. It was torn down in '81.

A.J. Foyt first tried his hand at stock car racing in 1963; by the time of the '71 Miller High Life 500 at Ontario (shown here), he was an old hand. Foyt picked up the winner's share of the richest purse to that date of any NASCAR race ($207,675) that day. It was only his third race in the Wood Brothers' number 21 car as well as his third straight top-five.

Chapter 4

ROAD COURSES

f asked to describe a stock car race, most fans would paint the picture of a sleek Monte Carlo or Taurus on the high banks of a superspeedway or perhaps an old Modified coupe sliding around a dirt track. But for almost all of NASCAR's history, its stock cars have slalomed through the chicanes and negotiated the hairpins of road courses as well.

Nowadays there are certainly far fewer road courses in the United States than half-milers, so by far the majority of races are run on ovals. But the road courses offered unique opportunities to the fledgling NASCAR. Today, road courses give NASCAR the opportunity to penetrate new markets that otherwise might not have access to a superspeedway. For instance, the addition of Watkins Glen and Sears Point (in New York and California, respectively) put two of the nation's biggest states back in the schedule.

Early in the sport's history the road courses gave it a touch more credibility in the broader world of auto racing. Many in that elite stratum saw stock car racing as just a bunch of good ol' boys going around in circles, so road racing gave the NASCAR hotshots a chance to demonstrate their skills in "European style" racing as well. In line with the international flavor of the events, most of the early NASCAR road races were open to foreign cars as well as domestics. Jaguars and MGs hadn't done well against Oldsmobiles and Hudsons on oval courses (there were a few of those races open to them as well), but once the right-hand turns were added, the story changed.

Road racing is different than running on oval tracks in many ways. As you'd expect, car setups are unique for road-course cars (since they turn right as well as left), and a team might field a different driver at a road-course event. While most of NASCAR's stars are as proficient on the twisty courses as on ovals, there are some who have expressed a clear dislike (or not displayed much skill) for those events. Some teams will sub a road-course specialist from USAC, CART, or SCCA for their usual driver to gain a better chance at a win or top finish. Of these, Dan Gurney (the most successful, with five NASCAR wins), Irv Hoerr, Tom Kendall, and Dorsey Schroeder have all filled in on the road courses over the years.

Pit strategies change quite a bit on a road course, too. As every fan knows, if you pit under green on an oval track you usually lose a lap or more to the leaders. If a yellow flag comes out before everyone cycles through their stops, you can end up stuck a lap down. That's not the case in the road races, where the track is so long and speeds low enough that pitting normally doesn't cost you a lap. So if you pit early and a caution flag flies, your car is left in the lead as everyone else pits.

Even the direction the cars go around the track is different on road courses. Oval track races in this country all run counterclockwise (that is, they turn left). The most sensible guess at how that tradition started is that it puts the driver (on the left side of a U.S.-made car) as far from the retaining wall as possible. This is not an issue on road courses, so the traffic moves clockwise from the start/finish line.

For NASCAR fans used to lots of side-by-side racing and constant passing, the nose-to-tail parade of a road race may seem less than exciting. As any driver will confirm, road races are by no means less competitive, though this may be less obvious to the fans. The races themselves are much less visible to spectators, for one thing. If you can get the good seats you can watch the action all around the track at even the biggest oval tracks, but at a road course the track is sprawling, and sight lines are often interrupted by trees, hills, and buildings.

Road-course events are still an important part of the NASCAR racing portfolio and provide a welcome change a couple of times a year. The limitations of the venue, to NASCAR's strong fan-centric orientation, are such that the percentage of road courses on the schedule will likely not go up much in near future.

ROAD AMERICA

LOCATION: *Elkart Lake, Wisconsin*
RACE LENGTH: *258.3 miles (413.3km) on a 4.1-mile (6.6km) road course*
NUMBER OF RACES RUN: *One Grand National, held on August 12, 1956*
SPEED RECORD (AVERAGE FOR AN ENTIRE RACE): *51.429 mph (82.3kph), set on August 12, 1956*

Carl Kiekhafer's number 300 Chrysler and Tim Flock were a match made in racing heaven. Flock hooked up with Wisconsin businessman and scientist Kiekhafer in 1955 at Daytona. Flock had quit NASCAR the previous year but couldn't resist the allure of the Kiekhafer machine. The team won together in their very first race, at Daytona Beach, and that was just the beginning. The two tallied eighteen wins that season—an unparalleled feat at the time—on their way to the '55 Grand National championship.

The following year could easily have been a repeat performance for the team but Kiekhafer had loftier goals—winning eighteen races wasn't enough. As Flock put it, "He wanted to win every race"—and went about achieving it in deliberate fashion. While Kiekhafer was

PAGES 124–125: A gorgeous view of the ess turns at Watkins Glen, New York. Team number 34 owners Frank Cicci and Scott Welliver are from the area and enter the Glen Winston Cup race each year. The team earned a surprise pole position in the 1997 race with Todd Bodine behind the wheel. PAGE 125: Tony Stewart in 1999, his amazing rookie NASCAR season. Among the many astounding feats the up-and-comer pulled off his freshman season was a victory in the inaugural Winston Cup race at the new Miami-Dade Homestead Motorsports Complex.

generous in his compensation, driving for him was by no means an easy task. He had a very detail-oriented, and controlling, approach to racing, which he applied not only to the cars but to his drivers as well. Despite their phenomenal success, Flock suffered stomach ulcers throughout his championship season, which he blamed on the owner's boot camp–like rules (including 6 a.m. reveilles and the separation of drivers and their wives in different hotel rooms the weekend of a race).

For the 1956 season, the Mercury Outboards owner took the approach of running multiple teams in each race, bringing six cars to Daytona Beach and running no fewer than two or three in each event. Flock was the most successful in the early part of the season, with three wins, but couldn't stand the routine the owner required of him. In April, after winning the North Wilkesboro race, he quit the team.

Kiekhafer continued to run multiple cars and the strategy seemed to work. In all his teams earned thirty wins that year and Buck Baker went on to the 1956 championship. Flock picked up rides with several teams, but wasn't burning up the circuit. He only had one other win that year, but it was a sweet one.

The 1956 258-Miler at Road America

August 12, 1956, was the one and only time the Grand National circuit visited the Road America course in Elkhart Lake, Wisconsin. Carl Kiekhafer's Mercury Outboard factory and headquarters were in Wisconsin, so the race was something of a homecoming for his teams. He invited friends and associates to the track, along with several thousand of his employees to watch his cars dominate the race. Kiekhafer did his best to stack the deck for the event, entering his three top drivers—Speedy Thompson, Buck Baker, and Frank Mundy (in cars numbered 500, 502, and 300, respectively). He wasn't the only owner with multiple teams in the race, though. Pete DePaolo outdid him with five entries. Joe Weatherly, Curtis Turner, Bill Amick, Junior Johnson, and

Fireball Roberts all drove factory-backed Fords out of DePaolo's garage. Tim Flock made the race in his first ride in Bill Stroppe's number 15 Mercury.

Buck Baker put one of Kiekhafer's Dodges on the pole for the race and jumped out to an early lead. He didn't stay there long, though, as Flock moved up from his sixth-place start to take the lead on lap six. He hung to the point for a handful of laps before starting to fade back, while Marvin Panch, the outside pole sitter, took over the top spot.

The DePaolo contingent was beset by mechanical woes early on. Junior Johnson, who joined the team for that race, went out after only one lap with a busted clutch. Teammate "Red" Amick soon followed. Ralph Moody made fifty-six laps before he was sidelined as well. Speedy Thompson inherited the lead at the halfway point when Marvin Panch's Ford developed rear-end trouble that took him out of the race. It looked like the Kiekhafer Express was on its way to the win.

Many drivers had trouble negotiating the winding course, which was even more challenging due to rain (NASCAR cars then had treaded tires so could run on wet surfaces). Curtis Turner, another DePaolo driver, slid off course after only twenty-one laps, ending up stuck on top of the hay bales lining the track. Tim Flock had no such trouble, though, and began making his way back to the front of the field from mid-pack. By lap fifty-three, he had worked his way back to second place when the engine in Thompson's number 500 Dodge let go. Flock was in the catbird seat and hung on to the lead to win by 17 seconds over Billy Myers. Fireball Roberts, one of the few DePaolo cars still on the track, charged up to third place from his seventeenth-position start.

Flock, who was still not on amicable terms with Kiekhafer, said it was his biggest win. "To come up here in Kiekhafer's backyard is special to me. This was one he wanted badly, and I won it."

The 1956 race was the only event NASCAR held at the Wisconsin road course, though Road America is still in operation and hosts races in various other classes.

Tim Flock may have won the battle by beating Carl Kiekhaefer's Dodges on the businessman's home turf in 1956 (in the only Grand National race to take place at Road America), but Kiekhafer won the war by putting his drivers in the top two championship spots that year.

Bobby Allison, seen here with the cup of victory, took the checkered flag in the 1979 Tuborg 400 at Riverside. Allison inherited the lead after Cale Yarborough's number 11 Chevy blew its engine and Richard Petty tagged the retaining wall. The road course win was one of only two that season for Allison, who was back on his own that year after leaving Junior Johnson's team.

RIVERSIDE INTERNATIONAL RACEWAY

LOCATION: *Riverside, California*

RACE LENGTH: *100–500 miles (160–800km) on a 2.631-mile (4.2km) paved road course*

NUMBER OF RACES RUN: *Forty-eight Grand National and Winston Cup, between June 1, 1958, and June 12, 1988*

SPEED RECORD (AVERAGE FOR AN ENTIRE RACE): *107.820 mph (172.5kph), set on January 14, 1979*

Built in 1957 and hosting a Grand National race the next year, Riverside International Raceway saw more road course races than any other NASCAR track to date. NASCAR returned to the track again several years later, beginning a twenty-seven-year-long association. A second Riverside race was added to the schedule in '70. The track was dropped from the circuit after the first race in '88, when the course was razed so the real estate could be more profitably redeveloped.

Riverside's unique configuration provided some amazing racing action over the years, and some of the most enduring images in motorsports (in particular the long line of cars snaking uphill through the esses, heading to turn six). The layout of the course stayed pretty much the same over its thirty-year history. A short chute was added between turns six and eight to eliminate the hairpins,

and turn nine—at the end of the long, high-speed back-stretch—was eventually banked and broadened. The length of the course varied only slightly from 2.6 miles (4.2km) to 2.7 miles (4.3km).

The first NASCAR race, in 1958, was a 500-mile (800km) event. The promoters obviously wanted to give fans their money's worth, but at an average speed of less than 80 mph (128kph), the race took more than six hours to complete. With races scheduled in New Jersey the day before and in South Carolina a couple of days later, many of the Grand National regulars didn't bother to make the long trip westward. Lee Petty, on his way to a championship, was an exception; he picked up a fair number of points with a fourth-place finish that day. Parnelli Jones was perhaps the best-known name in the field. He took the pole and led much of the race but crashed on lap 147. Eddie Gray, a California native, took over and won his first race.

Road racers dominated the event in 1963 when Dan Gurney, all of whose NASCAR victories were at Riverside, started his streak of wins at the track. Driving the number 121 Wood Brothers Ford, Gurney dominated the events from '63 through '68, though his '64 victory was marred by tragedy. Joe Weatherly, in Bud Moore's number 8 Mercury, slapped the retaining wall in turn six after getting out of shape through the ess turns. The contact was on the driver's side and, with no window nets or shoulder harnesses (Weatherly's preference), Joe's head hit the wall.

The Bondy Long number 11 bursts into flames in the Riverside pits during the 1965 Motor Trend 500. The Riverside emergency crew rapidly extinguished the fire and Ned Jarrett was able to get the car back on track albeit well behind the lead pack. Jarrett put together an impressive thirteen wins that year to take his second championship.

The former champ was dead when rescue workers reached the car minutes later.

Though the open-wheel racers fared well at the track, starting with the November 1963 race, the USAC sanctioning body forbade its drivers from participating in the events. A.J. Foyt and others had qualified for the event but had to pull out at the last minute as a result of the ruling.

Riverside in the Modern Era

Riverside was the site of several first-time and surprise winners. Californian Ray Elders was the winner in the first Riverside race in 1971, finishing ahead of Bobby Allison and Benny Parsons. Elders' was the only car in the field on Firestone tires, which may have made the difference. The farmer-cum-racer was jubilant about the win but commented that the winnings ($18,000) would have to be paid right to the bank. He followed up the performance with a second-place finish in the subsequent race (this time behind Allison) and another win in '72.

Another unlikely winner was Mark Donohue, driving Roger Penske's AMC Matador to the front in 1973. Actually it was the Matador that was the more unlikely part of the equation (Donohue was an accomplished USAC racer). Experts in the garage scoffed at the make but it quickly proved its worth. One of Bobby Allison's victories at the track, in 1975, was in a Matador as well.

Ricky Rudd and Tim Richmond are other top drivers who earned their first NASCAR wins on the twisty road course. Richmond earned three other wins at Riverside, including an emotional victory (his second in a row) in 1987. He had returned to the circuit after a prolonged illness, and in the winner's circle that day it looked as though the charismatic racer had made a full recovery.

Since the fall Riverside race was at the tail end of the NASCAR schedule throughout the 1980s it was often the site of the last battle in each year's championship war. Bobby Allison holds the track record with six wins, but even a victory at the track wasn't enough to help him catch Darrell Waltrip for the '81 championship. There were three races at the track that year. Allison won the first and Waltrip the second. The third was the last race of the year and Allison did his best to overcome the 83-point lead Waltrip had going in. Bobby put his Ranier Buick on the point and kept it there for the victory, but Waltrip drove a defensive race and finished sixth, high enough in the standings to retain a 53-point lead and win the title.

The final race in 1982, also at Riverside, was "déjà vu all over again." Allison had lost an early season points lead and trailed Waltrip when the circuit rolled into the California desert in November. Tim Richmond had the best car that day, but Waltrip managed a third-place finish. Allison finished poorly, in sixteenth, and once again saw his championship hopes evaporate. The '83 finale finally reversed what had become a frustrating trend for Allison. He held the points lead over Waltrip that year going into the last Riverside race, but cut a tire early on and fell back as far as twenty-seventh. With only eight laps left, Waltrip was battling for the lead with Tim Richmond and the two tangled. Waltrip recovered but fell back to sixth place. Allison fought his way back up to ninth place and was able to hang on to a 46-point margin, winning his first and only Winston Cup championship.

Darrell Waltrip's top-ten finish at the track in the last race of 1985 put the exclamation point on another of his miraculous late-season comebacks. Bill Elliott had dominated the circuit that year, winning eleven races and the Winston Million award. After the September Southern 500 at Darlington, though, Elliott's team had hit a slump and Waltrip crept up in the points standings. Elliott saw an advantage of more than 200 points dwindle into a deficit of 100. The nail in the coffin was Elliott's thirty-first place finish at Riverside, due to transmission failure; Waltrip cruised to seventh place and his third title.

The last race at Riverside was in 1988. Rusty Wallace, fast earning a reputation as a master road racer, had won the previous fall race there. He repeated in '88, his third road-course win in a row.

As is the case with several defunct racetracks, the Riverside course is now the site of a shopping mall.

LOCATION: *Watkins Glen, New York*

RACE LENGTH: *101–219 miles (161.6–350.4km) on a 2.42-mile (3.9km) paved road course*

NUMBER OF RACES RUN: *Eighteen Grand National and Winston Cup, first on August 4, 1957, then between July 19, 1964, and August 13, 2000*

SPEED RECORD (AVERAGE FOR AN ENTIRE RACE): *103.3 mph (165.3kph), set on August 13, 1995*

Set in the beautiful woodlands of New York's Finger Lakes region, Watkins Glen has been a preeminent part of the U.S. racing scene since its inception in 1948. The first road race held in the United States after World War II took place on a 6.6-mile (10.6km) course laid out by law student Cameron Argetsinger on the paved and dirt roads around the small town. Over the next five years the races there drew increasingly large crowds. In '56, a permanent paved facility was built.

NASCAR paid its first visit to the 2.3-mile track the following year; it was the first professional auto race held in the area. Though two more races were run at the Glen, in '64 and '65, NASCAR didn't make it a regular stop until 1986.

In the meantime, the course had been through some ups and downs. Each autumn from 1961 through '80 it hosted the international Formula 1 series in the U.S. Grand Prix. Mario Andretti, Mark Donohue, and Jody Scheckter were among the winners in CART CamAm and TransAm races also conducted there in the '70s. When the track was dropped from the Formula 1 schedule after '80, it fell on hard times. The facility was virtually unused and unattended for several years, until it was purchased in '84 by the Corning Glass Works and reopened as Watkins Glen International. NASCAR returned to the Glen in '86.

The facility's biggest event is the annual Winston Cup race. The Busch Grand National series and Craftsman Truck series also race there in a weekend billed as a "Festival of Speed and Sound," featuring live musical performances. The Winston Cup race, known as the Bud at the Glen (sponsored by Budweiser) since '86, went techno in the '99 season. The Frontier Corporation (a technology company from nearby Rochester, New York) assumed sponsorship and changed the event's name to the Frontier @ the Glen.

The first NASCAR event at Watkins Glen, in 1957, saw Buck Baker win from the pole, padding his points lead on the way to a championship. Fireball Roberts took second place in the caution-free 100-miler. Texan Billy Wade hit his stride in '64, driving the number 1 Mercury for Bud Moore and winning four straight races, the last of those at the Glen, in only his second full season. Moore had lost his ace driver,

ABOVE: Flags fly high over the main grandstands for the 1995 Bud at the Glen. Mark Martin (number 6) was on the pole for the race, with Bill Elliott (number 94) starting second. Traffic moves in the opposite direction on road courses, so the pole-sitter is on the left side of the starting lineup. Martin ended up right where he started (in first) while Elliott faded to eleventh place. OPPOSITE: Jeff Gordon was the road-course master during the second half of the 1990s, including three wins in a row at the Glen, starting in '97. He was making moves at the start of the 2000 race as well, but contact with Tony Stewart took him out of contention. Steve Park got the victory, his first.

N ASCAR's very first road race was run on a temporary course set up on the runways at New Jersey's Linden Airport. Since road racing had something of an international flavor to it, the June 1954 event was open to foreign car models as well as the usual U.S. makes. This was the second time that NASCAR relaxed its "USA only" rule; the first had been the '53 International 200 at Langhorne, Pennsylvania, in which the Jaguars, Porsches, and Volkswagens faired relatively poorly. It was a different story with the right-hand turns added at the Linden course.

The event was fifty laps on a 2-mile (3.2km) course. Buck Baker was the pole-sitter, in an Olds 88. He took off from the green flag and led the first ten laps. Herb Thomas, driving his Hudson, then made its way up to contend for the lead, and the two swapped the front spot throughout the first half of the show. On lap twenty-three, Al Keller drove Paul Whiteman's number 4 Jaguar hardtop around Thomas and into the lead. He stayed there for the rest of the race, completely lapping all but second-place finisher Joe Eubanks (also in a Hudson). Baker finished third, while spots four through six were all filled by Jaguars. Of the forty-three-car field, twenty-one were foreign models, which were pretty well mixed in with the domestic entries in the finishing order.

Linden was the second Grand National win for Keller (the Buffalo, New York, native's first had come earlier the same year, in a Hudson) and also his last. Right after the race he announced that he was quitting NASCAR to race in the AAA series, hopefully on his way to an Indy 500 ride.

Joe Weatherly, earlier that year in a fatal crash at Riverside. Disaster struck the team again as it prepared for the '65 season: the team was testing at Daytona when Wade lost a tire at top speed. The promising driver was killed in the resulting crash

When the series returned to Watkins Glen in '86, Tim Richmond was the man on the move. He was having a spectacular second half of the season, finally melding with veteran crew chief Harry Hyde on the Hendrick number 25 team. The Glen was one of his seven wins. Over the next several years, Rusty Wallace and Ricky Rudd regularly swapped wins at Watkins Glen: Wallace in '87, Rudd in '88, Wallace again in '89, and Rudd in '90. Tommy Kendall, who'd had some solid runs in Winston Cup cars on the road courses, was battling Sterling Marlin for fifth place on the last lap of the '90 race when the two collided. Marlin's number 94 fell back to mid-pack while Kendall went on to finish in eighth place. The number 94's owner, Billy Hagan, was not a fellow to repress his feelings and chased Kendall around his car, swatting at him with his cane, to let him know how he felt about the incident.

The 1991 Bud at The Glen

In 1991, John Delphus "J.D." McDuffie was a racing anachronism, a holdover from the earlier days of the sport when a man built his own car, drove it to and from the track, and serviced it with the help of a handful of friends or a weekend crew. He had no big corporate sponsorship deal—

the few decals on the old number 70 advertised hometown businesses (for many years, for instance, Rumple's Furniture provided badly needed, if limited, funds). Independent drivers like McDuffie made do: if you wanted to race, you made do with used or spare parts, limited help (provided pro bono by friends or relatives), and without the dynos (used to test engine setups) and wind-tunnel sessions that the premier teams found indispensable.

McDuffie had been making do since 1963. In 653 races he'd never won, never finished second. One pole position in '78 at Dover, twelve top-fives, and a ninth-place points standing in '71 were the top marks in his career. But he was able to continue racing—not in every event, but in enough each year to remain an active, and surprisingly popular, part of the sport.

Since 1988, though, the North Carolinian had been having trouble making races—only two, seven, and eight from '88 to '90, respectively. By August '91, he'd made the field for only five events. He did qualify for the August 11 race in New York—thirty-fifth in a field of forty.

Terry Labonte, Mark Martin, and Ernie Irvan were the men up front that day. Labonte, long regarded as a top road racer, was especially hungry for a win. He'd not held a trophy since he left Junior Johnson's team in 1989, and his reunion season with Billy Hagan was not going well. Labonte took off to lead the early laps, but was reined back in by a caution on only the fifth lap.

Turn five was the most dangerous part of the old Glen configuration. Cars came into the turn after a long straightaway and had to brake hard to drop their speed going into the right-hander. As McDuffie's number 70 approached the turn, the drivers behind him noticed a puff of smoke from one wheel. It appeared that he'd lost a brake line, and blew a wheel as he tried to control his speeding car going into the turn. He bumped Jimmy Means' number 52 and the two slid off course. According to Means it seemed like McDuffie had no brakes—he didn't slow down at all as he caromed toward the tire barrier at the edge of the broad, grassy berm. McDuffie's car hit the tires and retaining fence hard enough to rebound his car up off the ground. Means slid in under the airborne Pontiac and came to a stop against the fence; the number 70 landed beside him on its roof.

Means quickly climbed from his car, indicating that he was okay but waving for emergency crews to attend to McDuffie. The race was yellow-flagged, then red-flagged when the severity of the crash became apparent. More than an hour later, an obviously distraught Chip Williams, Winston Cup's media coordinator, announced that the fifty-two-year old McDuffie had been killed in the crash.

The race eventually restarted, after repairs were made to the retaining fence, and Ernie Irvan went on to victory. Irvin dedicated the win to McDuffie.

Following the race, drivers and NASCAR reviewed concerns over the danger of that area with track officials. The

THESE PAGES: During the 1991 event at the Glen, tragedy struck. A tire flew loose as J.D. McDuffie tore into turn five at full speed (opposite, left). Spinning out of control, the number 70 Pontiac hit the tire-and-wire retaining wall hard on the right side (opposite, right), flipped up into the air, and landed on its roof (below, left). Jimmy Means, who had skidded into the barrier under the airborne Pontiac, anxiously summoned help for the trapped McDuffie (below, right), but the driver of the number 70 had been fatally injured in the crash.

Pit road and the whole Watkins Glen course run in the opposite direction of most other Winston Cup tracks, so crews need to adjust their usual pit stop routine to handle the left side of the car first. The Hot Wheels crew had no troubles with stops in the 1999 race, seen here; thanks to excellent pit support, Kyle Petty moved up from the twenty-fifth starting spot to eighth place, one of his best finishes that year.

track management consequently reconfigured the course, adding an inner loop to the straightaway well before turn five, forcing the cars to slow down to a safe speed. The change has been effective—no serious incidents have occurred on that part of the track in the years since.

McDuffie's passing seemed to be another step in the modernization of NASCAR. There are very few driver/owners like him left to carry on the old traditions of dirt-under-the-fingernails stock car racing.

Watkins Glen Today

Kyle Petty got his first road-course win, and his first win in eighteen months, at the Glen in 1992. He started in second place and led several times during the race, but took the win by being at the front when the event was red-flagged due to rain. It looked like he might repeat in '93, but spun while in the lead, taking out second-place Dale Earnhardt and giving Mark Martin the opportunity to take the lead and the win.

Martin dominated the 1994 and '95 events in front of record crowds of more than 100,000. Wally Dallenbach came close to getting his first WC win in '95. He had a sizable lead on Martin until a late-race caution put Martin's Valvoline Ford on his bumper—but only briefly: Martin slipped around him to steal the win. From '97 to '99, the Bud at the Glen—now the Frontier @ the Glen—belonged exclusively to Jeff Gordon. Gordon demonstrated his racing prowess with five consecutive road-course wins (as of the end of '99), with three straight at the Glen. Gordon's attempt at four straight, however, was torpedoed in a first-lap incident with Tony Stewart.

SEARS POINT INTERNATIONAL RACEWAY

LOCATION: *Sonoma, California*
RACE LENGTH: *218 miles (348.8km) on a 1.95-mile (3.1km) paved road course*
NUMBER OF RACES RUN: *Twelve Winston Cup, held between June 11, 1989, and June 25, 2000*
SPEED RECORD (AVERAGE FOR AN ENTIRE RACE): *78.789 mph (126.1kph), set on June 25, 2000*

Riverside dropped from the Winston Cup circuit in 1988, but it wasn't long before NASCAR returned to a California road course. The following year, the Winston Cup cars roared into the lush wine country of Sonoma, just north of San Francisco.

The track was built in 1968 and originally hosted SCCA and USAC events. The racetrack has had a number of different owners and managers over the years as it's struggled financially. Under the management of one group, in '81, it was briefly renamed the Garden State Raceway. The addition of NHRA events in '87 and NASCAR Winston Cup in '89 brought new and much-needed stability to the facility and gave recent owners the cushion they needed to reinvest in and improve the tracks. In '96, Bruton Smith added Sears Point to his Speedway Motorsports, Inc. portfolio. Today, Sears Point International Raceway can brag that it's the busiest speedway in the country—and perhaps the world—with NHRA, NASCAR, AMA, and other series racing 340 days a year.

In 1998, the track layout was changed substantially to accommodate NASCAR events. A new high-speed chute was built between turns four and seven, a shortcut that reduced the track length by about ½ mile (0.8km), eliminated several of the most challenging turns, and improved the drivers' sight lines. The layout also improved visibility for fans. In fact, audiences can now see much of the course from seats on the surrounding hillsides. Spectators often arrive early to nab a good spot and enjoy the sun and scenery before the race.

Ricky Rudd and Rusty Wallace were the drivers to reckon with for the first several Cup races at the track. Rudd took the inaugural win, snatching the lead from Wallace in turn seven with a tap from behind that sent the number 27 sliding to the outside of the turn. Wallace got his chance to turn the tables the very next year, 1990, and picked the same spot to pull the same move on Rudd (with the same result).

The 1991 Banquet Frozen Foods 300

Last-lap contact again determined the outcome of the June 9, 1991, Banquet Foods 300. Rudd and Wallace were at the front of the field as usual, with the Tide number 5 on the pole and Wallace's new number 2 Pontiac starting in fourth. Rudd took the early lead but after a dozen laps started to fade back. Wallace had moved up to second and took over the lead on lap twelve. The Penske South driver looked like he was set to pick up another road-course win, easily outstripping the field for the next forty-eight laps. With fifteen to go, though, the Pontiac dropped a cylinder and his chances for winning were kaput.

Felix Sabates, owner of the number 42 car, had hired well-known road racer Tommy Kendall to sub for an injured Kyle Petty. Kendall took advantage of Wallace's mechanical misfortune and put the Mello Yello car at the front, on his way to a possible first win. Mark Martin's Folger's Ford was another strong car, though, and was running second to Kendall. With a handful of laps left, Martin tried a pass around the outside of the number 42. Kendall moved over to block and the two touched. The number 6 went spinning and Kendall blew the tire that he'd put into Martin's fender.

The Texaco team had worked throughout the weekend, making considerable changes on the number 28 to try and make that car more competitive for Davey Allison. They only managed a thirteenth starting spot and hadn't run up front at all, but Allison had slowly moved up through the pack and with Wallace, Kendall, and Martin out, was in position to lead the race. The early leader, Rudd, was right behind him. The hairpin turn eleven is the last corner before the flagstand at Sonoma, and as the two came through it on their way to the white flag, Rudd got up under the number 28, tapping him around. Rudd slipped by into the lead. Allison was able to recover quickly enough to hang on to second place, but had

With its open terrain, Sears Point proffers a wider field of view for spectators than other road courses do. Here, the crowd watches home-grown driver Jeff Gordon on his way to winning the 1999 Save Mart Kragen 250.

TOP: Davey Allison is congratulated in traditional NASCAR fashion after being declared winner of the 1991 Sears Point race. The talented young driver wasn't really known as a road racer—this was the only road course victory in his all-too-short career. ABOVE: The field climbs the hill at Sears Point in 1999. Teams often roll out new paint schemes for this West Coast race; Ricky Rudd's number 10 car, seen here, is an example.

Road Courses

fallen several seconds behind the Tide car. Rudd took the white flag as the leader.

NASCAR quickly decided to levy a stop-and-go penalty on Rudd for rough driving. The number 5 had already passed the pit road so would have to pull in the next time by—right before the checkered flag. While argument between the officials and the Tide crew ensued, Rudd drove around expecting to get the checkered flag. Instead he got the black flag. Allison was next, several seconds back, and Wallace managed third on seven cylinders.

Now what? Rudd had been black-flagged at the very finish of the race, but hadn't come in for the penalty. After several hours of review, NASCAR officials decided to penalize Rudd five seconds for the incident. Delaying his finishing time by that amount moved him from first place into second, and put Davey Allison (who had finished less than five seconds behind Rudd) into first. Allison was officially awarded the win and Rudd the runner-up spot.

As you might expect, Robert Yates and the number 28 team applauded NASCAR's fairness in giving them the win. Rudd and his crew chief Waddell Wilson were irate, and likened NASCAR to the World Wrestling Federation in regard to its objectivity in enforcing rulings.

Sears Point Moving Ahead

Ernie Irvan proved his mettle as a road racer with wins in Sonoma in 1992 and '94. The number 4 team's enthusiasm following the '92 win on June 7 was tempered by the sad news that NASCAR founder Bill France had died that day at age eighty-two. The '94 win was in the number 28 car (Irvan had replaced the late Davey Allison partway through the '93 season). The team worked well right from the start and Irvan already carried four wins coming into Sears Point. With that win, he remained in close contention for the championship with Earnhardt, right up until Irvan suffered critical injuries in a crash at Michigan.

Although Earnhardt is unquestionably one of the greatest stock car racers of all time, going into the 1995 Sears Point race, the Intimidator had a goose egg in the road-course wins column of his stats sheet. The '95 race started out with the usual faces at the front—Rudd, Martin, Wallace—and in usual fashion, Rudd was the leader from the green flag. Martin was just as strong, though, and hung close behind the Tide car. When Ricky missed a shift on lap five, Mark slid by and took off. It looked like Martin was untouchable until a late-race caution bunched the field back up. The Valvoline Ford was still out front but a very determined Dale Earnhardt was on Martin's back bumper when the race restarted with eight laps left. Perhaps sensing that this was his best chance for a road-course win, Dale drove those last laps with an unmatched intensity. At each turn he prodded and tested Martin's lead. Each time, Mark slammed the door on him with perfect execution through the corners. Then as the two headed into the carousel in turn six with two laps left, Martin got into a slick spot on the track that caused his back end to jump out. That was the break Earnhardt needed and he took advantage of it, darting under the number 6 and into the lead. Martin recovered quickly and glommed back onto the number 3's tail, but Earnhardt wasn't giving anything away. He drove the last two laps with precision and the seven-time champ earned his first road-course victory.

Sears Point changed in 1998, at least for NASCAR races, when turns four through seven were eliminated by a sweeping chute that connected the ends of the carousel. Jeff Gordon has been the only winner on the new configuration, capturing the '98, '99, and '00 events.

Racers often go up on two wheels as they negotiate the tight corners of Sears Point. Mark Martin shows how it's done in this 1999 photo, which shows the right side of the number 6 Valvoline Ford Taurus suspended over the hot asphalt.

Long gone are the days when a team took the same car to every race. The variety of tracks on the circuit and level of competition now demand specialized setups for each course to get the best performance. It used to be possible to categorize the vehicles as short-track, superspeedway, or road-course cars, but even that grouping is falling to the wayside as some teams build cars specifically for particular tracks. But there are basic differences in car setups for the three main types of tracks.

You have to consider several factors to deliver a solid package of speed: aerodynamics, braking, engine power, and handling all play more or less important roles at different types of tracks.

Aerodynamics—how a car moves through the air—is most critical at the fastest tracks: Daytona and Talladega. At the speeds achieved at these tracks, the car takes on the characteristics of a bullet, and its performance is subject to the flow of air over, around, and under the car. In wind-tunnel testing (conducted in large hangars equipped with a massive fan and smoke streams to help visualize the air moving around the vehicle) teams try to reduce the car's coefficient of drag (CD). That determines how much friction there is between the car and the air flowing by it at speed. The more friction (the higher the CD), the slower the car will be. The fascia of the car is carefully constructed to present no obstructions to the airflow. Grilles are partially taped to reduce the air going into rather than over the car. Bodywork is carefully trimmed to avoid any edges where air might catch. Even a small irregularity (or dent if a car has been involved in contact on the track) can cause air to swirl around in front of the car rather than flow smoothly over it, slowing it down.

One of the critical aspects of airflow is downforce. As air flows over the top of a car, it tends to go straight out past the rear edge of the roof, leaving a low-pressure area over the back end. Without the air pressing down on the back tires, the rear end is "loose", that is, it has less grip on the road and the car wants to spin around on the turns. At the fastest tracks, the cars use a big rear spoiler to "catch" as much air as possible on the rear deck and thereby hold the back end down. Spoiler angles (the angle between the spoiler and the ground) run around 70 degrees at superspeedways, which is nearly straight up. The driver likes as much "blade" as he can get

The angle of the spoiler, which can play a key role in determining a car's straightaway speed and handling at the big superspeedways, is strictly dictated by NASCAR rules. In fact, the angle is measured before and after the race to insure that it is the same at the end of the race as it was at the start. To ensure that the spoiler blade stays at the right angle, braces are added.

Here, a Pontiac's profile is checked using an official NASCAR template to insure that the car body has not been modified. NASCAR uses steel template strips to ensure that the body shape of every car conforms exactly to the approved measurements. Even a fraction of an inch variance may be cited, and if so, it must be remedied before the car can qualify or race. Gary Nelson, formerly a crew chief himself, joined the NASCAR inspection crew several years ago. He has defined the standards enforced, implemented rigorous and uniform verification processes, and made it clear that all cars must meet those standards.

because it provides better stability, but the higher the spoiler angle, the slower the car is on the straightaways; there is a balance that must be struck.

You've probably heard race broadcasters talk about a competitor getting up behind another car and "taking the air off his spoiler," causing the car in front to get loose and lose control. When cars run nose-to-tail, the train of cars has a different aerodynamic profile than a single car. The air tends to flow right over the top of the whole chain, with a lower CD than for a single car. This is called drafting, and it is the reason a pack of cars running single file at Daytona will always catch and pass a single car, or cars running side-by-side (which present more resistance to the airflow). Prior to the use of restrictor plates at certain tracks, cars had enough horsepower that the back car in a draft could pull out suddenly and slingshot past the leader. By pulling out from behind the front car, the challenger interrupts the airflow and creates a partial vacuum behind the lead car, actually slowing the leader down.

Braking is one of the most critical setup considerations at the short tracks and road courses, where drivers are hard on the brakes as they are repeatedly

forced to slow down from top speed to make the tight turns. The brakes quickly heat up, and once the brakes are gone, so are any chances of a decent finish. To prevent brake failure, grilles are left wide open and several "scoops" direct air from the grille and other openings in the body toward the brake assemblies to provide as much cooling as possible.

Engine setup is also a critical factor when preparing a stock car. Since 1988 a unique setup is used at Daytona and Talladega, the so-called restrictor-plate tracks, and in 2000 New Hampshire joined their ranks. NASCAR rules require that all teams install a special plate on the carburetor, called a restrictor plate. These plates are prepared and distributed solely by NASCAR for the express purpose of reducing the amount of air/fuel vapor that reaches the engine, cutting down the horsepower and thus the cars' speed.

Restrictor plates have been used at different times in NASCAR history, mostly to offset a particular engine's apparent advantage. In 1988 restrictor plates were decided on as a way to reduce the increasingly dangerous speeds of cars at the two fastest tracks. Since then, the restrictor plates have limited the power of any indi-

Through NASCAR's first decade, "stock car" meant exactly that. Nowadays, though, for reasons of safety and speed, Winston Cup cars have diverged to the point where the basic body shape is all that "stock cars" share with street cars. These body templates might fit reasonably well over your family's Monte Carlo, Taurus, or Grand Prix, but that's where the similarity ends.

vidual car at those two tracks, changing the strategy for winning there. Skillful drivers play the long trains of drafting cars, changing lanes to follow the fastest group to the front, then hoping that they can find a drafting partner when the time comes to pull out and pass.

Handling, a car's ability to negotiate turns, is less important at broad, sweeping tracks like Talladega or California, but it plays a critical role at the smaller tracks, where the turns are much tighter. At Dover and Darlington, for instance, intermediate-sized tracks with demanding turns, handling is everything.

Handling is affected by many factors, including springs, shock absorbers, sway bars, and tire pressures. If a car is tight (also called understeer), the front end doesn't want to turn in the corners; if a car is

loose (oversteer), it turns just fine, but the back end tends to fishtail. To paraphrase the late Neil Bonnett, "when the car's tight you see the wreck coming!"

Handling adjustments are all about the distribution of weight. As a car goes around a turn, the amount of pressure on each tire varies. Turning left, the most pressure is on the right front, the least on the left rear. Teams must adjust setup parameters on the four corners of the car to compensate for those differences. In general, the more weight that's on a particular tire, the better that tire will grip the track. If a car's tight on an oval course, where drivers always turn left, crews adjust to redistribute weight to the right front tire; if loose, weight is distributed to the right rear. On road courses, since the cars turns both left and right, setup is often the same on the left and right sides.

Tire pressures are also important. At short tracks, tire pressure is generally lower than at superspeedways. At short tracks, the heavy braking causes heat buildup that actually raises the tire pressure over the course of a run. To counter this, tires are inflated at the start to lower than the recommended pressure.

The shock rigidity and spring rates (how much pressure a compressed spring exerts) are significantly higher at superspeedways to give the cars more stability; at such high speeds, and with the cars only inches off the ground, up-and-down movement in undesirable. For both springs and shocks, the right sides are tighter than the left.

Tire stagger, the difference in diameter between the tires on the right and left sides, is another way of improving a car's handling. On an oval course, the tires on the right side are slightly bigger than those on the left, which helps the car turn left. To get good grip from tires you also want to have as much of the tire surface on the track as possible. To that end, teams adjust the tires' camber, which is a measurement of how much a tire is leaning in or out from top to bottom.

By setting the left side tire with slight positive camber (leaning out) and the right side with negative camber (leaning in), the contact area between tire and track is maximized, especially on the banking in the left-hand turns. Too much camber will cause the car to ride on the edge of the tire, which defeats the purpose and can also cause excessive wear and, eventually, a blow-out.

Teams also choose between scuffed tires or "stickers" (brand-new tires, with the manufacturer's stickers still in place) to get the best grip. To scuff a tire a team will run a lap or two on it, just to wear off the newness. Stickers are often used in qualifying since they tend to be softer and get better grip over the first couple of laps. But that differs track-to-track. On very smooth tracks teams may go with scuffs. The surface of some tracks, like Rockingham and Darlington, are so abrasive and hard on tires that everyone goes with stickers.

With all of the various factors that can go into adjusting a car's handling, it's no wonder that crew chiefs keep notebooks for each track, detailing the setup parameters that have worked well, or not so well, in previous visits.

Goodyear is the sole distributor of tires for Winston Cup teams today. Here, you can see lug nuts pre-glued in place on each wheel. This trick speeds up the pit stops as tires can be slammed on the hubs with the nuts already in position to be tightened. Also, each tire is marked with its position on the car ("RR" indicates the right rear spot). Depending on the track and the conditions, different pressures and cambers are used at different positions, and a team can be fined for putting left-side tires on the right side of the car or vice versa.

Chapter 5

EXPANSION

The challenges of building a racetrack have changed dramatically in the modern era. With the immense popularity of Winston Cup races, tracks face a logistical nightmare as they have to facilitate the movement, seating, and comfort of a small city's worth of visitors. Not only must banking and track widths be planned, but the need for thousands of acres of parking, sufficient water supplies (especially in arid parts of the United States), and sanitation facilities must be taken into account. And all this is in addition to the basic problems of handling the influx and organization of the race teams and hundreds of vendors.

The economic pressures on a track are different today, too. The venue must be able to support purses totaling millions of dollars (the purse for the 1999 Daytona 500, for example, was more than $8 million). This means that, even factoring in the money paid to the track for the broadcast rights, a lot of tickets have to be sold to make a profit. Notice that none of the tracks added to the schedule over the last few years are shorter than 1.5 miles (2.4km)—anything smaller couldn't support the "miles of aisles" necessary for survival. The need for sufficient seating to support the financial base, and the package of speed and size that is now associated with major league racing, dictates that the trend toward "big Ds" (as these tracks are called) will continue. But while the new facilities in California, Texas, and Las Vegas support good racing, it's just one style of racing. NASCAR fans remain nearly unanimous that stock car racers need to be proficient at shoe-horning their car around a tight half-miler and managing their tires on a high-banked intermediate track as well as running at the big tracks.

There is also something of a speedway war underway within the sport. International Speedway Corporation, run by the France family, owns six of the tracks on the circuit. Long-time France rival O. Bruton Smith runs Speedway Motorsports, Inc., which now owns six tracks. Throw in the four covered by Penske Motorsports and almost all of the tracks are under the control of a very few individuals. The contest over who gets race dates is ruled by NASCAR, under the direction of the Frances, and Smith has been vocal about his feelings of being shortchanged. Smith has even suggested splitting the sport into two divisions, to facilitate running more races at more tracks. You need only look at the effect that tactic had on Indy car racing to see that there's a very real danger that NASCAR could trip over its own success.

As it has so often throughout its history, NASCAR stands at a crossroads. There is opportunity for a great leap forward, but a misstep could have disastrous consequences. At the beginning of 2000, controversy over upcoming changes in TV coverage and ownership rights of images associated with the sport raised fears that the yellow brick road the sport is racing down might lead to the cliff's edge.

Of course, the France family has led NASCAR through more than fifty years of these sorts of challenges and their track record is pretty impressive. The road has often been bumpy but the sport has always gone in the right direction. Current NASCAR COO Mike Helton is no newcomer to the workings of the organization. A man who is steeped in the NASCAR's culture and values, Helton will no doubt insure that stock car racing remains a healthy sport that will continue to serve the needs and interests of its fans.

NEW HAMPSHIRE INTERNATIONAL SPEEDWAY

LOCATION: *Loudon, New Hampshire*
RACE LENGTH: *317 miles (507.2km) on a 1.058-mile (1.7km) paved oval.*
NUMBER OF RACES RUN: *Twelve Winston Cup, held between July 11, 1993, and September 17, 2000*
SPEED RECORD (AVERAGE FOR AN ENTIRE RACE): *117.134 mph (187.4kph), set on July 11, 1997*

The addition of New Hampshire International Speedway to the Winston Cup circuit was special in many respects. It was the first time the circuit stopped in the state of New Hampshire, and marked the Cup's return to the New England area after a two-decade-long absence. This was also the first brand new track that NASCAR visited since Talladega in 1969.

The track was built by Bob Bahre in 1989. It's a true oval, 1.058-miles around. The turns are flat, with only 12 degrees of banking, and the straights are flatter, with no banking at all along the front. The 1,500-foot (456m) front- and backstretches make for tight, challenging turns—sort of like a big Martinsville. The owners almost had to drop their plans for the twenty-nine grandstand-topping suites, which brought seating capacity at the facility to 72,000. Local firefighters didn't have equipment tall enough to reach the top of the stands if needed. The Bahres resolved the issue by buying the necessary equipment for the fire department.

The track has hosted a Busch Grand National race each year starting in 1990, and was granted a Winston Cup date for the '93 season. In '96, Bahre, in partnership with O. Bruton Smith, purchased the North Wilkesboro

PAGES 142–143: On August 3, 1996, Dale Jarrett became the third NASCAR driver to win the Brickyard 400. Edging out Robert Yates Racing teammate Ernie Irvan six laps before the finish, Jarrett was thrilled with the win at one of the most famous tracks in motorsports. "To be in victory lane at [the Brickyard] is just overwhelming," said Jarrett. PAGE 143: Bobby Labonte is certainly not the first younger brother to follow his older sibling into Winston Cup racing, but he is one of the most successful. With Bobby's 2000 championship victory, Terry and Bobby Labonte are the only brothers to have won NASCAR titles.

TOP: The field roars through turn two at New Hampshire in 1998. A second race at the New England track was added to the schedule that year. A pair of Jeffs took the trophies at those races, first Burton in the July event and then Gordon in August. ABOVE: A wide-angle shot of New Hampshire Speedway in 2000 shows the view from the top row of the stands above turn one. Hope you brought your binoculars—the other end of the speedway is nearly a half-mile (0.8km) distant.

The DuPont number 24 team enjoyed a breakthrough year in 1995. Gordon and crew chief, Ray Evernham (right), took home seven trophies—including this one from New Hampshire, their fifth win of the season—and a Winston Cup championship. The '95 Slick 50 300 win put the team in first place in the points standings, ahead of Sterling Marlin.

Speedway and closed it, freeing up the site's two race dates. One date was added to Loudon starting in the fall of '97 and the other went to Smith's Texas Motor Speedway.

Memorable Moments at New Hampshire

The first Winston Cup race at Loudon saw Mark Martin and Sterling Marlin battling for the lead through much of the first half. Marlin looked to be strong enough to earn his first victory, but faded after contact with Dale Earnhardt, who was trying to make up a lap. Davey Allison took over the point and was on his way to victory when a caution flag was thrown late in the race due to debris. Rusty Wallace's pit crew earned their pay, getting him back on the track in first. Wallace was able to pull away for the inaugural victory. Allison lost second place in the closing laps to Mark Martin; Dale Jarrett came in fourth and Ricky Rudd in fifth. Sadly, it was Davey Allison's last race. The next day he flew his new helicopter to Talladega to watch buddy Neil Bonnett's son practice. The helicopter flipped over during the landing and Davey was fatally injured.

Ricky Rudd used the 1994 Slick 50 300 to extend his long consecutive-season winning streak. Ernie Irvan, in Robert Yates' number 28 car, took the pole with a new lap record. Irvan kept up the pace, leading the most laps in the caution-strewn race. Seventeen yellow flags flew as driver after driver lost his grip on the hot, slick track. With only twenty-four laps left, Irvan himself spun on the restart and fell to thirtieth. After yet another caution, Dale Earnhardt was at the point with Ricky Rudd in second. Rudd pulled under the number 3 in the first turn, traded some paint, and then went on to the win. It was his first win as the owner of his own number 10 team, formed that year.

Rusty Wallace and Dale Earnhardt conducted one of their signature side-by-side battles during much of the 1995 race, but Jeff Gordon, on the way to his first championship, slipped by both and took the victory. Ernie Irvan sealed his miraculous recovery from life-threatening injuries (sustained in a crash during practice in '94) by returning to the winner's circle in the Jiffy Lube 300 in '96.

New Englander Ricky Craven thrilled the hometown crowd during the inaugural second Loudon race, added in 1997, leading throughout much of the CMT 300. Craven earned the pole for the July '98 race. And "Front-row Joe" Nemechek celebrated his first Winston Cup victory in the September '99 race, shortly after being released from his ride in the Sabco number 42 car. Nemechek beat challenger Tony Stewart (who almost won his first race in July before running out of gas with only a few laps to go) with fast restarts after three consecutive cautions in the waning laps. "I don't know how to explain this. This is just an unbelievable feeling," exclaimed the emotional driver. The win helped Nemechek land a new ride for 2000, with Andy Petree's number 33 team.

Tragedy at the Track

In 2000, New Hampshire was the unlikely site of two tragic events. On May 12, while testing his Busch Grand National car at the track, Adam Petty, the nineteen-year-old scion of the Petty dynasty, lost control heading into the first turn and was killed in an inexplicable crash. The racing world, already mourning the passing of Adam's great-grandfather—and NASCAR pioneer—Lee Petty in April, was stunned. The outpouring of compassion from friends and fans could but little ease the anguish of Kyle, Richard, and their families.

In July, lightning struck a second time. During practice on the Friday before the July 9 race, Winston Cup driver Kenny Irwin Jr. hit the wall in the same spot and lost his life.

Once the NASCAR community caught its breath from the fresh tragedy, its full attention was focused on the safety issue. In both cases, it appeared that the cars' accelerators must have stuck going into the turns, and with no banking to slow the cars, the impact was crushing. Foam barriers and other means of reducing impact were discussed, but in the end NASCAR decided that slowing the cars down was the best move. New Hampshire thus earned the dubious distinction of becoming the third restrictor-plate track on the circuit. The July 9 race, then, was run without incident, albeit at a slower speed. Winner Tony Stewart remembered Irwin as a respected colleague who brought out the best racer in him.

INDIANAPOLIS MOTOR SPEEDWAY (THE BRICKYARD)

LOCATION: *Indianapolis, Indiana*
RACE LENGTH: *400 miles (640km) on a 2.5-mile (4km) paved rectangular course*
NUMBER OF RACES RUN: *Seven Winston Cup, held between August 6, 1994, and August 5, 2000*
SPEED RECORD (AVERAGE FOR AN ENTIRE RACE): *155.918 mph (249.5kph), set on August 5, 2000*

No track is more recognized or has a more illustrious history than the Brickyard, built by Indianapolis businessman Carl Fisher in 1909. Most racing fans know that Ray Harroun won the first Indy 500 in 1911, but there were actually quite a few races at the facility held prior to that event. The very first race was a balloon race that started from the infield in June '09. The first scheduled motorized event was a motorcycle race, but rain and poor track conditions reduced it to a two-man competition. Cars first ran on the track in August '09, when more than ten short races of various lengths took place over a three-day period.

It was clear that dirt was not the way to go with a track that size, so Fisher had it surfaced using 3.2 million bricks (hence the nickname). By 1911, Fisher had settled on 500

Daytona may have a lake, but Indianapolis has an infield golf course. Indy has the largest seating capacity of any American racetrack, with box-office totals of more than 400,000 for some events. Grandstands rise up on both the inside and outside of the track, in some places producing something of a tunnel for the drivers going around the track.

TOP: Darrell Waltrip (in the number 66) said goodbye to racing—behind the wheel at least—at the end of the 2000 season. DW had his best showing of the year at the Brickyard 400, running up front most of the day and finishing eleventh. ABOVE: One of the traditions of Indy: the race winner signs his name on the yard (.9m)-wide strip of bricks at the start/finish line. Here, Ricky Rudd adds his John Hancock to the collection following a surprise win in the 1996 Brickyard event. OPPOSITE: The Goody's Body Pain 500 seems like a fitting name for a short-track race. The action at the back of the pack (shown here) is often furious as drivers dig hard for every spot, both to advance and to keep from going a lap down. The '99 WC champion, Dale Jarrett (car 88), started near the back but worked his way up to eighth place by the end.

miles (800km) as the best length for a feature, and the famed Indy 500 began. On a historical note, the flags used in the first Indy 500 were quite a bit different than those displayed today during a race: only the meaning of the checkered was the same, while green was "last lap," white was "stop for penalty," blue was "caution," and red was "go."

The track was resurfaced with asphalt (right on top of the bricks) in the 1940s, except the front straight, which wasn't covered until '61. Only the signature "yard of bricks" at the start/finish line remains exposed today.

The 2.5-mile Indianapolis track is a rectangular track with two 3,000-foot (912m) -long straights, two short chutes, after turns one and three of 660 feet (200.1m) each, and four tight corners 1/4 mile (400m) in length. It's a very flat track, with only 9 degrees of banking in the turns. The track's not overly wide, only 50 feet (15.2m), but Winston Cup drivers have found lots of places to pass and redefined the concept of close racing at the hallowed speedway.

Throughout its history, NASCAR has raced on the biggest and best speedways across the United States. In all that time, though, it had never visited the nation's, if not the world's, most prestigious track. Perhaps it had something to do with an incident between longtime track owner Tony Hulman and NASCAR founder Bill France. Due to a misunderstanding, France was forcibly removed from the Indy garage prior to a 500-miler in the 1950s. Hulman later apologized for the error, but the two never warmed to each other. Whatever the reason, it wasn't until '92 that fans were able to see how stock cars would fare at the Brickyard.

Informal discussions between Bill France, Jr. and current track owner (and Hulman's grandson) Tony George led to a test session in June 1992. Nine NASCAR teams and 35,000

OPPOSITE: As a driver, this is one view of the 1999 Martinsville Goody Body Pain 500 you definitely don't want to have. John Andretti (not in this photo) started the race back with these guys and steadily worked his way forward, taking the lead from the 99 car with only three laps left and going on to the victory. ABOVE: Jeff Gordon took the inaugural victory at Indianapolis, the second win of his sophomore season, in 1994. He later became the first two-time winner at the track as well (with his '98 victory). As a youngster, Gordon had dreamt of running in races at the famous track, though he expected to be in open-wheel Indy cars instead of stock cars.

spectators arrived at the track on a Monday morning to see how the heavy racecars would run. Dale Earnhardt, Rusty Wallace, Darrell Waltrip, Mark Martin, Kyle Petty, Davey Allison, Ernie Irvan, Ricky Rudd, and Bill Elliott stopped in Indiana on the way home from the Michigan race. The results of the test were positive: the cars tracked well through the tight corners and the drivers were able to race competitively. Moreover, the Winston Cup stars were an immediate success with the fans. After an impromptu two-hour session at the track, fence fans commented that the NASCAR drivers had signed more autographs that day than the other drivers (that is, Indy car drivers) had in years.

There was no official word on that test session for quite a while, but in April 1993 George and France announced that a Brickyard race would be added to the '94 Winston Cup schedule.

🏁🏁 The 1994 Brickyard 400

Even non-race fans could tell that the inaugural Brickyard 400 was a special event. A quarter million seats were sold in just a few days, with a final tally in excess of 300,000 (the biggest crowd for a NASCAR event ever), and rookies and old-timers alike wore an "I can't believe I'm going to race here" look of delight.

More than seventy teams showed up to vie for forty-three starting spots. Indy car veterans Danny Sullivan and John Andretti made the field, and the venerable A.J. Foyt came out of NASCAR retirement to be part of the historical event. The best of the old guard and the new lions started up front. Dale Earnhardt was on the outside of the front row and Jeff Gordon lined up in third. The pole-sitter was a dark horse: with the help of a fast set of Hoosier tires and a change in the cloud cover during his qualifying run, Rick Mast put the number 1 Skoal Ford at the top of the scoring pylon. Points leader Ernie Irvan lost two engines in practice and ended up qualifying in mid-pack.

Prerace hoopla included perennial Indy 500 master of ceremonies Jim Nabors singing the national anthem. When the matriarch of the Hulman family, Mary Hulman, gave the

command to "start your engines" the facility vibrated for the first time to the deep-throated roar of a full field of NASCAR stock cars.

Dale Earnhardt made no bones about his intention to lead the first lap at Indy. Rick Mast was equally determined, though, and hung onto the inside lane and the lead, even as Earnhardt overdrove the fourth turn, slapping the wall. The sentimental favorite in the race was hometown hero Jeff Gordon, who grew up in Pittsboro, Indiana. The number 24 Chevy had muscle to match the sophomore's desire and he drove to the inside of Mast on lap two to take the lead. Gordon stayed near the front all day, leading seven times for a total of ninety-three of the 160 laps. Twelve other drivers took turns at the point, including Earnhardt, who led for two laps during the cycle of green-flag pit stops.

Six caution flags interrupted the event. Jimmy Spencer put the McDonald's Ford into the wall on lap twelve, Mike Chase and Dave Marcis collided on lap ninety-five, and Jimmy Hensley tangled with road racer Geoff Brabham on lap 131. The strangest incident was a spin by contender Geoffrey Bodine on lap 101 that also collected Dale Jarrett. On the previous restart, Geoffrey had lined up right behind his brother Brett. As they sailed into turn three, Geoffrey gave his younger sibling a tap and slid by him for the lead. Brett immediately returned the favor in turn four but hit Geoffrey's Exide Ford hard enough to send it spinning. In the pits Geoffrey lambasted his brother to the media, accusing him of carrying a family feud onto the track and deliberately wrecking him.

Despite a poor starting spot, Ernie Irvan moved up steadily through the race. As the event wore down, Irvan moved past Rusty Wallace to take second, then challenged Gordon for the lead. The two swapped turns at the front, with Irvan in the lead and seemingly with a win in hand with only five laps to go. Then bad luck hit the Texaco team once again and the right front tire on the number 28 let go. Irvan kept the car off the wall but was forced to pit. Gordon, not quite believing his good fortune, flew by and won his second Winston Cup race to the thunderous approval of the crowd.

The Brickyard Today

Earnhardt, who'd struggled to a fifth-place finish in the inaugural event, led only once in the 1995 race. But that stretch included the last lap. The turning point came during the last set of green-flag pit stops. Rusty Wallace looked to be the leader after the stops but was slowed on pit road when two cars collided in front of him. By the time he cleared the wreck he'd lost the lead to the number 3 and had to settle for second place. With characteristic mischievousness Earnhardt teased young defending winner Jeff Gordon by proclaiming himself the first *man* to win the Brickyard race.

Dale Jarrett beat teammate Ernie Irvan to the finish line to take the win in 1996. Irvan had been strong all day, leading thirty-nine laps (Johnny Benson, Jr., in the number 30 Pennzoil Pontiac, was the lap leader with seventy circuits to his credit), but drove over some fluid dropped by the smoking number 81 car on lap 154 and slid up a lane. Jarrett dove inside him and made the pass for the win.

Ricky Rudd added his name to the Brickyard winner's list in 1997. Gordon and Jarrett repeated their trips to victory lane in '98 and '99, respectively, and Bobby Labonte gave Pontiac its first Indy win in '00. Indianapolis had been added to the "No Bull 5" program in '98 and Gordon cashed in on a million-dollar paycheck with his Brickyard 400 win that year.

Champagne for everyone! Jeff Gordon celebrates his 1.6-million-dollar payday with a shaken-up bottle of bubbly after the 1998 Brickyard victory. It was the highest-paying one-day payoff in the sport to that date.

LOCATION: *Fort Worth, Texas*
RACE LENGTH: *400.5 miles (640.8km) on a 1.5-mile (2.4km) paved oval*
NUMBER OF RACES RUN: *Four Winston Cup, held between April 6, 1997, and April 2, 2000*
SPEED RECORD (AVERAGE FOR AN ENTIRE RACE): *144.276 mph (230.8kph), set on March 28, 1999*

O. Bruton Smith's Texas Motor Speedway, which opened in 1997, was embroiled in controversy even before opening day. Smith and Bob Bahre, owner of New Hampshire International Speedway, had jointly acquired ownership of North Wilkesboro Speedway in '96 expressly in order to redistribute the venerable track's two Winston Cup dates—one to New Hampshire and one to Texas. Fans and competitors alike were upset about the loss of the North Wilkesboro dates and focused their outrage on Mr. Smith and his new track.

The facility itself is state-of-the-art, capable of hosting more than 200,000 fans (second in capacity only to Indianapolis). The 1.5-mile track was fashioned after Charlotte Motor Speedway as a flattened D-shaped oval, but the straightaway lengths and turn radii are different. The shorter straightaways—2,250-foot (684m) front, 1,330-foot (404.3m) back—and large-radius turns allow cars to maintain higher speeds everywhere on the track. Texas has dual banking (8 degrees, going up to 24 degrees), to support both stock car and Indy car racing, and features a Musco lighting system to allow night racing.

Track Troubles at Texas

When the first racing weekend rolled around in April 1997, Mother Nature intervened and turned the glittering facility into a mud bath. Torrential rains prevented qualifying for the Winston Cup race, so the drivers' points standing determined the starting lineup. The grass around the track hadn't had time to take root, so the ground liquefied with the heavy rain. The fans persevered, though, packing the stands, and the rain abated in time for the inaugural Busch race and subsequent Winston Cup event.

Competitors had expressed concern about the narrowness of turn one and the potential for problems there. It didn't take long in the WC race to prove those concerns well-founded. A multicar accident in that turn on the first lap took out a number of solid contenders, including Dale Earnhardt and Bill Elliott. Pole-sitter Dale Jarrett struggled with transmission problems, and second-place starter Jeff Gordon was caught up in another accident. Jeff Burton and the Exide team, which had a string of top-fives going into the race, were able to convert that success into Burton's first Winston Cup win.

The field awaits the command to start their engines on pit road prior to the 1998 Texas 500 (Mark Martin took the win later that day). In '00, Dale Earnhardt, Jr. proved that there's more to him than just his famous name by winning his first Winston Cup race, at Texas, after only six starts in big-league NASCAR competition.

Following the race, many of the drivers openly criticized the track's configuration. Texas management rebutted, and the series moved on. The following year, 1998, saw more confrontation between the track owners and NASCAR. Prior to the Texas 500, water began seeping through the surface of the problematic first turn. Qualifying was again halted and track crews worked overnight to fix the problem. The surface seemed acceptable the following day and Jeremy Mayfield went on to win the pole. The field made it through the first lap without incident, but on the second lap another multicar pileup in turn one, along with multiple crashes in the Busch race the preceding day, proved the final straw for NASCAR. Texas management was told to fix the track's problems or it would lose the race date.

To TMS management's credit, they went to work and rebuilt the track for 1999. Rain again played a factor in the '99 Primestar 500, putting a halt to final practice, but the track surface held up and the race was run without a multi-car crash. The new surface was tough on right front tires, and there were numerous blowouts that eliminated some top teams. In the end "Texas" Terry Labonte took the trophy, his first win in his home state.

CALIFORNIA SPEEDWAY

LOCATION: *Fontana, California*
LENGTH: *500 miles (800km) on a 2-mile (3.2km) paved oval*
NUMBER OF RACES RUN: *Four Winston Cup, held between June 6, 1997, and April 30, 2000*
SPEED RECORD (AVERAGE FOR AN ENTIRE RACE): *155.012 mph (248kph), set on June 22, 1997*

NASCAR racing returned to southern California (which had previously hosted the series at Ontario and Riverside raceways) in 1997 with Roger Penske's California Speedway. In an unprecedented move, both NASCAR and CART committed to race dates before the track was even built.

The facility was built on the site of the defunct Kaiser Steel Mill, whose water tower still stands just outside the track. The area had been so bleak that it had been used to film scenes of industrial wasteland in *The Terminator*. Just clearing the land for the track proved a challenge: more than 21,000 tons (19,047t) of hazardous waste left over from the mill had to be removed from the locale before building could begin.

The 2-mile tri-oval mirrors the successful Michigan Speedway's layout. Banking is slightly less at California—14 degrees in the turns (to Michigan's 18 degrees), 11 degrees on the front stretch, and 3 degrees on the back. The track is wide, 75 feet (22.8m) across, and can accommodate four- or five-abreast competition.

An Auspicious Start for California

In contrast to opening-day problems at Texas Motor Speedway, California was a finished and polished gem when the series rolled in for the June 1997 weekend. Joe Nemechek and California native Ernie Irvan shared the front row for the start of the event. There were several strong contenders, but Jeff Gordon won the race on mileage. Gordon was able to run the final 100-lap segment on only one pit stop, while the others required a second gas-and-go with about ten laps left.

Mark Martin was the 1998 winner, sweeping the California weekend with an IROC victory the previous day as well. Several poor finishes leading into the '99 event didn't stop Jeff Gordon from repeating his win at the track. Gordon held off Jeff Burton, who had fought his way back to second place from being a lap down, to take the win by more than four seconds.

Jeremy Mayfield took his second checkered flag at California in 2000. The win turned out to be bittersweet for the team, though, when a postrace inspection uncovered an illegal fuel additive in the number 12 car—a major rules infraction. The team was severely penalized, both in dollars and points, and even though the win stood, the team went through a difficult time trying to repair its tarnished image.

The California track also hosts CART events. In the fall 1999 race in that series, driver Greg Moore tragically lost his life after a staggering impact to the inside retaining wall.

LOCATION: *Las Vegas, Nevada*
RACE LENGTH: *400 miles (640km) on a 1.5-mile (2.4km) paved tri-oval*
NUMBER OF RACES RUN: *Three Winston Cup, held on March 1, 1998, and March 5, 2000*
SPEED RECORD (AVERAGE FOR AN ENTIRE RACE): *146.554 mph (234.5kph), set on March 1, 1998*

The $200 million "Diamond in the Desert" is O. Bruton Smith's latest addition to the NASCAR schedule. Called the "Racing Capital of the West" by *Sports Illustrated*, the track is a 1.5-mile tri-oval, similar in shape to the Daytona and Talladega speedways. It's a flat track, with 12 degrees of banking in the turns, 9 on the front stretch, and 3 on the back straight. The track is wide and considered one of the most "raceable" on the circuit, but it is only one part of this remarkable facility, which also features a ⅜-mile (0.6km) paved oval, a road course, a dirt track, and a drag strip (under construction at this writing).

Las Vegas may not be the fastest track on the circuit, but it does hold one interesting speed record. It is the only speedway to have an exit ramp directly off a major interstate highway, and for the 1998 Winston Cup race crews were able to park more than 47,000 cars in less than three hours. With the wealth of hotel accommodations nearby, this track may be the only one on the circuit where you won't have a hard time finding a place to stay. Nevada is, of course, an arid state, but building codes require there to be a sizable quantity of water on hand for fire safety. The speedway has water in spades—a water tower holds 1 million gallons (3,785,000l) and a manmade pond holds 3.5 million gallons (13,247,500l).

PAGES 154-155: The Joe Gibbs Interstate Batteries Pontiac of 2000 Winston Cup champion Bobby Labonte. Labonte was the Busch Grand National champion in '91 before moving up to Winston Cup in '93. He moved to the Gibbs organization in '95, and immediately served notice of things to come, with three wins that season. Four wins and fifteen other top-fives in the '00 season kept him at the top of the points standing for almost the entire year. ABOVE: The pack fans out around the broad sweep of California Speedway's turns. The number 12 Mobil One team's 2000 win at the track, and indeed the team's whole season, was tainted by the discovery that illegal fuel additives had been used in the car during the race. The fines and suspensions were stiff and the deduction of series points pushed the team well down in the standings.

As of this writing, the Las Vegas track (seen here in March 2000) is the latest of the 1.5-mile (2.4km), D-shaped ovals added to the circuit. Though the tracks are well built and generally well liked by drivers, the spate of superspeedway additions has prompted many fans to petition for the next new venue to be a short track.

Las Vegas Motor Speedway is also unique for its commitment to motorsports education and training. It is home to the University of Motorsports, which offers ten specialized training schools both for professional drivers and fans. Courses run the gamut from BMX bikes to the Richard Petty Driving Experience.

The facility was built in 1996 by Ral Englestead and Bill Bennett. It hosted an Indy Racing League event that fall and NASCAR Busch Grand National and Craftsman Truck Series races the following year. Winston Cup came to the facility in '98. Smith's Speedway Motorsports, Inc. purchased the speedway in December '98.

So far, the Las Vegas 400 has been dominated by Rousch Racing, with teammates Mark Martin and Jeff Burton taking the first two events. The 1998 race was conducted with typical Las Vegas showmanship: there were pre-race shows, and several cars featured special paint schemes (Rusty Wallace's "Elvis" car and sequined racing suit were standouts). Dale Jarrett won the pole, but Mark Martin was the man to beat that Sunday. Martin took the number 6 Ford to the front early on and kept it there for most of the event. The Valvoline team was surprised that their car held

together through the whole 400 miles (640km)—it developed a transmission vibration early on that they thought could sideline them at any time. The anticipated problem never developed, though, and the low-key Mark Martin found himself looking a bit out of place wedged between towering, feather-bedecked showgirls in victory lane.

Las Vegas Motor Speedway became one of the Winston "No Bull 5" races in 1999, replacing Indianapolis; the race that year turned out to be an exciting showdown between the brothers Burton. Ward Burton's number 22 was a strong contender for the win, but his younger brother slipped past him with only nine laps left to go on for his first win of the year. On racing his brother for the win, Jeff commented, "That's awfully stressful. I'm a big fan of Ward Burton's. We always wanted to come down to the end like that—next time he'll get me."

For the second year in a row, a rookie contender earned a Winston Cup win when Dale Earnhardt Jr. took the 2000 Teams Trophy. Team owner and proud papa Dale Sr. joined his son for the celebration in victory lane. Junior later proved the victory was no fluke, following with wins at Richmond and in the Winston All-Star Race at Charlotte.

Expansion

What's not to smile about? Flanked by a pair of beautiful showgirls and holding a big trophy, Mark Martin basks in typical Las Vegas hoopla in the winner's circle after his 1998 Las Vegas 400 win. Martin and Rousch teammate Jeff Burton seem to have adapted quickly to the new tracks on the schedule, dominating the competition at California, Las Vegas, and Texas speedways at the dawn of the new millennium.

Expansion

MIAMI-DADE HOMESTEAD MOTORSPORTS COMPLEX

LOCATION: *Homestead, Florida*

RACE LENGTH: *400.5 miles (640.8km) on a 1.5-mile (2.4km) paved oval*

NUMBER OF RACES RUN: *Two Winston Cup, held on November 14, 1999, and November 12, 2000*

SPEED RECORD (AVERAGE FOR AN ENTIRE RACE): *140.335 mph (224.5kph), set on November 14, 1999*

The Miami-Dade facility had hosted Busch Grand National Craftsman Truck races since its opening in '95 and the CART FedEx Championship Series since '96 before becoming the latest track to be added to the Winston Cup schedule in '99. The architecture of the facility was carefully planned to match the Art Deco look of Miami's South Beach area—even the outside retaining walls of the track are painted a bright, Florida turquoise.

Miami is a true oval, with 1,760-foot (535m) straightaways and turns with 750-foot (228m) radii. It's a flat track, with only 6 degrees of banking in the turns and 3 on the straights. Unlike some flat tracks, which have slight banking nearer the outer wall, Miami is flat all the way out. So if a driver gets out of shape, he can find himself at the wall really quickly. The track is wide—60 feet (18.2m) on the straights and 80 feet (24.3m) in the turns—but the inside of the track is definitely the place to be. The most difficult portion of the track is the exit from turn four, and that's where most of the incidents occurred.

The debut Winston Cup race, on November 14, 1999, was the thirty-third and penultimate race of the season. Despite expectations of trouble, there was only one caution, when Ricky Rudd's engine blew. The long green-flag runs and changing track conditions as the afternoon wore on caused the field to get quite strung out. Bobby Labonte dominated the race, leading the most laps and leaving only eight cars on the lead lap. Labonte's teammate Tony Stewart was stout also, and pulled off a daring move coming out of the pits after the last stop to take the lead for the final segment. Stewart went on to win, the third in his record-breaking rookie season. Dale Jarrett, who had won the opening Busch race there in '95, locked up the '99 Winston Cup championship at Miami.

Tony Stewart, shown here pitting during the 1999 Pennzoil 400, won both of the first two Winston Cup races at Homestead speedway, opened in 1999. The '00 race was especially sweet for the Joe Gibbs organization: not only did the number 20 team win the race, but Bobby Labonte (in the number 18) secured the '00 championship title.

1949

Charlotte Speedway
(See pages 25–7)

Daytona Beach & Road Course
(See pages 13–21)

Occoneechee Speedway (Orange Speedway)
LOCATION: Hillsboro, North Carolina
RACE LENGTH: 200 miles (320km) on a 1-mile (1.6km) (re-measured to 0.9 mile [1.44km] in 1956) dirt oval
NUMBER OF RACES RUN: 32 Grand National, between August 7, 1949, and September 15, 1968
SPEED RECORD (AVERAGE FOR AN ENTIRE RACE): 90.663 mph (145.1kph), on March 14, 1965

The third race of the Strictly Stock division's opening season was held at this track.

Langhorne Speedway
(See pages 27–9)

Hamburg Speedway (Erie County Fairgrounds)
LOCATION: Hamburg, New York
RACE LENGTH: 100 miles (160km) on a 1/2-mile (0.8km) dirt oval
NUMBER OF RACES RUN: 2 Grand National, on September 18, 1949, and August 27, 1950
SPEED RECORD (AVERAGE FOR AN ENTIRE RACE): 50.747 mph (81.2kph), on August, 27, 1950

Hamburg Speedway was the fifth race of the first Strictly Stock season.

Martinsville Speedway
(See pages 29–35)

Heidelberg Speedway
LOCATION: Pittsburgh, Pennsylvania
RACE LENGTH: 100 miles (160km) on a 5/8-mile (1km) dirt oval, paved in 1966
NUMBER OF RACES RUN: 4 Grand National, between October 2, 1949, and July 10, 1960

SPEED RECORD (AVERAGE FOR AN ENTIRE RACE): 67.450 mph (107.kph), on July 10, 1960

North Wilkesboro Speedway
(See pages 36–7)

1950

Canfield Motor Speedway
LOCATION: Canfield, Ohio
RACE LENGTH: 100 miles (160km) on a 1/2-mile (0.8km) dirt oval
NUMBER OF RACES RUN: 3 Grand National, between May 30, 1950, and May 30, 1952
SPEED RECORD (AVERAGE FOR AN ENTIRE RACE): 49.308 mph (78.9kph), on May 30, 1951

The Grand National races were held on Memorial Day—the same day as the Indianapolis 500—and were humorously declared the "Poor Man's 500."

Vernon Fairgrounds
LOCATION: Vernon, New York
RACE LENGTH: 100 miles (160km) on a 1/2-mile (0.8km) dirt oval
NUMBER OF RACES RUN: 2 Grand National, on June 18, 1950, and October 1, 1950
SPEED RECORD (AVERAGE FOR AN ENTIRE RACE): No average speed was recorded

Dayton Speedway
LOCATION: Dayton, Ohio
RACE LENGTH: 100 miles (160km) on a 1/2-mile (0.8km) dirt oval, paved in 1951
NUMBER OF RACES RUN: 6 Grand National, between June 25, 1950, and September 21, 1952
SPEED RECORD (AVERAGE FOR AN ENTIRE RACE): 65.526 mph (104.8kph), on May 18, 1952

Monroe County Fairgrounds
LOCATION: Rochester, New York
RACE LENGTH: 100 miles (160km) on a 1/2-mile (0.8km) dirt oval

NUMBER OF RACES RUN: 8 Grand National, between July 2, 1950, and July 25, 1958
SPEED RECORD (AVERAGE FOR AN ENTIRE RACE): 59.990 mph (96kph), on July 25, 1958

Darlington Raceway
(See pages 60–9)

Winchester Speedway
LOCATION: Winchester, Indiana
RACE LENGTH: 100 miles (160km) on a 1/2-mile (0.8km) dirt (oiled) oval
NUMBER OF RACES RUN: One Grand National, on October 15, 1950
SPEED RECORD (AVERAGE FOR AN ENTIRE RACE): 63.875 mph (102.2kph)

The Winchester track has a long history. It was originally opened by Frank Funk in 1914 and is still active today. Only 1 Grand National race was run on the high-banked track, prior to it being paved in 1951. The race attracted only 13 entries since it was scheduled on the same day as the Grand National race in Martinsville, Virginia! Only 6 cars finished the race, lead by Lloyd Moore.

1951

Lakeview Speedway
LOCATION: Mobile, Alabama
RACE LENGTH: 112.5 miles (180km) on a 3/4-mile (1.2km) dirt oval
NUMBER OF RACES RUN: 2 Grand National, on April 8, 1951, and November 25, 1951
SPEED RECORD (AVERAGE FOR AN ENTIRE RACE): 50.260 mph (80.4kph), on April 8, 1951

The race was organized by Fonty Flock who also ran in it, and finished second to his brother, Tim.

Carrell Speedway (Gardena Bowl)
LOCATION: Gardena, California
RACE LENGTH: 100 miles (160km) on a 1/2-mile (0.8km) dirt oval
NUMBER OF RACES RUN: 4 Grand National, between April 8, 1951, and May 30, 1954
SPEED RECORD (AVERAGE FOR AN ENTIRE RACE): 61.047 mph (97.7kph), on April 8, 1951

This was the first Grand National race on the west coast!

Arizona State Fairgrounds (Phoenix Fairgrounds)
LOCATION: Phoenix, Arizona
RACE LENGTH: 150 miles (240km) on a 1-mile (1.6km) dirt oval
NUMBER OF RACES RUN: 4 Grand National, between April 22, 1951, and April 3, 1960
SPEED RECORD (AVERAGE FOR AN ENTIRE RACE): 71.899 mph (115kph), on April 3, 1960

Columbus Speedway
LOCATION: Columbus, Georgia
RACE LENGTH: 100 miles (160km) on a 1/2-mile (0.8km) dirt oval
NUMBER OF RACES RUN: 1 Grand National, on June 10, 1951
SPEED RECORD (AVERAGE FOR AN ENTIRE RACE): No average speed was recorded

It first opened in 1910 and closed in 1963.

Columbia Speedway
(See pages 40–1)

Grand River Speedrome
LOCATION: Grand Rapids, Michigan
RACE LENGTH: 100 miles (160km) on a 1/2-mile (0.8km) dirt oval
NUMBER OF RACES RUN: 2 Grand National, on July 1, 1951, and July 11, 1954
SPEED RECORD (AVERAGE FOR AN ENTIRE RACE): 52.090 mph (83.3kph), on July 11, 1954

Bainbridge Fairgrounds
LOCATION: Bainbridge, Ohio
RACE LENGTH: 100 miles (160km) on a 1 mile (1.6km) dirt oval
NUMBER OF RACES RUN: 1 Grand National, on July 8, 1951
SPEED RECORD (AVERAGE FOR AN ENTIRE RACE): 65.753 mph (105.2kph)

Asheville-Weaverville Speedway (Skyline Speedway)
(See pages 41–2)

Altamont Speedway (Albany-Schenectady Fairgrounds)
LOCATION: Altamont, New York
RACE LENGTH: 100 miles (160km) on a 1/2-mile (0.8km) dirt oval

Number of races run: 2 Grand National, on August 1, 1951, and July 29, 1955

Speed record (average for an entire race): No average speed was recorded

The track closed right after the second Grand National race. That race was red-flagged and ended early after a car crashed through the fence, which was irreparably damaged. Cautious over safety issues (the Le Mans accident that killed over 80 people had occurred just weeks earlier), officials halted the race rather than run it with the fence down.

Michigan State Fairgrounds

Location: Detroit, Michigan
Race length: 250 miles (400km) on a 1-mile (1.6km) dirt oval
Number of races run: 2 Grand National, on August 12, 1951, and June 29, 1952
Speed record (average for an entire race): 59.908 mph (95.9kph), on June 29, 1952

Fort Miami Speedway

Location: Toledo, Ohio
Race length: 100 miles (160km) on a 1/2-mile (0.8km) dirt oval
Number of races run: 2 Grand National, on August 19, 1951, and June 1, 1952
Speed record (average for an entire race): 50.847 mph (81.4kph), on August 19, 1951

Morristown Speedway

Location: Morristown, New Jersey
Race length: 100 miles (160kph) on a 1/2-mile (0.8km) dirt oval
Number of races run: 5 Grand National, between August 24, 1951, and July 15, 1955
Speed record (average for an entire race): 69.417 mph (111.1kph), on July 10, 1953

Greenville-Pickens Speedway

Location: Greenville, South Carolina
Race length: 100 miles (160km) on a 1/2-mile (0.8km) dirt oval, paved in 1970
Number of races run: 29 Grand National, between August 25, 1951, and June 26, 1971

Speed record (average for an entire race): 78.159 mph (125.1kph), on April 10, 1971

Greenville-Pickens was a staple on the Grand National scene up to the winnowing of tracks for the Winston Cup schedule. The race held in 1971 was the first Grand National points race ever televised in its entirety!

Central City Speedway (Macon Speedway, Georgia State Fairgrounds)

Location: Macon, Georgia
Race length: 100 miles (160km) on a 1/2-mile (0.8km) dirt oval
Number of races run: 7 Grand National, between September 8, 1951, and September 12, 1954
Speed record (average for an entire race): 56.417 mph (90.3kph), on April 26, 1953

The track was closed in 1956.

Wilson County Speedway

Location: Wilson, North Carolina
Race length: 100 miles (160km) on a 1/2-mile (0.8km) dirt oval
Number of races run: 12 Grand National, between September 30, 1951, and April 17, 1960
Speed record (average for an entire race): 58.065 mph (92.904kph), on June 20, 1959

Thompson Speedway

Location: Thompson, Connecticut
Race length: 100 miles (160km) on a 1/2-mile (0.8km) paved oval
Number of races run: 3 Grand National, between October 12, 1951, and July 9, 1970
Speed record (average for an entire race): 89.498 mph (143.2kph), on July 10, 1969

Thompson International Speedway was the only track run by NASCAR in Connecticut! The first Grand National race was in 1951, but another was not held there until 1969.

Pine Grove Speedway

Location: Shippenville, Pennsylvania
Race length: 100 miles (160km) on a 1/2-mile (0.8km) dirt oval

Number of races run: 1 Grand National, on October 14, 1951
Speed record (average for an entire race): No average speed was recorded

Oakland Speedway

Location: Oakland, California
Race length: 150 miles (240km) on a 0.625-mile (1km) dirt and paved oval
Number of races run: 1 Grand National, between October 14, 1951, and August 1, 1954
Speed record (average for an entire race): 78.748 mph (126kph), on October 14, 1951

Oakland Stadium had something for everyone. The track originally opened in the 1930s as a 1-mile (1.6km) high-banked dirt track. It hosted 500-mile events, rare outside of Indianapolis, through that decade. A 0.625 mile (1km) track, on which the Grand National races were run, was built inside the larger track with turns that sloped up to 45 degrees! The last race in 1954 used another course there that featured paved straightaways, but dirt turns.

Hanford Motor Speedway (Marchbanks Speedway)

Location: Hanford, California
Race length: 100 miles (160km) on a 1/2-mile (0.8km) dirt oval, paved and expanded to 250 miles (400km) on a 1.4-mile (2.24km) oval in 1960
Number of races run: 3 Grand National, between October 28, 1951, and March 12, 1961
Speed record (average for an entire race): 95.621 mph (153kph), on March 12, 1961

Hanford underwent a dramatic transformation between the 1951 race and the next Grand National event in 1960. The track was orginally a 1/2-mile (0.8km) dirt track, but was reconfigured to a 1.4-mile (2.2km), high-bank paved course. It was really the first high-banked superspeedway run by NASCAR. Fireball Roberts won the last race in 1961 and led every lap from start to finish—the only time this has been done in Grand National or Winston Cup in a superspeedway event. The complex (there were actually several tracks there) was closed in 1984.

Speedway Park (Jacksonville Speedway)

Location: Jacksonville, Florida
Race length: 100 miles (160km) on a 1/2-mile (0.8km) paved oval
Number of races run: 6 Grand National, between November 4, 1951, and December 1, 1963
Speed record (average for an entire race): 69.031 mph (110.5kph), on February 13, 1955

Wendell Scott's only win was there in 1963.

Lakewood Speedway

Location: Atlanta, Georgia
Race length: 100–150 miles (160–240km) on a 1-mile (1.6km) dirt oval
Number of races run: 11 Grand National, between November 11, 1951, and June 14, 1959
Speed record (average for an entire race): 79.016 mph (126.4kph,) on April 13, 1958

1952

Palm Beach Speedway (Southland Speedway)

Location: West Palm Beach, Florida
Race length: 100 miles (160km) on a 1/2-mile (0.8km) dirt oval, paved in 1955
Number of races run: 7 Grand National, between January 20, 1952, and March 4, 1956
Speed record (average for an entire race): 68.990 mph (110.4kph), on March 4, 1956

Hayloft Speedway (Augusta Speedway)

Location: Augusta, Georgia
Race length: 100 miles (160km) on a 1/2-mile (0.8km) dirt oval
Number of races run: 1 Grand National, on June 1, 1952
Speed record (average for an entire race): No average speed was recorded

Stamford Park

Location: Niagara Falls, Ontario, Canada
Race length: 100 miles (160km) on a 1/2-mile (0.8km) dirt oval
Number of races run: 1 Grand National, on July 1, 1952
Speed record (average for an entire race): 45.610 mph (73kph)

This was the first NASCAR race held outside of the United States. Only one event was held there, but the series raced again in Toronto, Canada, in 1958. Buddy Shuman was one of the few survivors at the end of the race. Only 3 of the 17 starters were still at full speed at 200 laps, and Shuman took the win.

Wine Creek Race Track (Shangri-La Speedway)

LOCATION: Oswego, New York
RACE LENGTH: 100 miles (160km) on a 1/2-mile (0.8km) dirt oval
NUMBER OF RACES RUN: 1 Grand National, on July 4, 1952
SPEED RECORD (AVERAGE FOR AN ENTIRE RACE): 56.603 mph (90.6kph)

The surface of the track was so rough that some racers ran out of tires and had to park their cars. Tim Flock helped Hudson on its way to domination of the season with the win.

Monroe Speedway

LOCATION: Monroe, Michigan
RACE LENGTH: 100 miles (160km) on a 1/2-mile (0.8km) dirt oval
NUMBER OF RACES RUN: 1 Grand National, on July 6, 1952
SPEED RECORD (AVERAGE FOR AN ENTIRE RACE): 44.499 mph (712kph)

Playland Park Speedway

LOCATION: South Bend, Indiana
RACE LENGTH: 100 miles (160km) on a 1/2-mile (0.8km) dirt oval
NUMBER OF RACES RUN: 1 Grand National, on July 20, 1951
SPEED RECORD (AVERAGE FOR AN ENTIRE RACE): 41.889 mph (67kph)

Only 8 cars were left running at the end of this yellow flag–intensive race. Tim Flock took the win, his seventh of that season.

1953

Harnett Speedway

LOCATION: Spring Lake, North Carolina
RACE LENGTH: 100 miles (160km) on a 1/2-mile (0.8km) dirt oval
NUMBER OF RACES RUN: 1 Grand National, on March 8, 1953
SPEED RECORD (AVERAGE FOR AN ENTIRE RACE): 48.826 mph (78.1kph)

Herb Thomas led the entire 200 laps from the pole on his way to the 1953 championship.

Richmond International Raceway (Fairgrounds Speedway, Strawberry Hill Speedway, Atlantic Rural Exposition Fairgrounds)

(See pages 43–6)

Hickory Speedway

LOCATION: Hickory, North Carolina
RACE LENGTH: 100–138 miles (160–220.8km) on a 1/2-mile (0.8km) (re-measured to 0.4 miles [0.6km] in 1956) dirt oval (paved in 1967)
NUMBER OF RACES RUN: 35 Grand National, between May 16, 1953, and August 28, 1971
SPEED RECORD (AVERAGE FOR AN ENTIRE RACE): 82.827 mph (132.5kph,) on June, 1954

Powell Motor Speedway

LOCATION: Columbus, Ohio
RACE LENGTH: 100 miles (160km) on a 1/2-mile (0.8km) dirt oval
NUMBER OF RACES RUN: 1 Grand National, on May 24, 1953
SPEED RECORD (AVERAGE FOR AN ENTIRE RACE): 56.127 mph (89.8kph)

Raleigh Speedway (Dixie Speedway)

LOCATION: Raleigh, North Carolina
RACE LENGTH: 100–300 miles (160–480km) on a 1-mile (1.6km) paved oval
NUMBER OF RACES RUN: 7 Grand National, between May 30, 1953, and July 4, 1958
SPEED RECORD (AVERAGE FOR AN ENTIRE RACE): 79.822 mph (127.7kph), on July 4, 1956

Louisiana Speedway

LOCATION: Shreveport, Louisiana
RACE LENGTH: 100 miles (160km) on a 1/2-mile (0.8km) dirt oval
NUMBER OF RACES RUN: 1 Grand National, on June 7, 1953
SPEED RECORD (AVERAGE FOR AN ENTIRE RACE): 53.199 mph (85.1kph)

Five Flags Speedway

LOCATION: Pensacola, Florida
RACE LENGTH: 100 miles (160km) on a 1/2-mile (0.8km) dirt oval

NUMBER OF RACES RUN: 1 Grand National, on June 14, 1953
SPEED RECORD (AVERAGE FOR AN ENTIRE RACE): 63.316 mph (101.3kph)

The sole race at the track was red flagged after 140 laps due to rain.

High Point Motor Speedway

LOCATION: High Point, North Carolina
RACE LENGTH: 100 miles (160km) on a 1/2-mile (0.8km) dirt oval
NUMBER OF RACES RUN: 2 Grand National, on June 26, 1953, and November 7, 1954
SPEED RECORD (AVERAGE FOR AN ENTIRE RACE): 62.882 mph (110.6kph), on November 7, 1954

Piedmont Interstate Fairgrounds

LOCATION: Spartansburg, South Carolina
RACE LENGTH: 100 miles (160km) on a 1/2-mile (0.8km) dirt oval
NUMBER OF RACES RUN: 22 Grand National, between July 4, 1953, and June 4, 1966
SPEED RECORD (AVERAGE FOR AN ENTIRE RACE): 66.367 mph (106.2kph), on February 27, 1965

Rapid Valley Speedway

LOCATION: Rapid City, South Dakota
RACE LENGTH: 100 miles (160km) on a 1/2-mile (0.8km) dirt oval
NUMBER OF RACES RUN: 1 Grand National, on July 22, 1953
SPEED RECORD (AVERAGE FOR AN ENTIRE RACE): 57.270 mph (91.6kph)

Herb Thomas won the only race held in the Dakotas. The track is still open.

Lincoln City Fairgrounds (North Platte Speedway)

LOCATION: North Platte, Nebraska
RACE LENGTH: 100 miles (160km) on a 1/2-mile (0.8km) dirt oval
NUMBER OF RACES RUN: 1 Grand National, on July 26, 1953
SPEED RECORD (AVERAGE FOR AN ENTIRE RACE): 54.380 mph (87kph)

Davenport Speedway

LOCATION: Davenport, Iowa
RACE LENGTH: 100 miles (160km) on a 1/2-mile (0.8km) dirt oval

NUMBER OF RACES RUN: 1 Grand National, on August 2, 1953
SPEED RECORD (AVERAGE FOR AN ENTIRE RACE): 62.500 mph (100kph)

NASCAR continued its tour through the mid-west in 1953 with its sole visit to Iowa. The track was originally opened in the 1920s and is still active today.

Princess Anne Speedway

LOCATION: Norfolk, Virginia
RACE LENGTH: 100 miles (160km) on a 1/2-mile (0.8km) dirt oval
NUMBER OF RACES RUN: 1 Grand National, on August 23, 1953
SPEED RECORD (AVERAGE FOR AN ENTIRE RACE): 51.040 mph (81.7kph)

Herb Thomas took the win at the fancifully named speedway. The track closed in the mid-1950s and is now a shopping center.

Bloomsburg Fairgrounds

LOCATION: Bloomsburg, Pennsylvania
RACE LENGTH: 100 miles (160km) on a 1/2-mile (0.8km) dirt oval
NUMBER OF RACES RUN: 1 Grand National, on October 3, 1953
SPEED RECORD (AVERAGE FOR AN ENTIRE RACE): No average speed was recorded

1954

Oglethorpe Speedway

LOCATION: Savannah, Georgia
RACE LENGTH: 100 miles (160km) on a 1/2-mile (0.8km) dirt oval
NUMBER OF RACES RUN: 2 Grand National, on March 28, 1954, and March 6, 1955
SPEED RECORD (AVERAGE FOR AN ENTIRE RACE): 60.150 mph (96.2kph), on March 8, 1955

Sharon Speedway

LOCATION: Hartford, Ohio
RACE LENGTH: 100 miles (160km) on a 1/2-mile (0.8km) dirt oval
NUMBER OF RACES RUN: 1 Grand National, on May 23, 1954
SPEED RECORD (AVERAGE FOR AN ENTIRE RACE): There is no speed record for the race due to frequent interruptions for rain (including a red flag after 160 of the 200 scheduled laps).

Linden Airport

LOCATION: Linden, New Jersey
RACE LENGTH: 100 miles (160km) on a 2-mile (3.2km) paved road course
NUMBER OF RACES RUN: 1 Grand National, on June 13, 1954
SPEED RECORD (AVERAGE FOR AN ENTIRE RACE): 77.569 mph (124.1kph)

Williams Grove Speedway

LOCATION: Mechanicsburg, Pennsylvania
RACE LENGTH: 100 miles (160km) on a 1/2-mile (0.8km) dirt oval
NUMBER OF RACES RUN: 1 Grand National, on June 27, 1954
SPEED RECORD (AVERAGE FOR AN ENTIRE RACE): 51.085 mph (81.7kph)

The small track hosted only 1 NASCAR race, but that event attracted over 21,000 spectators. It also featured a field of 41 cars—huge for a 1/2-mile (0.8km) track. Unfortunately, NASCAR only paid prize money for the top 20 finishers, so most of the field went unpaid. Herb Thomas was the predictable winner.

Santa Fe Speedway

LOCATION: Willow Springs, Illinois
RACE LENGTH: 100 miles (160km) on a 1/2-mile (0.8km) dirt oval
NUMBER OF RACES RUN: 1 Grand National, on July 10, 1954
SPEED RECORD (AVERAGE FOR AN ENTIRE RACE): 72.216 mph (115.5kph)

NASCAR's first race in the Chicago area took place here.

Charlotte Fairgrounds

LOCATION: Charlotte, North Carolina
RACE LENGTH: 100 miles (160km) on a 1/2-mile (0.8km) dirt oval
NUMBER OF RACES RUN: 17 Grand National, on August 13, 1954, and November 6, 1960
SPEED RECORD (AVERAGE FOR AN ENTIRE RACE): 59.435 mph (95.1kph), on November 6, 1960

The perennial Herschel McGriff (who has raced in NASCAR from 1950 well into the 1990s) earned 2 of his 4 career wins at this venue in 1954, helping him to a sixth place points finish—by far his best showing.

Bay Meadows Speedway

LOCATION: San Mateo, California
RACE LENGTH: 250 miles (400km) on a 1-mile (1.6km) dirt oval
NUMBER OF RACES RUN: 3 Grand National, between August 22, 1954, and August 19, 1956
SPEED RECORD (AVERAGE FOR AN ENTIRE RACE): 68.571 mph (109.7kph), on August 22, 1954

Corbin Speedway

LOCATION: Corbin, Kentucky
RACE LENGTH: 100 miles (160km) on a 1/2-mile (0.8km) dirt oval
NUMBER OF RACES RUN: 1 Grand National, on August 29, 1954
SPEED RECORD (AVERAGE FOR AN ENTIRE RACE): 63.080 mph (100.9kph)

Although it's the home of horse racing, only one Grand National race was ever held in the state of Kentucky!

Memphis-Arkansas Speedway

LOCATION: LeHi, Arkansas
RACE LENGTH: 250 miles (400km) (remeasured to 200 miles [320km] in 1957) on a 1.5-mile (2.4km) dirt oval
NUMBER OF RACES RUN: 5 Grand National, between October 10, 1954, and July 14, 1957
SPEED RECORD (AVERAGE FOR AN ENTIRE RACE): 89.892 mph (143.8kph), in August 1955

1955

Montgomery Motor Speedway (Montgomery International Raceway)

LOCATION: Montgomery, Alabama
RACE LENGTH: 100 miles (160km) on a 1/2-mile (0.8km) dirt oval
NUMBER OF RACES RUN: 6 Grand National, between April 17, 1955, and December 8, 1968
SPEED RECORD (AVERAGE FOR AN ENTIRE RACE): 73.200 mph (117.1kph), on December 8, 1968

The track is still in operation.

Tucson Rodeo Grounds

LOCATION: Tucson, Arizona
RACE LENGTH: 100 miles (160km) on a 1/2-mile 0(.8km) dirt oval
NUMBER OF RACES RUN: 1 Grand National, on May 15, 1955

SPEED RECORD (AVERAGE FOR AN ENTIRE RACE): 51.429 mph (82.3kph)

North Carolina State Fairgrounds (Raleigh Speedway)

LOCATION: Raleigh, North Carolina
RACE LENGTH: 100 miles (160km) on a 1/2-mile (0.8km) dirt oval
NUMBER OF RACES RUN: 3 Grand National, on May 28, 1955, June 26, 1969, and September 30, 1970
SPEED RECORD (AVERAGE FOR AN ENTIRE RACE): 68.376 mph (109.4kph), on September 30, 1970

Winston-Salem Fairgrounds

LOCATION: Winston-Salem, North Carolina
RACE LENGTH: 100 miles (160km) on a 1/2-mile (0.8km) dirt oval
NUMBER OF RACES RUN: 2 Grand National, on May 29, 1955, and August 7, 1955
SPEED RECORD (AVERAGE FOR AN ENTIRE RACE): 50.583 mph (80.9kph), on May 29, 1955

Lincoln Speedway

LOCATION: New Oxford, Pennsylvania
RACE LENGTH: 100 miles (160km) on a 1/2-mile (0.8km) dirt oval
NUMBER OF RACES RUN: 7 Grand National, between June 10, 1955, and September 14, 1965
SPEED RECORD (AVERAGE FOR AN ENTIRE RACE): 82.607 mph (132.2kph), on September 14, 1965

Fonda Speedway

LOCATION: Fonda, New York
RACE LENGTH: 100 miles (160km) on a 1/2-mile (0.8km) dirt oval
NUMBER OF RACES RUN: 4 Grand National, between June 18, 1955, and July 11, 1968
SPEED RECORD (AVERAGE FOR AN ENTIRE RACE): 65.826 mph (105.3kph), on July 13, 1967

The Grand National circuit didn't get around to the Fonda track until the third time it had closed and re-opened. One race was run in 1955 and the next didn't occur until 1967. The track is still in operation.

Plattsburg Speedway

LOCATION: Plattsburg, New York
RACE LENGTH: 100 miles (160km) on a 1/2-mile (0.8km) dirt oval
NUMBER OF RACES RUN: 1 Grand National, on June 19, 1955
SPEED RECORD (AVERAGE FOR AN ENTIRE RACE): 59.074 mph (94.5kph)

New York State Fairgrounds

LOCATION: Syracuse, New York
RACE LENGTH: 100 miles (160km) on a one-mile (1.6km) dirt oval
NUMBER OF RACES RUN: 3 Grand National, between July 30, 1955, and September 5, 1957
SPEED RECORD (AVERAGE FOR AN ENTIRE RACE): 86.179 mph (137.9kph), on May 30, 1956

The New York Fairgrounds was an early site for auto racing. The track first opened in 1880, and was used for auto racing as early as 1909. Tim Flock won the first race—leading the entire event from the pole.

Las Vegas Park Speedway

LOCATION: Las Vegas, Nevada
RACE LENGTH: 200 miles (320km) on a one-mile (1.6km) dirt oval
NUMBER OF RACES RUN: 1 Grand National, on October 16, 1955
SPEED RECORD (AVERAGE FOR AN ENTIRE RACE): 44.449 mph (71.1kph)

This was the site of the only Nevada race, until the circuit's recent return to Las Vegas' new facility. The track was located on the current site of the Hilton Hotel. A multi-car wreck slowed the race and delayed it so long that it was red-flagged at just over half-way for darkness.

1956

Willow Springs Speedway (Kern County Speedway)

LOCATION: Lancaster, California
RACE LENGTH: 200 miles (320km) on a 2.5 mile (4km) oiled dirt road course
NUMBER OF RACES RUN: 2 Grand National, on November 20, 1955, and November 11, 1956
SPEED RECORD (AVERAGE FOR AN ENTIRE RACE): 78.648 mph (125.8kph), on November 11, 1956

The timing on the Willow Springs races was unusual. The 1955 race was actually the third race in the 1956 season. The 1956 race was the first race of the 1957 season. Drivers had to choose between that race and one at Hickory Speedway held on the same date, which was at the end of the 1956 season (the schedules for the two seasons overlapped by a couple of weeks between 1956 and 1957).

Concord Speedway

LOCATION: Concord, North Carolina
RACE LENGTH: 100 miles (160km) on a 1/2-mile (0.8km) dirt oval
NUMBER OF RACES RUN: 12 Grand National, between May 6, 1956, and June 11, 1964
SPEED RECORD (AVERAGE FOR AN ENTIRE RACE): 66.352 mph (106.2kph,) on June 11, 1964

Portland Speedway

LOCATION: Portland, Oregon
RACE LENGTH: Various lengths on a 1/2-mile (0.8km) paved oval
NUMBER OF RACES RUN: 7 Grand National, between May 27, 1956, and July 14, 1957
SPEED RECORD (AVERAGE FOR AN ENTIRE RACE): 64.574 mph (103.3kph), on April 28, 1957

This was an unusual venue for several reasons. Although there were 7 races run at the track, they occurred in only 2 seasons. The 1956 schedule featured 4 visits to Portland, and the 1957 schedule, 3. Further, every event had a different length—from 50 miles (80km) (one of the shortest races ever run by NASCAR) to 125 miles (200km). The facility was also used for more than racing—the infield served as a drive-in movie lot (the screen was along the backstretch).

Redwood Speedway (Eureka Speedway)

LOCATION: Eureka, California
RACE LENGTH: 100 miles (160km) on a 0.625-mile (1km) dirt oval
NUMBER OF RACES RUN: 2 Grand National, on May 30, 1956, and May 30, 1957
SPEED RECORD (AVERAGE FOR AN ENTIRE RACE): 55.957 mph (89.5kph), on May 30, 1957

Neither of the NASCAR races went to completion. The first was halted due to poor track conditions—holes in the surface and thick dust. The second was red-flagged when a car crashed through the fence, which couldn't be repaired.

Merced Fairgrounds Speedway

LOCATION: Merced, California
RACE LENGTH: 100 miles (160km) on a 1/2-mile 0(.8km) dirt oval
NUMBER OF RACES RUN: 1 Grand National, on June 3, 1956
SPEED RECORD (AVERAGE FOR AN ENTIRE RACE): 47.325 mph (75.7kph)

The original 2-mile (3.2km) oval was replaced by a 1/2-mile (0.8km) circuit for NASCAR, then later by a 1/4-mile (0.4km) track.

Sacramento Fairgrounds (California State Fairgrounds)

LOCATION: Sacramento, California
RACE LENGTH: 100 miles (160km) on a one-mile (1.6km) dirt oval
NUMBER OF RACES RUN: 6 Grand National, between July 8, 1956, and September 10, 1961
SPEED RECORD (AVERAGE FOR AN ENTIRE RACE): 74.074 mph (118.5kph), on July 8, 1956

Lloyd Dane earned the first of his 4 NASCAR wins in the 1956 race here. The track was replaced by a shopping center in 1970.

Soldier Field

LOCATION: Chicago, Illinois
RACE LENGTH: 100 miles (160km) on a 1/2-mile (0.8km) paved oval
NUMBER OF RACES RUN: 1 Grand National, on July 21, 1956
SPEED RECORD (AVERAGE FOR AN ENTIRE RACE): 61.037 mph (97.7kph)

The track was built around the inside of the famous football stadium. The track was removed following protests over funding in 1970.

Cleveland County Fairgrounds (Shelby Motor Speedway)

LOCATION: Shelby, North Carolina
RACE LENGTH: 100 miles (160km) on a 1/2-mile (0.8km) dirt oval

NUMBER OF RACES RUN: 6 Grand National, between July 27, 1956, and August 5, 1965
SPEED RECORD (AVERAGE FOR AN ENTIRE RACE): 64.748 mph (103.6kph), on August 5, 1965

The track was the site of much controversy in 1956. The second race there (October 23rd) was added to the schedule just 10 days beforehand at the express desire of car owner Carl Kiekhafer, who leased the track for the event. The reason for this move was to give one of his drivers (Buck Baker) another chance to catch up to points leader Herb Thomas. Thomas had quit Kiekhafer's team earlier that year and Mr. K. didn't want to see him go on to the championship. He got that and more as Kiekhafer's other driver, Speedy Thompson, wrecked Thomas partway through the race. As a result of the wreck, Thomas was seriously injured and his racing career effectively ended. Baker went on to win the championship.

Oklahoma State Fairgrounds

LOCATION: Oklahoma City, Oklahoma
RACE LENGTH: 100 miles (160km) on a 1/2-mile (0.8km) dirt oval
NUMBER OF RACES RUN: 1 Grand National, on August 3, 1956
SPEED RECORD (AVERAGE FOR AN ENTIRE RACE): 60.100 mph (96.2kph)

Only 12 cars started and 7 finished the only event in Oklahoma.

Road America

(See pages 126–27)

Old Bridge Stadium

LOCATION: Old Bridge, New Jersey
RACE LENGTH: 100 miles (160km) on a 1/2-mile (0.8km) paved oval
NUMBER OF RACES RUN: 6 Grand National, between August 17, 1956, and July 9, 1965
SPEED RECORD (AVERAGE FOR AN ENTIRE RACE): 73.891 mph (118.21kph), on July 10, 1964

Norfolk Speedway

LOCATION: Norfolk, Virginia
RACE LENGTH: 100 miles (160km) on a 0.4-mile (0.64) dirt oval

NUMBER OF RACES RUN: 2 Grand National, on August 22, 1956, and July 24, 1957
SPEED RECORD (AVERAGE FOR AN ENTIRE RACE): 56.408 mph (90.3kph), on August 22, 1956

Coastal Speedway

LOCATION: Myrtle Beach, South Carolina
RACE LENGTH: 100 miles (160km) on a 1/2-mile (0.8km) dirt oval
NUMBER OF RACES RUN: 2 Grand National, on August 25, 1956, and August 26, 1957
SPEED RECORD (AVERAGE FOR AN ENTIRE RACE): 50.782 mph (81.3kph), on August 26, 1957

Points leader Herb Thomas suffered a setback in this race in 1956. Running near the front of the field halfway through the race, he stopped during a caution flag for tires and gas. A rule change in place for the race prohibited teams from getting gas during yellow flag stops. NASCAR stopped scoring Thomas at that point, and he fell to thirteenth place.

Chisolm Speedway

LOCATION: Montgomery, Alabama
RACE LENGTH: 100 miles (160km) on a 1/2-mile (0.8km) dirt oval
NUMBER OF RACES RUN: 1 Grand National, on September 9, 1956
SPEED RECORD (AVERAGE FOR AN ENTIRE RACE): 60.893 mph (97.4kph)

Only 2,000 spectators showed up for the event, won by Buck Baker. The track closed after the event.

Newport Fairgrounds

LOCATION: Newport, Tennessee
RACE LENGTH: 100 miles (160km) on a 1/2-mile (0.8km) dirt oval
NUMBER OF RACES RUN: 2 Grand National, on October 7, 1956, and June 15, 1957
SPEED RECORD (AVERAGE FOR AN ENTIRE RACE): 61.475 mph (98.4kph), on October 7, 1956

Fireball Roberts won both races at Newport; the second despite having just lost factory backing.

1957

Titusville-Cocoa Speedway

LOCATION: Titusville, Florida
RACE LENGTH: 89.6 miles (143.4km) on a 1.6-mile (2.6km) paved road course
NUMBER OF RACES RUN: 1 Grand National, on December 30, 1956
SPEED RECORD (AVERAGE FOR AN ENTIRE RACE): 69.106 mph (110.6kph)

The course used runways at the Titusville-Cocoa airport. A decent crowd of 16,000 attended although there were only 15 cars in the field. Peter DePaolo's Ford factory team swept the top 4 spots.

Central Carolina Fairgrounds (Greensboro Fairgrounds)

LOCATION: Greensboro, North Carolina
RACE LENGTH: 83.25 miles (133.2km) on a 1/3-mile (0.53km) dirt oval
NUMBER OF RACES RUN: 3 Grand National, between April 28, 1957, and May 11, 1958
SPEED RECORD (AVERAGE FOR AN ENTIRE RACE): 49.905 mph (79.8kph), on April 28, 1957

The 1958 race was only 50 miles.

Lancaster Speedway

LOCATION: Lancaster, South Carolina
RACE LENGTH: 100 miles (160km) on a 1/2-mile (0.8km) dirt oval
NUMBER OF RACES RUN: 2 Grand National, on June 1, 1957, and July 30, 1957
SPEED RECORD (AVERAGE FOR AN ENTIRE RACE): 66.543 mph (10.5kph), on July 30, 1957

The second race, won by Speedy Thompson, was never recorded in official NASCAR records. Thompson is thus credited with one fewer win (19 instead of 20) than he deserves.

Ascot Stadium (Los Angeles Speedway)

LOCATION: Los Angeles, California
RACE LENGTH: Various lengths on a 0.4-mile (0.64km) dirt oval
NUMBER OF RACES RUN: 3 Grand National, between June 8, 1957, and May 27, 1961

SPEED RECORD (AVERAGE FOR AN ENTIRE RACE): 68.833 mph (110.1kph), on May 30, 1959

The 1959 race was a special event—200 miles (320km), and featuring Grand National, Convertible, and Short Track division cars competing together. In fact, Harlan Richardson was the lone Grand National competitor. Most entries, including winner Parnelli Jones, were driving short track cars.

Capitol Speedway

LOCATION: Sacramento, California
RACE LENGTH: 100 miles (160km) on a 1/2-mile (0.8km) dirt oval
NUMBER OF RACES RUN: 1 Grand National, on June 22, 1957
SPEED RECORD (AVERAGE FOR AN ENTIRE RACE): 59.890 mph (95.8kph)

A scoring error ended the race after 199 laps.

Jacksonville Speedway

LOCATION: Jacksonville, North Carolina
RACE LENGTH: 100 miles (160km) on a 1/2-mile (0.8km) dirt oval
NUMBER OF RACES RUN: 2 Grand National, on June 30, 1957, and November 8, 1964
SPEED RECORD (AVERAGE FOR AN ENTIRE RACE): 57.535 mph (92.1kph), on November 8, 1964

The Jacksonville race was the season finale for NASCAR's longest year—62 races in 1964. No one raced the whole schedule—Petty and Pearson each entered 61 of the events.

Kitsap County Airport

LOCATION: Bremerton, Washington
RACE LENGTH: 72 miles (115.2km) on a 0.9-mile (1.4km) paved road course
NUMBER OF RACES RUN: 1 Grand National, on August 4, 1957
SPEED RECORD (AVERAGE FOR AN ENTIRE RACE): 58.959 mph (94.3kph)

The Washington site featured a 1.25-mile (1.8km) dirt oval as well as 3 road courses using different configurations of airport runways. The 0.9-mile (1.4km) course, NASCAR's shortest road course, had tight turns requiring heavy braking.

Watkins Glen International

(See pages 130–34)

Santa Clara Fairgrounds (San Jose Fairgrounds)

LOCATION: San Jose, California
RACE LENGTH: 100 miles (160km) on a 1/2-mile (0.8km) dirt oval
NUMBER OF RACES RUN: 1 Grand National, on September 15, 1957
SPEED RECORD (AVERAGE FOR AN ENTIRE RACE): No average speed was recorded

A major pileup half-way through the race depleted the 22-car field so much that officials red-flagged the race at 116 laps. Only 4 cars remained on track!

Newberry Speedway

LOCATION: Newberry, South Carolina
RACE LENGTH: 100 miles (160km) on a 1/2-mile (0.8km) dirt oval
NUMBER OF RACES RUN: 1 Grand National, on October 12, 1957
SPEED RECORD (AVERAGE FOR AN ENTIRE RACE): 50.398 mph (80.6kph)

The race set the all-time low for attendance at a NASCAR event. Only 900 spectators showed up for the race despite a solid field of 23 entries.

1958

Champion Speedway

LOCATION: Fayetteville, North Carolina
RACE LENGTH: 50 miles (80km) on a 1/3-mile (0.53km) paved oval
NUMBER OF RACES RUN: 4 Grand National, between November 3, 1957, and November 9, 1958
SPEED RECORD (AVERAGE FOR AN ENTIRE RACE): 59.170 mph (94.7kph), on November 3, 1957

Champion Speedway was built by Harold Brasington, the owner of Darlington Raceway. This track was less successful, and only operated through 1959. Three of its 4 NASCAR dates were in the same season (1958). In fact, all 4 races occurred within a 1-year period.

Old Dominion Speedway

LOCATION: Manassas, Virginia
RACE LENGTH: Various lengths on a 0.375-mile (0.6km) paved oval
NUMBER OF RACES RUN: 7 Grand National, between April 25, 1958, and July 7, 1966
SPEED RECORD (AVERAGE FOR AN ENTIRE RACE): 70.275 mph (112.4kph), on May 18, 1963

Starkey Speedway

LOCATION: Roanoke, Virginia
RACE LENGTH: 37.5 (60km) and 50 miles (80km) on a 1/4-mile (0.4km) paved oval
NUMBER OF RACES RUN: 4 Grand National, between May 15, 1958, and August 23, 1964
SPEED RECORD (AVERAGE FOR AN ENTIRE RACE): 51.165 mph (81.9kph), on August 15, 1962

It was hardly worth the bother. The brief 1958 race resulted in almost the same finishing order as the qualifying order! The race was increased to 50 miles in 1962.

Bowman-Gray Stadium

(See pages 46–8)

Trenton Speedway

LOCATION: Trenton, New Jersey
RACE LENGTH: Various lengths on a 1-mile (1.6km) and 1.5-mile (2.4km) paved oval
NUMBER OF RACES RUN: 8 Grand National and Winston Cup, between May 30, 1958, and July 16, 1972
SPEED RECORD (AVERAGE FOR AN ENTIRE RACE): 121.008 mph (193.6kph), on July 13, 1969

Riverside International Raceway

(See page128–29)

New Bradford Speedway

LOCATION: Bradford, Pennsylvania
RACE LENGTH: 50 miles (80km) on a 1/3-mile (0.53km) dirt oval
NUMBER OF RACES RUN: 1 Grand National, on June 12, 1958
SPEED RECORD (AVERAGE FOR AN ENTIRE RACE): 59.840 mph (95.7kph)

The race was notable in that 3 of the contestants were disqualified in post-race inspections as NASCAR cracked down on cheating.

Reading Fairgrounds

LOCATION: Reading, Pennsylvania
RACE LENGTH: 100 miles (160km) on a 1/2-mile (0.8km) dirt oval
NUMBER OF RACES RUN: 2 Grand National, on June 15, 1958, and April 26, 1959
SPEED RECORD (AVERAGE FOR AN ENTIRE RACE): 53.763 mph (86kph), on June 15, 1958

This was a well-known track in the mid-Atlantic region that had run auto races since the 1920s. Both NASCAR events were won by Junior Johnson.

McCormick Field

LOCATION: Asheville, North Carolina
RACE LENGTH: 37.5 miles (60kph) on a 1/4-mile (0.4km) paved oval
NUMBER OF RACES RUN: 1 Grand National, on July 12, 1958
SPEED RECORD (AVERAGE FOR AN ENTIRE RACE): 46.440 mph (74.3kph)

The small track was laid out around a baseball field (home of the Asheville Tourists). In one of the most unusual accidents in racing, Lee Petty's No. 42 took a detour through the team dugout that lined one section of the track, after a bump from competitor Cotten Owens.

State Line Speedway

LOCATION: Busti, New York
RACE LENGTH: 50 miles (80km) on a 1/3-mile (0.53km) dirt oval
NUMBER OF RACES RUN: 1 Grand National, on July 16, 1958
SPEED RECORD (AVERAGE FOR AN ENTIRE RACE): 47.110 mph (75.4kph)

Canadian National Exposition Speedway

LOCATION: Toronto, Canada
RACE LENGTH: 33.3 miles (53.3km) on a 1/3-mile (0.53km) paved oval
NUMBER OF RACES RUN: 1 Grand National, on July 18, 1958
SPEED RECORD (AVERAGE FOR AN ENTIRE RACE): 43.184 mph (69.1kph)

This was one of the 2 races held in Canada and is notable as Richard Petty's first Grand National race. His car, no? No, not No. 43—it was the No. 142 Olds. Petty was knocked into the wall, taking him out of the race after only 55 laps. The culprit was his father, Lee.

Buffalo Civic Stadium

LOCATION: Buffalo, New York
RACE LENGTH: 25 miles (40km) on a 1/4-mile (0.4km) paved oval
NUMBER OF RACES RUN: 1 Grand National, on July 19, 1958
SPEED RECORD (AVERAGE FOR AN ENTIRE RACE): 46.972 mph (75.2kph)

Well, this is it—the shortest race ever run by the Grand National or Winston Cup division. The race took only half and hour to run. Jim Reed, master of short sprints, was the winner.

Wall Stadium

LOCATION: Bellmar, New Jersey
RACE LENGTH: 100 miles (160km) on a 1/3-mile (0.53km) paved oval
NUMBER OF RACES RUN: 1 Grand National, on July 26, 1958
SPEED RECORD (AVERAGE FOR AN ENTIRE RACE): 65.395 mph (104.6kph)

Rookie, Richard Petty, picked up his first top 10 finish in the No. 42A Olds.

Bridgehampton Raceway

LOCATION: Bridgehampton, New York
RACE LENGTH: 100 miles (160km) on a 2.85-mile (4.6km) paved road course
NUMBER OF RACES RUN: 4 Grand National, between August 2, 1958, and July 10, 1966
SPEED RECORD (AVERAGE FOR AN ENTIRE RACE): 87.707 mph (140.3kph), on July 12, 1964

Richard Petty and David Pearson earned their first road course wins at Bridgehampton in 1963 and 1966 (respectively).

Nashville Speedway

(See pages 49–51)

Rambi Race Track (Myrtle Beach Speedway)

LOCATION: Myrtle Beach, South Carolina
RACE LENGTH: 100 miles (160km) on a 1/2-mile (0.8km) dirt oval
NUMBER OF RACES RUN: 9 Grand National, between August 23, 1958, and June 24, 1965
SPEED RECORD (AVERAGE FOR AN ENTIRE RACE): 64.171 mph (102.7kph), on July 21, 1962

No, not Sylvester Stallone's home track. "Rambi" was an acronym for Racing Association of Myrtle Beach, Incorporated. The track is notable as the only one on which Lee, Richard and Kyle Petty have all run (though Kyle was in a short-track event after the Winston Cup had dropped the track from its schedule).

Fairgrounds Speedway (Birmingham Super Speedway)

LOCATION: Birmingham, Alabama
RACE LENGTH: 100 miles (160km) on a 1/2-mile (0.8km) dirt oval
NUMBER OF RACES RUN: 8 Grand National, between September 7, 1958, and June 8, 1968
SPEED RECORD (AVERAGE FOR AN ENTIRE RACE): 89.153 mph (142.6kph), on June 8, 1968

"Home" track for Alabama Gang leader Bobby Allison, who was credited with the win in 1967 after a scoring error was corrected. The Allisons were actually from Florida, but raced and won so often in Alabama that they acquired that moniker.

Gastonia Fairgrounds

LOCATION: Gastonia, North Carolina
RACE LENGTH: 66.7 miles (106.7km) on a 1/3-mile (0.53km) dirt oval
NUMBER OF RACES RUN: 1 Grand National, on September 12, 1958
SPEED RECORD (AVERAGE FOR AN ENTIRE RACE): 47.856 mph (76.6kph)

Salisbury Super Speedway

LOCATION: Salisbury, North Carolina
RACE LENGTH: 100 miles (160km) on a 0.625-mile (1km) dirt oval
NUMBER OF RACES RUN: 1 Grand National, on October 5, 1958
SPEED RECORD (AVERAGE FOR AN ENTIRE RACE): 58.271 mph (93.3kph)

They may have called it a super-speedway, but it ranks with the dirt bullrings.

1959

Daytona International Speedway

(See pages 70–80)

1960

Lowe's Motor Speedway (Charlotte Motor Speedway)

(See page 90–5)

Montgomery Air Base

LOCATION: Montgomery, New York
RACE LENGTH: 200 miles (320km) on a 2-mile (3.2km) paved course
NUMBER OF RACES RUN: 1 Grand National, on July 17, 1960
SPEED RECORD (AVERAGE FOR AN ENTIRE RACE): 88.626 mph (141.8kph)

The Montgomery course was laid out on the runways of an airforce base. The track was originally a road course, set in a triangular shape. Most drivers cut across the dirt inside the course to "round out" the tight turns. In fact the only caution was to repair the hay bale wall that had been clipped by that action.

Atlanta Motor Speedway

(See pages 80–90)

Dixie Speedway

LOCATION: Birmingham, Alabama
RACE LENGTH: 50 miles (80km) on a 1/4-mile (0.4km) paved oval
NUMBER OF RACES RUN: 1 Grand National, on August 3, 1960
SPEED RECORD (AVERAGE FOR AN ENTIRE RACE): 54.463 mph (87.1kph)

South Boston Speedway

LOCATION: South Boston, Virginia
RACE LENGTH: Various lengths on a 1/4-mile (0.4km), then 0.375-mile (0.6km) dirt oval
NUMBER OF RACES RUN: 10 Grand National, between August 20, 1960, and May 9, 1971
SPEED RECORD (AVERAGE FOR AN ENTIRE RACE): 76.906 mph (127.8kph), on August 21, 1969

It's still in operation today—running NASCAR Busch Grand National races on a 0.4-mile (0.64km) circuit.

Gamecock Speedway (Rebel Speedway, Sunter Speedway)

LOCATION: Sunter, South Carolina
RACE LENGTH: 50 miles (80km) on a 1/4-mile (0.4km) dirt oval

NUMBER OF RACES RUN: 1 Grand National, on September 15, 1960
SPEED RECORD (AVERAGE FOR AN ENTIRE RACE): 41.208 mph (65.9kph)

Gamecock was where Cale Yarborough first got his start in racing, although he did not participate in the Grand National race there in the 1960s.

1961

Norwood Arena
LOCATION: Norwood, Massachusetts
RACE LENGTH: 125 miles (200km) on a 1/4-mile (0.4km) paved oval
NUMBER OF RACES RUN: 1 Grand National, on June 17, 1961
SPEED RECORD (AVERAGE FOR AN ENTIRE RACE): 53.827 mph (86.1kph)

Hartsville Speedway
LOCATION: Hartsville, South Carolina
RACE LENGTH: 50 miles (80km) on a 1/3-mile (0.53km) dirt oval
NUMBER OF RACES RUN: 1 Grand National, on June 23, 1961
SPEED RECORD (AVERAGE FOR AN ENTIRE RACE): 46.234 mph (74kph)

Bristol Motor Speedway (Bristol International Speedway)
(See pages 52–7)

Southside Speedway
LOCATION: Richmond, Virginia
RACE LENGTH: Various lengths on a 1/4-mile (0.4km) then 1/3-mile (0.53km) paved oval
NUMBER OF RACES RUN: 4 Grand National, between August 18, 1961, and May 19, 1963
SPEED RECORD (AVERAGE FOR AN ENTIRE RACE): 67.747 mph (108.4kph,) on May 4, 1962

The races varied between 37.5 (60km) and 100 miles (160km). In a "tortoise vs. hare" scenario, Jimmy Pardue won the May, 1962, event despite having to hard-wire his car into third gear just to start the race. His unspectacular but steady pace kept him advancing as competitors wore out or fell to the wayside with mechanical problems.

1962

Savannah Speedway
LOCATION: Savannah, Georgia
RACE LENGTH: 100 miles (160km) on a 1/2-mile (0.8km) dirt oval (paved in 1969)
NUMBER OF RACES RUN: 10 Grand National, between March 17, 1962, and March 15, 1970
SPEED RECORD (AVERAGE FOR AN ENTIRE RACE): 82.418 mph (130.3kph), on March 15, 1970

Augusta Speedway (Augusta International Speedway)
LOCATION: Augusta, Georgia
RACE LENGTH: 100 (160km) and 150 miles (240km) on a 1/2-mile (0.8km) dirt oval (paved in 1964)
NUMBER OF RACES RUN: 12 Grand National, between June 19, 1962, and October 19, 1969
SPEED RECORD (AVERAGE FOR AN ENTIRE RACE): 78.740 mph (126kph), on October 19, 1969

The spectators voiced loud complaints after the April, 1963, event, which was abbreviated from 200 laps to 112 laps due to heavy dust. The fans felt that seeing Cale Yarborough win his first pole and watching half a race was not enough excitement for their $4 entry fee. Darel Dieringer gave Mercury its final win in its final NASCAR race (the Mercury division had announced it would pull out of racing after that season) in November 1964. Elm Langley got a scare in practicing for the 1965 event. He got out of the groove and ended up riding on top of the guardrail through the third and fourth turn. The car had turned around so he got a good look at the nearly 100-foot drop outside the turns. Luckily his Ford slid back down onto the track instead of falling "out into space."

New Asheville Speedway
LOCATION: Asheville, North Carolina
RACE LENGTH: 100 miles (160km) on a 0.4-mile (0.64km) paved oval
NUMBER OF RACES RUN: 8 Grand National, between July 13, 1962, and May 21, 1971
SPEED RECORD (AVERAGE FOR AN ENTIRE RACE): 78.294 mph (125.8kph), on July 13, 1962

New Asheville seemed to bring out the roudy in even the most gentlemanly competitors. Normally restrained Ned Jarrett and Richard Petty got into it in 1963 after a hard-fought 100-miler. David Pearson's crew was in a scuffle with Stan Meserve's team after the lapped Meserve tangled with Pearson and took him out of the race. Petty won the 1971 race, but finished ahead of only 4 other cars. All but 5 cars boycotted the race just before the green flag when track owner George Ledford refused to pay appearance money to anyone but Richard Petty. "We've got who we need," said the promoter, who resigned shortly after that last NASCAR race at the track.

Boyd Speedway (Chattanooga Raceway Park)
LOCATION: Chattanooga, Tennessee
RACE LENGTH: 100 miles (160km) on a 1/3-mile (0.53km) paved oval
NUMBER OF RACES RUN: 2 Grand National, on August 3, 1962, and June 19, 1964
SPEED RECORD (AVERAGE FOR AN ENTIRE RACE): 71.145 mph (113.8kph), on July August 3, 1962

Huntsville Speedway
LOCATION: Huntsville, Alabama
RACE LENGTH: 50 miles (80kph) on a 1/4-mile (0.4km) paved oval
NUMBER OF RACES RUN: 1 Grand National, on August 8, 1962
SPEED RECORD (AVERAGE FOR AN ENTIRE RACE): 54.644 mph (87.4kph)

Valdosta 75 Speedway
LOCATION: Valdosta, Georgia
RACE LENGTH: 100 miles (160km) on a 1/2-mile (0.8km) dirt oval
NUMBER OF RACES RUN: 3 Grand National, between August 25, 1962, and June 27, 1965
SPEED RECORD (AVERAGE FOR AN ENTIRE RACE): 61.454 mph (98.3kph), on August 25, 1962

Cale Yarborough claimed his first Grand National win in the 100-miler in June 1965. He almost hadn't made the race—it was scheduled for the previous evening and Yarborough was fogged in at another airport. Sam McQuagg started his car instead. The race was stopped after only 25 laps due to rain. Officials decided to restart the whole race the next day and Yarborough took the seat.

Dog Track Speedway
LOCATION: Moyock, North Carolina
RACE LENGTH: 100 miles (160km) on a 1/4-mile 0(.4km) dirt oval (expanded to .333-mile [0.53km] in 1964)
NUMBER OF RACES RUN: 7 Grand National, between September 11, 1962, and May 29, 1966
SPEED RECORD (AVERAGE FOR AN ENTIRE RACE): 63.965 mph (102.3kph), on August 13, 1964

Gloria "Goldie" Parsons drove as a teammate to Buddy Baker in her only Grand National appearance, at Moyock in 1965. Despite spinning out twice, she finished fourteenth in the field.

1963

Golden Gate Speedway
LOCATION: Tampa, Florida
RACE LENGTH: 66.7 miles (106.7km) on a 1/3-mile (0.53km) dirt oval
NUMBER OF RACES RUN: 1 Grand National, November 11, 1962
SPEED RECORD (AVERAGE FOR AN ENTIRE RACE): 57.167 mph (91.5kph)

The 1962 race was actually at the start of the 1963 season.

Tar Heel Speedway
LOCATION: Randleman, North Carolina
RACE LENGTH: 50 miles (80km) on a 1/4-mile (0.4km) dirt oval
NUMBER OF RACES RUN: 5 Grand National, between November 22, 1962, and October 5, 1963
SPEED RECORD (AVERAGE FOR AN ENTIRE RACE): 48.605 mph (77.8kph), on May 5, 1963

The "Turkey Day 200" was held on Thanksgiving in 1962 (the third race of the 1963 season). Petty Enterprises won all 3 of the races held on this home-town track, though King Richard only got the last of those. Jim Paschal drove Petty Plymouths to wins in the first 2. An interesting note—the 1963 race records show Paschal driving the No. 43 car, while Richard was in the No. 41.

West Virginia International Speedway (Dick Clark's International Raceway Park)

LOCATION: Huntington, West Virginia
RACE LENGTH: 112.5 miles (180km) on a 0.375-mile (0.6km) paved oval (remeasured to 0.437-mile [0.7km] and extended to 218.75 [350km] miles in 1964)
NUMBER OF RACES RUN: 4 Grand National, between August 18, 1963, and August 8, 1971
SPEED RECORD (AVERAGE FOR AN ENTIRE RACE): 83.805 mph (134.1kph), on August 8, 1971

The sole track run by NASCAR in West Virginia was owned by television personality Dick Clark. The West Virginia races were characterized by frequent cautions. In the initial race the pavement came apart in large pieces, which caused most of the cautions. The track closed in 1972.

1964

Augusta International Raceway

LOCATION: Augusta, Georgia
RACE LENGTH: 417 miles (667.2km) on a 3-mile (4.8km) paved road course
NUMBER OF RACES RUN: 1 Grand National, on November 17, 1963
SPEED RECORD (AVERAGE FOR AN ENTIRE RACE): 86.320 mph (138.1kph)

The race was originally scheduled for 510 miles (816km), but qualifying speeds showed that there would be insufficient time to complete the race before darkness set in, so it was abbreviated to 417 miles (667.2km). Still, it was the longest road course race ever in NASCAR history. Fireball Roberts was one of the 16 cars remaining on track at the end, and won the event—the only race ever held at the facility!

Langley Field Speedway

LOCATION: Hampton, Virginia
RACE LENGTH: 100 miles (160km) on a 0.4-mile (0.64km) dirt oval (paved in 1968)
NUMBER OF RACES RUN: 9 Grand National, between May 15, 1964, and November 22, 1970
SPEED RECORD (AVERAGE FOR AN ENTIRE RACE): 75.789 mph (121.3kph), on May 17, 1969

The first couple of "Tidewater 250's" were run without cautions. In 1966, Bill Seifert's car struck a guardrail and pushed the nose of the car through it. Another car, losing control behind him, struck Seifert and pushed his car through the railing and over the embankment. Seifert was shaken up but not seriously injured.

Islip Speedway

LOCATION: Islip, New York
RACE LENGTH: 60 miles (96km) on a 0.2-mile (0.32km) dirt oval
NUMBER OF RACES RUN: 6 Grand National, between July 15, 1964, and July 15, 1971
SPEED RECORD (AVERAGE FOR AN ENTIRE RACE): 49.925 mph (79.9kph), on July 15, 1971

Islip was the shortest track run by the Grand National series. Billy Wade and Ned Jarrett excited the crowds with a fender-banging duel in the first race there, with Wade earning his third consecutive win.

Harris Speedway (Tri-City Motor Speedway)

LOCATION: Harris, North Carolina
RACE LENGTH: 100 miles (160km) on a 1/3-mile (0.53km) paved oval
NUMBER OF RACES RUN: 2 Grand National, on October 25, 1964, and May 30, 1965
SPEED RECORD (AVERAGE FOR AN ENTIRE RACE): 59.009 mph (94.4kph), on October 25, 1964

1965

Smokey Mountain Raceway

LOCATION: Maryville, Tennessee
RACE LENGTH: 100 miles (160km) on a 1/2-mile (0.8km) dirt oval (paved in 1968)
NUMBER OF RACES RUN: 12 Grand National, between August 13, 1965, and April 15, 1971
SPEED RECORD (AVERAGE FOR AN ENTIRE RACE): 88.697 mph (141.9kph), on April 15, 1971

Beltsville Speedway (Baltimore-Washington Speedway)

LOCATION: Beltsville, Maryland
RACE LENGTH: 100–150 miles (160–240km) on a 1/2-mile (0.8km) paved oval
NUMBER OF RACES RUN: 10 Grand National, between August 25, 1965, and May 15, 1970
SPEED RECORD (AVERAGE FOR AN ENTIRE RACE): 77.253 mph (123.6kph), on July 15, 1969

Tiny Lund earned 1 of his 5 victories at this track in 1966, beating rookie James Hylton in a photo finish. David Pearson almost lost his 1968 championship bid at Beltsville when he was disqualified after the September race that year. Inspectors found that his car was 200 pounds underweight and stripped him of the money and points that went with his second place finish. Bobby Isaac, whose team filed the protest against Pearson, won the race and pulled to within 55 points in the title contest. He would regardless finish second to the Silver Fox in the points race. Pearson again came out on the losing end of an official ruling in the July 1969 event. He was flagged the winner, but it was determined that he was nearly a lap behind Richard Petty.

North Carolina Motor Speedway

(See pages 95–8)

1966

Starlite Speedway

LOCATION: Monroe, North Carolina
RACE LENGTH: 125 miles (200km) on a 1/2-mile (0.8km) dirt oval
NUMBER OF RACES RUN: 1 Grand National, on May 13, 1966
SPEED RECORD (AVERAGE FOR AN ENTIRE RACE): 60.140 mph (96.2kph)

In a year of conflict between NASCAR and the auto manufacturers, Chrysler teams were instructed to boycott the sole race at Starlite in May of 1966. Independent Darel Dieringer won the race. Early leader John Sears was later killed at the facility (in 1973). The track closed shortly thereafter.

Middle Georgia Raceway (Peach State Fairgrounds)

LOCATION: Macon, Georgia
RACE LENGTH: 100–250 miles (160–400km) on a 1/2-mile (0.8km) paved oval
NUMBER OF RACES RUN: 9 Grand National, between May 10, 1966, and November 7, 1971
SPEED RECORD (AVERAGE FOR AN ENTIRE RACE): 85.121 mph (136.2kph), on November 17, 1968

The track was built in 1966 on the site of the former Central City Speedway and it had one feature that no other NASCAR racetrack has ever offered (that we know of anyhow). The track held the 1968 season-opener (in November 1967) despite a furor just weeks before. Federal sheriffs had discovered a suspicious trapdoor in the floor of a ticket booth at the north end of the facility. From the trapdoor a ladder led down to a tunnel. The tunnel went 125 feet to an underground chamber—the cleverly hidden location of a moonshine still! The still was huge—capable of producing 200 gallons of moonshine every couple of days! Sheriffs said this was one of the best-concealed arrangements they had ever seen. Track owner, H. Lamar Brown was indicted (since it was assumed that the tunnels had to be dug during the original construction of the track) but acquitted by jury.

Oxford Plains Speedway

Location: Oxford, Maine
Race length: 100 miles (160km) on a 1/3-mile (0.53km) paved oval
Number of races run: 3 Grand National, between July 12, 1966, and July 9, 1969
Speed record (average for an entire race): 63.717 mph (101.9kph), on July 9, 1968

Bobby Allison broke Chevy's 3-year winless streak at Oxford, using a lightweight car with a small, 327 c.i. engine. He won again in 1967 in his own Chevy, when his Dodge team owner, Cotten Owens decided not to run the race. Chrysler wasn't thrilled with Allison's boost to the rival marque and he was released from his Dodge ride!

1968

Jeffco Speedway (Peach State Speedway)

Location: Jefferson, Georgia
Race length: 100 miles (160km) on a 1/2-mile (0.8km) paved oval
Number of races run: 2 Grand National, on November 3, 1968, and November 2, 1969
Speed record (average for an entire race): 85.106 mph (136.2kph), on November 2, 1969

Jeffco won the honor of being the fastest 1/2-mile (0.8km) track in the country with Cale Yarborough's pole qualifying speed of 90.694 mph (145.1kph) for the 1968 race.

1969

Michigan International Speedway

(See pages 109–12)

Kingsport Speedway

Location: Kingsport, Tennessee
Race length: 100 miles (160km) on a 0.4-mile (0.64km) paved oval (remeasured to 0.337 mile [0.54km] in 1970)
Number of races run: 3 Grand National, between June 19, 1969, and May 23, 1971
Speed record (average for an entire race): 73.619 mph (117.8kph), on June 19, 1969

Dover Downs International Speedway

(See pages 105–9)

Talladega Superspeedway (Alabama International Motor Speedway

(See pages 98–105)

Texas International Speedway (Texas World Speedway)

Location: College Station, Texas
Race length: 400–500 miles (640–800km) on a 2-mile (3.2km) paved oval
Number of races run: 8 Grand National and Winston Cup, between December 7, 1969, and June 7, 1981
Speed record (average for an entire race): 159.046 mph (254.5kph), on June 1, 1980

1970

Albany-Saratoga Speedway

Location: Malta, New York
Race length: 90.5 miles (144.8km) on a 0.362-mile (0.58km) paved oval
Number of races run: 2 Grand National, on July 7, 1970, and July 14, 1971
Speed record (average for an entire race): 68.589 mph (109.7kph), on July 7, 1970

Richard Petty won both NASCAR events at the track, coming back from a lap deficit for the second win.

1971

Ontario Motor Speedway

Location: Ontario, California
Race length: 500 miles (800km) on a 2.5-mile (4km) paved, rectangular course
Number of races run: 9 Grand National and Winston Cup, between February 28, 1971, and November 15, 1980
Speed record (average for an entire race): 140.712 mph (225.1kph), on November 23, 1975

Meyer Speedway

Location: Houston, Texas
Race length: 150 miles (240km) on a 1/2-mile (0.8km) dirt oval
Number of races run: 1 Grand National, on June 23, 1971
Speed record (average for an entire race): 73.489 mph (117.6kph)

Only 14 teams made the trip to Texas for the sole running at Meyer. The stress of keeping up a long season was telling on race teams—Mario Rossi announced that he was folding his operation, and L.G. DeWitt temporarily pulled out of the circuit prior to the Meyer race. Meyer has the dubious distinction of being the last facility added to the NASCAR schedule that is no longer on the circuit.

1974

Pocono Raceway

(See pages 112–18)

1988

Phoenix International Raceway

(See pages 118–20)

1989

Sears Point International Raceway

(See pages 134–37)

1993

New Hampshire International Speedway

(See pages 144–47)

1994

Indianapolis Motor Speedway (The Brickyard)

(See pages 147–52)

1997

Texas Motor Speedway

(See pages 152–53)

California Speedway

(See pages 153–56)

1998

Las Vegas Motor Speedway

(See pages 156–58)

1999

Miami-Dade Homestead Motorsports Complex

(See page 159)

Books

25th Anniversary of Talladega Superspeedway. Charlotte, NC: UMI Publications, 1994.

Bongard, Tim, and Bill Coulter. *Richard Petty: The Cars of the King.* Champaign, IL: Sports Publishing, Inc., 1997.

Darlington Raceway 50th Anniversary. Charlotte, NC: UMI Publications, 1999.

Fielden, Greg. *Charlotte Motor Speedway.* Osceola, WI: MBI Publishing, 2000.

Fielden, Greg. *Forty Years of Stock Car Racing, Volumes 1–4.* Surfside Beach, SC: Galfield Press, 1989, 1990, 1992, 1992.

Fielden, Greg. *Forty Years of Stock Car Racing Plus Four.* Surfside Beach, SC: Galfield Press, 1994.

Golenbock, Peter, and Greg Fielden. *The Stock Car Racing Encyclopedia.* New York: Macmillan Press, 1997.

Hunter, Don, and Al Pearce. *The Illustrated History of Stock Car Racing.* Osceola, WI: MBI Publishing, 1998.

Hunter, Don, and Ben White. *American Stock Car Racers.* Osceola, WI: Motorbooks International, 1997.

Kirkland, Tom, and David Thompson. *Darlington International Raceway 1950–1967.* Oscoela, WI: MBI Publishing, 1999.

Latford, Bob. *Built for Speed.* Philadelphia, PA: Courage Books, 1999.

Moriarty, Frank. *The Encyclopedia of Stock Car Racing.* New York: MetroBooks, 1998.

NASCAR Association. NASCAR: *The Thunder of America, 1948–1998.* Del Mar, CA: Tehabi Books, 1998.

NASCAR Winston Cup Yearbooks: 1973–2000. Charlotte, NC: UMI Publications.

Pierce, Al, and Ben White. *Brickyard 400: Five Years of NASCAR at Indy.* Osceola, WI: MBI Company, 1999.

Riggs, Randy D. *Flat-Out Racing.* New York: Friedman/Fairfax Publishers, 1995.

The Official NASCAR Preview and Press Guide: 1991–2001. Charlotte, NC: UMI Publications, 2001.

Thomy, Al. *Bill Elliott—Fastest Man Alive.* Atlanta, GA: Peachtree Publishers, 1988.

Vehorn, Frank. *The Intimidator.* Asheboro, NC: Down Home Press, 1991.

Zeller, Bob. *Mark Martin— Driven to Race.* Phoenix, AZ: David Bull Publishing, 1997.

Internet Sites

AMC NASCAR Matador: *www2.dsu.nodak.edu/users/mberg/Matador/AMC_NASCAR_Matador.html.com*

Atlanta Motor Speedway: *www.atlantamotorspeedway.com*

Automotive Racing Legends: *www.automuseum.com/Depalma.html*

Bristol Motor Speedway: *www.bristolmotorspeedway.com*

California Speedway: *www.californiaspeedway.com*

Darlington Raceway: *www.darlingtonraceway.com*

Daytona International Speedway: *www.daytonainternationalspeedway.com*

Greenville-Pickens: *www.greenvillepickens.com*

Holman Moody History: *www.holmanmoody.com/history*

Homestead-Miami: *www.homesteadmiamispeedway.com*

Indianapolis Motor Speedway: *www.brickyard.com*

International Motorsports Hall of Fame: *www.motorsportshalloffame.com*

International Speedway Corporations: *www.iscmotorsports.com*

Jayski's NASCAR Silly Season Site: *www.jayski.com*

Las Vegas Motor Speedway: *www.lvms.com*

Living Legends of Racing: *www.lloar.com*

Lowe's Motor Speedway: *www.lowesmotorspeedway.com*

Martinsville Speedway: *www.martinsvillespeedway.com*

Michigan Speedway: *www.mispeedway.com*

NASCAR On-line: *www.nascar.com*

Nashville Raceway: *www.nashvillespeedway.com*

North Carolina Motor Speedway: *www.northcarolinaspeedway.com*

Phoenix Raceway: *www.phoenixintlraceway.com*

Racing History: *www.racinghistory.com*

Richmond Raceway: *www.richmondracewaycomplex.com*

Sears Point Raceway: *www.searspoint.com*

Speed Fx: 50 Years of NASCAR History: *www.speedfx.com/history/history_index.shtml*

Speedway Motorsports, Inc.: *http://199.230.26.96/trk/officers.html*

Talladega Superspeedway: *www.talladegasuperspeedway.com*

Texas Motor Speedway: *www.texasmotorspeedway.com*

That's Racin': *www.thatsracin.com*

Watkins Glen: *www.theglen.com*

Winged Warriors: *www.superbird.com/wingedwarriors*